GW00976024

PC Dictionary

WAVE

THOMSON LEARNING

WAVE-PCDC-7104A
Revision 2.0

PC Dictionary
WAVE-PCDC-7104A
Revision 2.0
©1988-2001 Wave Technologies International, Inc.,
a Thomson Learning company.
Thomson Learning™ is a trademark used herein under license.
All rights reserved.

Printed in the United States of America. No part of this book may be used or reproduced in any form or by any means, or stored in a database or retrieval system, without prior written permission of the publisher. Making copies of any part of this book for any purpose other than your own personal use is a violation of United States copyright laws. For information, contact Wave Technologies International, Inc., 10845 Olive Blvd., Suite 250, St. Louis, Missouri 63141.

This book is sold as is, without warranty of any kind, either express or implied, respecting the contents of this book, including, but not limited to, implied warranties for the book's quality, performance, merchantability, or fitness for any particular purpose. Neither Wave Technologies International, Inc., nor its dealers or distributors shall be liable to the purchaser or any other person or entity with respect to any liability, loss, or damage caused or alleged to be caused directly or indirectly by this book.

Trademarks

Trademarks and registered trademarks of products mentioned in this book are held by the companies producing them. Use of a term in this book should not be regarded as affecting the validity of any trademark or service mark.

The Wave Technologies International, Inc. logo is a registered trademark of Wave Technologies International, Inc., St. Louis, Missouri.

Copyrights of any screen captures in this book are the property of the software's manufacturer.

Mention of any products in this book in no way constitutes an endorsement by Wave Technologies International, Inc.

10 9 8 7 6 5 4 3 2 1

Contents

Symbols

16-bit application

An application native to Windows 3.1 or Windows for Workgroups 3.11.

2000rkst.msi

Source file for installing Windows 2000 Support Tools. This file is located in the \Support\Tools\ directory of the Windows 2000 Installation CD-ROM.

32-bit application

An application native to Windows NT or Windows 95.

3x box

The OS/2 application environment that emulates an 8086-based PC running DOS version 3.x.

56k line

A digital phone-line connection (leased line) that can carry 56,000 bps. At this speed, a megabyte will take approximately 3 minutes to transfer, making it four times as fast as a 14,400-bps modem.

#

1. Symbol used by SQL Server to identify a local temporary table.
2. Symbol used in Linux and UNIX to begin a comment within a script.

##

Symbol used by SQL Server to identify a global temporary table.

$DISPLAY

In Linux, a shell variable containing the current user's default display for the X Window System.

$HOME

In Linux, a shell variable containing the path to the current user's home directory.

$PATH

In Linux, a shell variable containing a list of directories that will be searched for a command or program upon execution.

$TERM

In Linux, a shell variable containing the current user's default terminal type.

.bash_profile

In the user's home directory in Linux, a file containing commands to be executed at login after the execution of the systemwide /etc/profile. Available for user customization.

.bashrc

In the user's home directory in Linux, a file containing commands to be executed to initialize each new shell. Under some circumstances, this is a default name; other circumstances may require the name of this file to be stored in a global variable $ENV or $BASH_ENV.

.rhosts

In UNIX, this is a file located in a user's home directory that grants or denies password-free access to the "r" network services (e.g., rlogin, rsh, rcp). This file creates a trust relationship.

.xhosts

In UNIX, this is a file located in a user's home directory that grants or denies access to his/her X server from other hosts. This file creates a trust relationship.

/

In Linux, the root directory of a file system is referred to as /. The / character is also used to separate directory names in a path.

/etc

In Linux, the directory containing system configuration files and directories and some configuration commands.

/home

By convention in Linux, directory containing users' home directories.

/mnt

By convention in Linux, location for temporarily mounting removable drive directory trees.

/proc

In Linux, the directory containing a pseudo file system. It provides information on currently running processes, system statistics such as memory availability and processor usage, and hardware information, including interrupts and addresses used by adapters.

/var/log

By convention in Linux, the directory containing log files for system processes. The /var portion of the pathname indicates files that vary frequently.

@

Symbol used by SQL Server to identify a local variable.

@@

Symbol used by SQL Server to identify a global variable.

[PUBLIC] trustee

This is a special trustee that can be added to any object, directory, or file in NetWare. [PUBLIC] includes the Read and File Scan rights by default. By making [PUBLIC] a trustee of an object, directory, or file, all objects in NDS have rights to that object, directory, or file. [PUBLIC] is only used in trustee assignments and can be added or deleted like any other trustee. It must be entered within the square brackets. An Inherited Rights Filter blocks inherited rights for [PUBLIC] in the same way it would for any other trustee.

[ROOT] object

An object in the directory tree that provides the highest point to access different Country and Organization objects and allow trustee assignments granting rights to the entire directory tree. Country, Organization, and Alias objects are created at the [ROOT] object. It is a place holder and contains no information.

A

Abbreviated addressing

Addressing in which a simple mnemonic code is used in lieu of the complete addressing information. The reference to the complete address is stored in the PAD.

Abnormal end (Abend)

When the NetWare operating system detects a serious problem, for example, a hardware or software failure, it issues this message and stops the NetWare server.

Abstract class

An abstract class is used to define common features contained by a subclass.

Abstract method

A method that does not contain an implementation.

Abstract syntax

A description of a data structure that is independent of machine-oriented structures and encodings.

Abstract Syntax Notation One (ASN.1)

The OSI language for describing abstract syntax.

Abstract Window Toolkit (AWT)

A package containing classes that enable you to construct Graphical User Interfaces (GUIs).

Abstraction

The process of refining away the unimportant details of an object. According to your perception, you abstract characteristics of a real-world object and use them to represent the object on a computer.

AC-3 compression

Dolby digital compression. AC-3 is one of the primary compression technologies supported by DVD.

Accelerated Graphics Port (AGP)

A bus specification that allows 3D graphics to be displayed rapidly and smoothly on personal computers.

Accelerator board

1. A circuit board containing one or more 680x0, PowerPC, or other processors used to upgrade the CPU and/or graphics performance of a Macintosh computer.

2. Circuit board upgrading performance in a particular area of PC funtionality, typically graphics.

Acceptable Use Policy (AUP)

These rules define data network usage and, based on the usage definition, allow or restrict access for certain uses.

Access

Ability to use a computer or network service based on user authentication.

Access code

This is a password or code that allows a user to gain access to a service. It is established by the service provider.

Access control

The method of authenticating user accounts when users log on to a Windows 2000 or NT domain. Users are granted or denied access to network resources through the use of security descriptors.

Access Control Entry (ACE)

An access privilege assigned to a user or group. With Windows NT/2000 Server, the ACE is stored with the object being protected.

Access Control List (ACL)

A security mechanism used in Windows, Novell, and some UNIX systems that lists users and groups with access to given computer resources.

1. A list of trustees who have been granted rights to an object or rights to the properties of an object. Each object in the NDS contains an Access Control List.

2. Under Windows NT/2000, the Access Control List contains user and group Access Control Entries.

Access Control List and Access Control Entry

When discussing Windows NT Server security, the discretionary Access Control List (ACL) contains an entry for each user or group for which access privileges or restrictions have been defined. The format of each Access Control Entry (ACE) is that of an access mask containing all values appropriate for the type of resource.

The order in which the entries are listed is significant. SIDs (Security IDs) that have a permission of "No Access" assigned are listed first. This is to ensure that any users or groups specifically restricted from the resource do not accidentally gain access.

Access control right

A NetWare file system right allows the user to change the Access Control List (ACL) trustee assignments and Inherited Rights Filter for a directory or file.

Access group

All stations that have identical rights to make use of computer networks or data PBX resources.

Access mask

A value passed that describes the privilege requirements for a user's access request. This is compared against the user's access privileges to determine access.

Access method

1. In IBM environments, it is a host program managing the movement of data between the main storage and an input/output device of a computer system. BTAM, TCAM, and VTAM are common data communications access methods.

2. In LAN technology, it is a means to allow stations to gain access to make use of the network's transmission medium, which is classified as a shared access or discrete access method.

Access path

This is the route between two communicating computers. An access path on the Internet is routed through nodes on the network.

Access protection

The ability to protect a block of memory by setting flags. The flags determine how the information stored at that memory location can be used.

Access specifiers

Keywords that control access to variables by other classes. In Java, access specifiers are private, public, protected, and default.

Access time

A measurement of the average time it takes from when the PC issues a command to get data from a disk drive. This is a combination of several factors. The major determining factor is drive seek time. Moving the read/write heads is the slowest, single operation for a hard disk. The faster it can move the head array during seek time, the faster the disk access time.

Access Token

A Windows NT object describing a user account and group memberships. The Access Token is used in access validation.

Access unit

The electronic mail component responsible for transferring messages between dissimilar mail systems.

Accessibility

The level at which the application's user interface supports interaction by users with special needs.

Accessories

Microsoft Windows or Windows NT applets.

Account balance

In NetWare, the cost and payment status of a network user. Typically, a dollar amount is credited to a network user's account. Network charges, such as connection time, disk space, and logins, are deducted, leaving the unspent balance. The network supervisor or account manager controls account balances using the Account Balance option in the SYSCON (in older versions of NetWare), NETADMIN, or NWADMIN User Information menu.

Account SID

A unique value identifying a Windows NT or NT Server user, group account, or object.

Accounting

In networking, a method of allocating space, time, and costs to users. In NetWare, user accounts are created by using the SYSCON supervisor option. The accounts keep track of connection time, logins, and network use. They also calculate and apply charges, and withdraw charge privileges, when necessary.

Accunet

AT&T data-oriented digital services, including the following: Accunet T1.5 terrestrial wideband at 1.544 megabits per second used primarily for video teleconferencing applications, Accunet packet-switching services, and Accunet Dataphone Digital Services (DDS).

ACK packet

An acknowledgment packet, sent as a response to a SYN packet.

Acknowledgment (ACK)

A response by the receiver of a communications message indicating the message was received correctly.

ACONSOLE

Asynchronous CONSOLE. A NetWare 3.x or 4.x utility for remote management of file servers by supervisors and remote console operators. ACONSOLE transfers information between a remote station and a file server. It also allows the use of a stand-alone computer as a remote console for asynchronous communication with a file server via a modem.

Action event

An event that is generated by a mouse-click on a button, menu, or listbox.

Active Channel

A technology that enables Active Channel Web sites to push changes to the desktop.

Active Desktop

A technology that allows you to integrate HTML with the operating system's desktop.

Active Directory

The Windows 2000 directory service. Active Directory treats users, files, directories, applications, and other items as objects. It allows system administrations to modify the properties of objects. Objects and their properties are described in the Active Directory schema.

Active Directory service

Microsoft incorporated its automated directory service into Windows 2000. Active Directory service is a highly integrated set of APIs and protocols that extends its services across multiple servers and namespaces. It also will collect and show resource information that is across LAN and WAN connections.

Active Directory Services Interface (ADSI)

A COM-based service that allows applications to communicate with Active Directory and provides the means for directory service clients to use one set of interfaces to communicate with any namespace that provides an ADSI implementation. ADSI also allows developers to create Web-based applications that interact with and manage Active Directory from a single interface.

Active Directory-integrated

One of the zone name server options supported by Windows 2000 DNS. Zone database storage and replication are supported through Active Directory storage.

Active monitor

Any station on a Token Ring network that originates a free token. There can be only one active monitor at a time. The active monitor is also responsible for making sure the same frame doesn't keep circulating around the ring.

Active Scripting Language

Any language that can be hosted by the ActiveX Script engine. Both VBScript and JScript are Active Scripting Languages.

Active Server Pages

A script that can be compiled and run by Internet Information Server. It is written using an ActiveX scripting language, such as VBScript or JScript. Its output is usually plain HTML that can be displayed by any browser.

Active window

The window that is currently selected in a desktop environment, such as the Macintosh desktop, Windows desktop, or the desktops in Linux–X, KDE, or GNOME.

ActiveX

A technology, based on the Component Object Model (COM) standard, that allows developers to create reusable objects, including ActiveX controls, ActiveX components, and ActiveX Documents.

ActiveX component

A server that exposes a COM interface. The interface contains methods, properties, and events that consumers can call to use the services provided by the server. ActiveX components are sometimes called OLE Automation servers.

ActiveX control

A special type of ActiveX component that must be sited in a container. An ActiveX control has both design-time behavior and run-time behavior.

ActiveX Data Objects (ADO)

A data access technology. It works in conjuction with OLE DB to provide universal data access for both relational and nonrelational data sources.

ActiveX document

An ActiveX component that can negotiate with an ActiveX container to display menus on the menubar. Like an ActiveX control, it can be sited in a container. However, an ActiveX Document does not have design-time behavior. Some applications, like Microsoft Word, can run as stand-alone applications or as ActiveX Documents.

Ad hoc query

1. A SQL Server query designed for immediate execution.

2. An SMS ad hoc query is designed for immediate execution. It is not stored in the SMS system database and does not affect existing queries.

Adapter

A piece of hardware, usually with a type of interface port, added to a system to perform a specific funtion. Commonly used in reference to video and network cards.

Adaptive bridge

Sometimes referred to as a *learning bridge* because it learns the node address of workstations on the LAN. This type of bridge builds its own table of address, which frees the administrator or installer of this task.

ADD NAME SPACE

A NetWare 3.x and 4.x internal command that allows multiple platforms to more easily share files. When this command is used, the specified name space may be added to the specified volume, so files may be read in another operating system. NetWare automatically provides DOS and OS/2 name spaces. Any other file type, such as Macintosh, must have a name space loaded before it can be copied to the file server.

Add or Delete Self right

A NetWare property right that allows a trustee to add or remove itself as a value of the property.

Add-on board

A circuit board that changes or improves a personal computer's capabilities. For example, a memory board increases the amount of RAM in a computer. A network board (also called an NIC or network adapter card) lets workstations communicate with each other and the NetWare server. These boards are connected by cabling or some other transmission medium.

Add/Remove Hardware Wizard

Wizard launched by the Control Panel's Add/Remove Hardware utility that lets you install, uninstall, and troubleshoot hardware devices.

Address

A unique designation for the location of data, the identity of an intelligent device, or a logical or physical network address.

Address mask

A bit mask used to select bits from an Internet (TCP/IP) address for subnet addressing. The mask is 32 bits long and selects the network portion of the Internet address and two or more bits of the local portion. It is sometimes called subnet mask.

Address resolution

A means for mapping logical addresses to physical addresses.

Address Resolution Protocol (ARP)

A protocol used to determine the MAC or OSI Physical layer (hardware) address when the Network layer (IP) address is known.

Address space

A block of addresses that a process can assign to a particular block of data. The memory allocated from an address space must be backed by physical memory.

Addressing

The method by which numbers are assigned to identify hardware resources or disk channels. Each controller must have a unique address. The documentation shipped with the controller will list the physical address settings.

Addressing space

1. The range of addresses that a processor can access. This usually depends on the width of the processor's address bus and address registers. Address space can be either physical or virtual.

2. This is the total amount of RAM available to a NetWare 4 server operating system. It can be divided into domains. The maximum addressing space is 4 gigabytes (GB) in a NetWare 4 operating system, however, practical hardware limits are much lower.

adduser

Originally, a script that performed the tasks necessary to add a user account to the system. It has been superceded by the useradd program. Many Linux distributions still provide both methods, although some have begun to remove adduser and create a symbolic link to useradd in place of it.

ADMINCFG

The program shipped with Windows for Workgroups 3.11 that allows system administrators to put global restrictions on how Windows for Workgroups workstations can share and access network resources.

Administrative Management Domain (ADMD)

An X.400 Message Handling System public service carrier. Examples: MCImail and ATTmail in the U.S., British Telecom Gold 400mail in the U.K. The ADMDs worldwide provide the X.400 backbone.

Administrative Domain (AD)

This is a single NetWare administrative unit that has authority over hosts, links, and networks.

Adminpak.msi

Source file for installing additional Administrative Tools on a Windows 2000 system. This file is located in the \%systemroot%\system32 folder.

Advanced Communications Function/Virtual Telecommunications Access Method (ACF/VFTAM)

The most basic and widespread element in IBM's mainframe networking software.

Advanced Configuration and Power Interface (ACPI)

The system interface that enables a motherboard to describe its power management interface, as well as attached devices and their configuration, to the operating system.

Advanced Encryption Standard (AES)

An encryption standard, completed October 2000, meant to replace Data Encryption Standard (DES). The Rijndael encryption algorithm was selected by the National Institute of Standards and Technology (NIST).

Advanced Power Management (APM)

The specification that enables a computer's BIOS to monitor battery status and report when battery power is getting low. BIOS chips that are written to this specification can also turn off devices and put a computer to *sleep* when a specified amount of time has elapsed without activity, such as user input or interrupt requests.

Advanced Program-to-Program Communications (APPC)

An Application Programming Interface (API) developed by IBM for its Systems Network Architecture (SNA).

Advanced Research Projects Agency (ARPA)

The government agency that started the Internet.

Advanced Research Projects Agency Network (ARPANET)

A packet-switched network developed in the early 1970s. The *grandfather* of today's Internet. ARPANET was decommissioned in June 1990.

AFP Server object

Represents an AppleTalk Filing Protocol file server on the network.

AFP.NLM

The AFP.NLM is the NetWare Loadable Module loaded on the file server to provide AppleTalk Filing Protocol (AFP) services.

Agent

In the client-server model, the part of the system that performs information preparation and exchange on behalf of a client or server application.

Aggregate functions

Microsoft SQL Server TRANSACT-SQL functions that generate one summary value from a group of values in a specified column. The functions are AVG, COUNT, COUNT(*), SUM, MIN, and MAX.

Alert

1. An error message sent to the system control point at the host system.
2. A defined response to an event occurring in SQL Server.
3. Windows 2000 method for monitoring and detecting performance counter limits.

Alert box

A dialog box used to display warning or error messages.

Alerter

A component within the SMS Executive service that evaluates alert conditions and triggers alert actions when specific query conditions are detected.

Algorithm

The steps that must be performed in order to complete a particular action.

Alias

1. In SQL, an alias is a temporary name given to a table and specified in the FROM clause of a select statement. It eliminates extra typing and allows self joins.

2. A SQL Server mechanism allowing a server login ID to assume the identity of another database user. Use an alias when temporary access is required or to allow database creators to create all objects with the same owner name.

3. This is the MS-DOS filename associated with a long filename in Windows 95 or Windows NT.

4. On a Macintosh, an alias is a shortcut to a volume, folder, or file.

Alias object

This type of object is used to point to another object located in another branch of NetWare's NDS directory tree.

All Points Addressable (APA)

In computer graphics, pertaining to the ability to address and display or not display each picture element on a display surface.

Alloc memory

An expandable section of memory in NetWare 3.11 that is not required for DOS or the NetWare operating system. Alloc memory is used to store network status information, such as drive mappings, loadable module tables, and locked files. In addition, it stores current operations, including user connections, queue manager tables, service request buffers, and messages to be broadcast on the network.

Allocation

Associating a memory address with a block of data and setting aside physical memory to back it.

Allocation granularity

The size of the memory page, as defined by the particular processor.

Allocation page

The first page of an allocation unit that describes how the remaining pages within the allocation unit are used. Allocation pages have logical page numbers that are multiples of 256, starting 0, 256, 512, and so on.

Allocation unit

Set of 32 SQL Server extents, representing 0.5 MB of disk space.

Alt

A category in USENET for newsgroups on alternative topics.

American National Standards Institute (ANSI)

A group of committees formed to establish voluntary commercial and government standards. The committee responsible for computing, data processing, and information technology is ANSI-X3, formerly named USASI (United States of America Standards Institute). ANSI is a member of the International Standards Organization (ISO).

American Standard Code for Information Interchange (ASCII)

The character set used to translate a byte into a character or number. Devised in 1968, ASCII is used for the purpose of standardizing the transmission of data to achieve hardware and software compatibility.

ASCII has 128 Characters and uses 7 of the 8 bits to form these characters. The eighth bit is used for error checking.

IBM developed the Extended Character Set, which contains 256 characters. In this character set, the eighth bit is used for special symbols, such as bullet points, fractions, and copyright or trademark symbols.

American Wire Gauge (AWG)

A standard for determining wire diameter. The diameter varies inversely to the gauge number.

Amplitude modulation

A method of encoding, enabling the frequency of the carrier wave to remain constant while the information it carries changes in strength. This system changes the strength (size) of an analog signal (wave) from the zero line to a positive peak, and then to an equal negative peak. The stronger the voltage, the higher the wave. Often abbreviated as AM.

Analog

The representation of a continuously changing physical variable (sound, for example) by another physical variable (such as electrical current).

Analog adapter

On an analog video board, intensity information is transmitted across separate lines, one for each of the three primary colors (red, green, and blue). In theory, the possible number of variations of each of the basic colors could allow for an infinite number of displayed color variations. VGA, Super VGA, MCGA, and 8514/A monitors require analog adapters.

Analog signal

A smoothly varying value of voltage or current. The signal varies continuously in amplitude and time.

Anchor

An anchor is a marker inserted in a Web page so the point in the page can be referred to. It can also be called a hyperlink.

Anonymous FTP

An Internet utility that allows a user to connect to a remote computer as a guest to retrieve documents, files, programs, and other archived data without having a user ID or password on the host system. Users identify themselves as anonymous and skip local security checks.

Anonymous pipe

A data storage buffer that an operating system maintains in RAM. Used for interprocess communications.

Anonymous subscription

A pull subscription where the Subscriber is only recognized by the Publisher for the length of the connection.

ANSI character set

The American National Standards Institute 8-bit character set containing 256 characters.

ANSI-92 SQL

Current standard for "generic" SQL.

Answer file

A text file containing answers to Setup prompts for a Windows NT or Windows 2000 unattended installation. Answer files can be created by using the Windows 2000 Setup Manager Wizard found in the Windows 2000 Resource Kit Deployment Tools.

Apache

An extremely popular Web server product. The name is from "A patchy Web server" since the server was originally derived by patching the NCSA Web server. A major successful example of open software.

Apartment neutral threading

A threading model provided in COM+ that will allow objects to be created on the same thread as their creator, regardless of the creator's threading model. This threading model is very fast but cannot be used by components that require thread affinity, such as those created with Visual Basic or MFC.

Apartment threading

The threading model in which each thread has an apartment where it stores its own copy of global data for the instances of components it creates.

Apple Desktop Bus (ADB)

The expansion bus used to connect Macintosh keyboards and input devices.

Apple events

A Macintosh OS System 7 (and later) feature that allows an application to call another application on the same computer or across a network.

Apple Guide

The online help system built into Macintosh OS System 7.5 and later.

Apple menu

The pull-down menu available at the top left corner of the Macintosh Finder menu bar. Disk drives, files, folders, and program aliases located in the Apple Menu Items folder inside the System Folder appear in this menu.

AppleScript

The native scripting language built into the Macintosh OS. Similar in function to the DOS batch language.

AppleShare

The software that allows a Macintosh computer to share file system resources with other networked Macs. This is also the name of the extension (utilized by the Chooser) that allows a Mac to connect to other shared file system resources via AppleTalk.

AppleShare software

A Macintosh computer can function as a file server in an AppleTalk network using this networking software. As Macintosh workstation software, it allows access to an AppleShare server.

Applet

A Java program that is embedded in an HTML page and run in a Java-enabled browser.

Applet viewer (appletviewer)

A tool that allows you to execute an applet from the command line.

AppleTalk

Protocols for a network of Macintosh computers.

AppleTalk is based on the ISO/OSI Reference Model and incorporates the SPX protocol. AppleTalk networks may be configured in Ethernet and Token-Ring topologies. AppleTalk networks use various kinds of cables. The AppleTalk Filing Protocol (AFP), for client server architecture, runs on VAX and other non-Macintosh servers. AppleTalk and AFP are compatible with NetWare and are available as VAPs (2.x) and NLMs (3.x) in NetWare for Macintosh.

AppleTalk Data Stream Protocol (ADSP)

Responsible for providing a simple transport method for data across the network.

AppleTalk Echo Protocol (AEP)

Responsible for checking for communications between different nodes on the network.

AppleTalk Filing Protocol (AFP)

This is the AppleTalk protocol that allows communication and data transmission between file servers and clients in an AppleShare network. If AFP.NLM is loaded on a NetWare server that is running NetWare for Macintosh, the AFP lets Macintosh users share files by interacting directly with the NetWare file system. It operates on the same level as NetWare Core Protocol (NCP).

AppleTalk Phase I

AppleTalk Phase I networks are limited to one network number per cable segment as well as 256 nodes.

AppleTalk Phase II

AppleTalk Phase II networks exceed the 254-device limitation by allowing the assignment of multiple network numbers on the same network segment. Phase II networks allow the creation of larger, more open networks with the introduction of TokenTalk and EtherTalk.

AppleTalk Print Services module

A NetWare Loadable Module (NLM) that allows Macintosh users to print to NetWare print queues and non-Macintosh users to print to AppleTalk printers.

AppleTalk protocols

The forms and rules that regulate communication between nodes on an AppleTalk network. They also control the Apple Talk network from the network board to the application software. The protocols are Link Access Protocols (LAPs), Datagram Delivery Protocol (DDP), Routing Table Maintenance Protocol (RTMP), AppleTalk Update-Based Routing Protocol (AURP), Name Binding Protocol (NBP), Printer Access Protocol (PAP), and Zone Information Protocol (ZIP).

AppleTalk Remote Access (ARA)

Allows Macintosh computers to remotely connect via modems.

AppleTalk Session Protocol (ASP)

Responsible for maintaining all sessions between the workstation and the file server. Some of these tasks may include session initiation, maintenance, and termination.

AppleTalk Transaction Protocol (ATP)

Responsible for handling network messaging. Unlike DDPm, ATP requires an acknowledgment of delivery.

Application

The use to which an information processing system is put. For example, a payroll application, an airline reservation application, or a network application.

Application layer

OSI Layer 7 providing an interface with user or application programs.

Application log

Windows NT log that application errors and events, including SQL Server errors and events, are recorded to.

Application menu

The pull-down menu available at the top-right corner of the Macintosh Finder menu bar. It is used to switch between loaded applications. This menu is found in Macintosh OS System 7 and later.

Application Programming Interface (API)

An interface application developers use to invoke the services provided by the operating system or another application. For example, the ODBC API allows developers to use call functions provided by the ODBC library. The WIN32 API allows developers to call functions to interface with 32-bit Windows operating systems.

Application role

SQL Server security role defining application access permissions.

Application server mode

Terminal Services server mode optimized for support of multiuser applications.

Applications Manager

A component within the SMS Executive service that distributes application configuration information.

Archie

Acts as a catalog and index of anonymous FTP sites on the Internet. It was developed by the McGill University School of Computer Science. Archie client sites can be publicly queried, and Archie searches Internet FTP sites by program or document name (names appearing on FTP menus). It displays a list of all files containing the search string, as well as the computer address and directories holding the requested information. A user needs to know the exact filename or a substring of it to utilize Archie.

Architecture

The specific design and construction of a computer. Architecture usually refers to the hardware makeup of the central processing unit and the size of the byte or set of bytes it processes, such as 8-bit, 16-bit, or 32-bit architecture.

Archive

Storing files on a long-term medium, such as optical disks or magnetic tape.

Archive Needed attribute

A file system attribute indicating that a file has been changed since the last time it was backed up.

Archive sites

Computer sites that provide access to a group of files on the Internet. Many popular sites can be reached using anonymous FTP and provide information, freeware, and shareware that can be transferred to the users' computers.

Argument

A value passed with a procedure containing values needed for procedure execution. The term "command option" or parameter may also be used.

ARP table

A table maintained by the operating system matching IP addresses to physical device addresses.

Array

A collection of like elements that can be accessed serially or by index. A series of variables having the same name and data type. Each item in an array is called an element.

Article

SQL Server table or portion of a table published for replication. Articles can only be defined on published databases.

ASCII terminal

A terminal that uses ASCII. Usually synonymous with asynchronous terminal and dumb terminal.

Asia and Oceania Workshop (AOW)

One of the three regional OSI Implementors Workshops and is equivalent to OIW and EWOS.

Aspect ratio

The ratio between the horizontal and vertical pixels. By convention, horizontal is written first. Most VGA, Super VGA, and 8514/A follow a 4:3 ratio.

Association Control Service Element (ACSE)

The method used in OSI for establishing a call between two applications. Checks the identities and contexts of the application entities and can apply an authentication security check.

Asymmetric Digital Subscriber Line (ADSL)

ADSL is a technology that increases the amount of data that can be transmitted in a single direction over Plain Old Telephone Service (POTS) lines. It relies on the fact that multimedia communication involves transmitting a large amount of data in one direction and only small amounts (for control) in the other.

Asymmetric Multiprocessing (ASMP)

Multiprocessor management method where one processor supports the operating system and any additional processors support process threads.

Asynchronous

1. A form of communication where each transmitted character is preceded by a start bit and followed by a stop bit. This eliminates the need for a particular spacing or timing scheme between characters. Personal computers communicate asynchronously via a serial port.

2. An adjective used to describe a method that returns control to the consumer before it completes execution. An asynchronous component cannot return a value.

Asynchronous modem

A modem that cannot supply timing signals and requires all the timing information to be supplied by the associated Data Terminal Equipment (DTE).

Asynchronous Transfer Mode (ATM)

A high-speed (155 to 162 Mbps) communications transport facility capable of carrying voice, data, and video signaling. ATM forms the backbone for broadband ISDN networks.

Asynchronous transmission

In computer communications, data (binary digits) can be transmitted in asynchronous mode or synchronous mode. When the mode is asynchronous, the binary digits are not orderly, meaning they are out of synchronization and sent at irregular intervals in characters, words, or blocks. To ensure that the receiving device is ready, a special *start bit* is sent ahead of each character and a stop bit at the end of each character, a process which continues until the final character is sent.

In ASCII, where 8 bits form a character or byte, 10 bits must be sent for each character. Asynchronous transmission is sometimes known as start-stop transmission.

ATCON

A NetWare utility that allows the network manager to monitor AppleTalk routing on the MultiProtocol Router product.

ATPS.NLM

The ATPS.NLM is the NetWare Loadable Module which is loaded on the file server to provide print services to an Apple LaserWriter.

ATTACH

A NetWare command-line utility that allows a user already logged in to a file server to log in to one or more additional servers.

Attached Resource Computer Network (ARCNET)

A token-passing network that can utilize both star and bus topologies. ARCNET is not an IEEE standard but was developed by the Datapoint Corporation in 1977.

Although generally considered old technology, ARCNET originally used coaxial cable and transmitted at 2.5 Mbps.

Several vendors announced ARCNET Plus, a 20-Mbps version compatible with the 2.5-Mbps ARCNET standard. Both versions can run on the same LAN. Each node advertises its capabilities, and faster nodes slow their speed to communicate with slower nodes.

Some of the newer ARCNET cards operate at speeds of 100 Mbps and use twisted-pair or fiber-optic cable.

With ARCNET, active hubs can support cable lengths up to 2,000 feet.

ARCNET is a reliable system that is not as susceptible to failure as coaxial-cabled Ethernet. If a cable is cut or comes loose, only the workstation goes down, not the entire network. The token-passing protocol requires that every transaction be acknowledged, so there is little chance for errors.

The tradeoff is that ARCNET data throughput is much slower than with other networking schemes.

Attachment Unit Interface (AUI)

Standard Ethernet connector.

Attribute

A characteristic that defines an Active Directory (AD) object. Most AD objects are defined by a set of attributes that make the object unique.

Audio Interchange File Format (AIFF)

A common format used on the Macintosh platform for sound files.

Audit trail

The complete series of traces left by system-level actions; used to evaluate damage from an attack or to gather information on the attacker.

Authentication

1. A way to verify that an object sending messages or requests is who or what the requests declare them to be. This is commonly done with login or resource access validation through a username and password.

2. A way to verify that requests for a connection or service are coming from a trusted source.

Authentication (connection)

The process by which connection credentials are verified before accepting the connection.

Author mode

Microsoft Management Console (MMC) mode that allows users to modify MMC custom consoles.

Authorization (connection)

The process by which a connection attempt is verified to ensure that it is allowed.

Autoexec.bat

The DOS environment is set up and configured by loading device drivers. This is done through the system configuration files Autoexec.bat and Config.sys. When DOS is booted, these files are executed.

Autoexec.bat is a text batch file that must be located at the root directory of the boot drive. The Autoexec.bat file is executed by Command.com after the Config.sys file and is used to customize the environment and automatically start applications.

It is a good idea to make a backup of this file prior to installing a new application. Many applications will make changes to this file during their installation. It is wise to make note of the changes in case of system errors or problems. Applications that alter this file typically make a backup copy. Refer to the application's documentation for details.

Changes to the Autoexec.bat file will not take effect until the system is rebooted.

Mistakes in the Autoexec.bat file may cause system startup errors. You can bypass the execution of Autoexec.bat by pressing the *F5* key when you see the "Starting DOS" message.

Autoexec.bat is still supported with Windows 95 to provide backward compatibility with DOS.

AUTOEXEC.NCF

NetWare batch file (for 3.x and 4.x) loaded into the file server after the operating system that initiates file execution for startup.

Autoexec.nt

The replacement for Autoexec.bat for DOS programs running under Windows NT.

Automatic Baud Rate Detection (ABR)

Sometimes referred to as Autobaud, it is a process by which a receiving device determines the speed, code level, and stop bits of incoming data by examining the first character, which is usually a pre-selected sign-on character. ABR allows the receiving device to accept data from a variety of transmitting devices operating at different speeds, without the need to establish data rates in advance.

Automatic recovery

During automatic recovery, SQL Server uses the transaction logs to ensure database consistency. Automatic recovery will occur every time you launch SQL Server.

During normal operations, all changes to a database are recorded in the transaction log unless specifically instructed not to do so. Automatic recovery uses the transaction log as reference, and all completed transactions are written to the database file. All uncommitted transactions are *rolled back* so they are not reflected in the database.

Automatic recovery occurs in a specific order. The master database is recovered, then the model database is recovered. Next, the tempdb database is cleared, and the pubs database is recovered if it is installed. On distribution servers, the distribution database is recovered. Finally, each user database is recovered.

Even though users may log on as soon as SQL Server has finished recovering the system databases, any user database that has not yet been recovered will not be available for access.

Automatic Repeat-Request (ARQ)

A type of send/receive procedure in which each message must be either positively or negatively acknowledged. ARQ is a popular form of error control.

Automatic rollback

A feature of TTS that returns a database to its original state. The database returns, or rolls back, to its latest complete state if it fails during a transaction when the network is running under TTS. This feature prevents an incomplete transaction from causing corruption.

Automatic Skip Driver Agent (ASD)

A Windows 98 program that automatically detects which drivers are preventing Windows 98 from starting.

Automatic synchronization

The process by which subscription databases are initially synchronized with a published database through use of a Snapshot of the published database.

Autonomous system

Internet (TCP/IP) terminology for a collection of gateways (routers) that fall under one administrative entity and cooperate using a common Interior Gateway Protocol (IGP).

A/UX

A UNIX operating system version designed to run on Macintosh computers.

Availability

The amount of time particular components of the application need to be accessible. This characteristic also involves the application's ability to handle planned and unplanned downtime.

Average access time

The average time between the instant of request and the delivery from a storage device.

awk

A pattern-matching text processing utility that applies regular expressions to the data stream. The name is derived from the initials of the authors: Aho, Weinberger, and Kernigan. Due to its unique pattern-matching syntax, it is often used in data retrieval and data transformation.

B

Back door

A hidden feature of software allowing abnormal access to the software features, bypassing normal authentication channels.

Back up

To copy information, usually onto diskette or tape, for safekeeping.

Backbone

The primary connectivity mechanism of a hierarchical distributed system. All systems that have connectivity to an intermediate system on the backbone are assured connectivity to each other. This does not prevent systems from setting up private arrangements with each other to bypass the backbone for reasons of cost, performance, or security.

Background application

An application that is running but does not have focus and cannot receive user input.

Background category

A classification of processes that consists of those associated with a screen group not currently being displayed.

Background printing

A feature that allows a computer to print in the background while other applications execute in the foreground.

Background process

A process that is not the focus of user input. A currently running process can be moved into the background by pressing *CONTROL+z*, which will suspend the process. You may then run the **bg** command, which will move the suspended process into the background. You may also choose to have a program run in the background by appending the & character to the end of the execution line. The process will be started in the background.

Background task

An active process that is not receiving interactive user input.

BackOrifice

In Windows, this is a very dangerous remote control program disguised as a device driver, allowing clandestine access to machine resources in a way that bypasses security features.

Backup

Pertaining to a system, device, file, or facility that can be used to recover data in the event of a malfunction or loss of data.

Backup device

A file, tape, or named pipe defined for use in backup and restore operations.

Backup Domain Controller (BDC)

Windows NT domain controller that serves as a backup/failover to the Primary Domain Controller (PDC).

Backup file

A file that stores the contents of a backup.

Backup hosts and target

A NetWare server with a storage device and storage device controller attached is called a backup host. The server, workstation, or database data is being backed up from or restored to is the target.

Backup media

Disk, tape, or named pipe used for storage of a backup set.

Backup set

The contents of a single backup operation.

Balanced transmission

A transmission mode in which signals are transmitted as a current that travels down one conductor and returns on the other. For digital signals, this technique is known as differential signaling, with the binary value depending on the voltage difference.

Bandwidth

1. The range of frequencies that can be transmitted through a particular circuit.

2. The speed at which data travels over a particular media. Bandwidth is measured in bits per second, kilobits per second, or megabits per second. Commonly used when referring to network interfaces; today's standard network cards run at 10 and 100 megabits per second.

Bandwidth throttling

Limiting the amount of network or Internet connection bandwidth that will be made available to a Web site or Web server.

Base memory address

The bit where a block of allocated memory begins.

Base priority

The thread priority level within the priority class of the process before any dynamic priority modifiers have been applied.

Base tables

A permanent (or underlying) database table on which a view is based.

Baseband

Characteristic of any network technology that uses a single carrier frequency and requires all stations attached to the network to participate in every transmission.

bashrc

In the /etc directory, a part of the shell initialization sequence.

Basic disk

A hard disk configured for industry-standard disk storage. Basic disks are supported by MS-DOS, all Windows *X* versions, all Windows NT versions, and Windows 2000.

Basic Encoding Rules (BER)

Standard rules for encoding data units described in ASN.1. Sometimes incorrectly lumped under the term ASN.1, which properly refers only to the abstract syntax description language, not the encoding technique.

Basic Input/Output System (BIOS)

A set of routines stored in ROM (Read-Only Memory), embedded in chips on the circuit board, that provide basic access to hardware devices independently of the operating system. The BIOS also contains the instructions to start the operating system. Often, the BIOS code is used only to start the operating system, which then takes over hardware management with its own code. Some BIOS manufacturers are IBM, Compaq, AMI, Award, and Phoenix.

Basic Rate ISDN

ISDN connection using two 64-Kbps channels.

Basic Telecommunications Access Method (BTAM)

An IBM software routine; the basic access method for 3270 data communications controls.

Bastion host

A highly secured, hardened server exposed to the outside network, typically as part of a border network.

Batch

A method of computer job processing where input is collected and run through the processing programs all at once and outputs are produced in the form of files and reports. Batch is the opposite of interactive job processing in which an operator at a terminal interacts with the processing program directly during data entry. Most personal computers employ interactive processing. Mainframes use batch processing.

Batch program

A text file that contains operating system commands. When you run a batch program, the operating system carries out the commands in the file as if you had typed them at the command prompt.

Baud

1. Abbreviation for Baudot, which gets its name from J. M. Emile Baudot (1845-1903), who invented the code. The Baudot code is a special set of binary characters using 5 bits per character to form 32 combinations. The number of combinations was increased to 62 through the use of two special shift characters. The Baudot code was mainly used to handle telex messages by common communications carriers such as Western Union. The main disadvantage of the Baudot code is its lack of an error-checking bit.

2. Used commonly to refer to transfer rates on dial-up lines.

Baud rate

The data transmission speed setting of a serial device. Typical rates include 300, 1,200, 2,400, and 9,600. Higher speeds, 19,200, 38,400, and 57,600 baud, are achieved through data compression. Sometimes referred to simply as baud.

Beacon

Sent when Token Ring failure occurs. Used to identify ring failures.

Bearer mode

The type of compression that can be performed on a particular telephone network. For example, a voice bearer mode indicates that the data can be compressed. A data bearer mode indicates that the telephone network should leave it uncompressed.

Because It's Time Network (BITNET)

BITNET is an academic computer network originally based on IBM mainframe systems that were interconnected via leased 9600 bps lines. BITNET has merged with the Computer+Science Network (CSNET) to form the Consortium for Research and Educational Network (CREN).

Bell 103

An AT&T, 0-300-bps modem providing asynchronous transmission with originate/answer capability. Also, often used to describe any Bell 103-compatible modem.

Bell 113

An AT&T, 0-300-bps modem providing asynchronous transmission with originate/answer capability (but not both). Also, often used to describe any Bell 113-compatible modem.

Bell 201

An AT&T, 2,400-bps modem providing synchronous transmission; Bell 201 B was designed for leased-line applications; Bell 201 C was designed for public telephone network applications. Also, often used to describe any Bell 201-compatible modem.

Bell 202

An AT&T, 1,800-bps modem providing asynchronous transmission that requires a 4-wire circuit for full-duplex operation. Also, often used to describe any Bell 202-compatible modem.

Bell 208

An AT&T, 4,800-bps modem providing synchronous transmission; Bell 208 A was designed for leased-line applications; Bell 208 B was designed for public telephone network applications. Also, often used to describe any Bell 208-compatible modem.

Bell 209

An AT&T, 9,600-bps modem providing synchronous transmission. Also, often used to describe any Bell 209-compatible modem.

Bell 212

An AT&T, 1,200-bps, full-duplex modem providing asynchronous transmission or asynchronous transmission for use on the public telephone network. Also, often used to describe any Bell 212-compatible modem.

Bell 43401

Bell Publication that defines requirements for transmission over telco-supplied circuits having DC continuity (that are metallic).

Bell Operating Company (BOC)

More commonly referred to as RBOC for Regional Bell Operating Company. The local telephone company in each of the seven U.S. regions.

Berkeley Sockets

The standard TCP/IP programming model.

Berkeley Software Distribution (BSD)

BSD UNIX, developed by the Computer Systems Research Group of University of California at Berkeley from 1979 to 1993. Distributed free (copying costs only), much of the BSD code includes code from Bell's UNIX System Laboratories (USL) and requires a valid USL license. Berkeley Systems Design, founded in 1991, continues to develop BSD code. An open variant of BSD is also available as OpenBSD.

Big-endian

A format for storing or transmitting binary data in which the most significant bit (or byte) comes first. From a story in Gulliver's Travels (Swift) in which two warring factions disputed over which end of an egg should be opened. The reverse convention is called little-endian.

Binary

Having two components or possible states. Usually represented by a code of zeros and ones.

Binary access

File access method used for access of binary data files.

Binary digit (bit)

A computer only knows two states: ON and OFF. Each bit is either a one (1) or zero (0). The Binary Digit 1 represents "ON," while the number 0 represents "OFF." The term "bit" is derived from Binary digIT. Eight bits make up a byte.

The American Standard Code for Information Interchange (ASCII) character set is used to translate bits into characters and numbers. In this standard, 1 byte is used to represent each letter of the alphabet, for example, "01000001" represents the letter "A."

Binary stream

An unstructured series of ones and zeros.

Binary Synchronous Communications (BSC)

A type of synchronous communications control procedure set up by IBM as a line control procedure in which the sending and receiving stations are synchronized before a message is sent. The synchronization is checked and adjusted during the transmission, using a defined set of control characters.

Binary tree (B-tree)

An efficient method of storing data that will be used in search operations.

BIND

A NetWare 3.x and 4.x console command that links an installed network board's communication protocol to its LAN driver loaded in the file server. It is used to bind one or several protocols to a board, or a protocol to one or several boards.

Bindery

In NetWare 3, the bindery stores information about users, groups, file servers, print servers, and other logical and physical entities on the network. Network information, such as passwords, account balances, and trustee assignments, are also kept in the bindery.

The bindery files, NET$OBJ.SYS, NET$PROP.SYS, and NET$VAL.SYS, are stored in the SYSTEM directory on the SYS volume. The files are system files and do not appear in a normal directory search.

BINDFIX is a utility that rebuilds the bindery files, purges deleted users and groups, and then removes their mail directories and trustee rights. The original bindery files are copied to NET$OBJ.OLD, NET$PROP.OLD, and NET$VAL.OLD.

BINDFIX runs without other parameters. One should be logged in as SUPERVISOR and have SYS:SYSTEM as the default directory before running the utility. Ensure there is no other activity on the system before running BINDFIX.

BINDREST is a utility used to restore the original bindery files should BINDFIX fail for any reason. BINDREST runs without additional parameters.

Bindery context

A server's bindery services is enabled in this container object.

Bindery context path

A path statement that sets bindery context in up to 16 containers. The SET parameter can specify bindery contexts, with multiple contexts separated by semicolons.

Bindery emulation

A process by which NetWare 4.x emulates bindery functions to support legacy clients.

Bindery objects

An object placed in the Directory tree by an upgrade or migration utility and is represented by this leaf object. NDS cannot identify the object, and it provides backward compatibility with bindery-oriented utilities.

Bindery queue object

A leaf object representing a print queue placed in the Directory tree by an upgrade or migration utility. NDS cannot identify this object, but it provides backward compatibility with bindery-oriented utilities.

Bindery services

Bindery-based utilities (a NetWare 4 feature) that allow clients and applications to coexist with NetWare Directory Services (NDS) on a network. Objects listed in the server's bindery exist in a flat database. Bindery services create a flat structure for a server, using the bindery relevant leaf objects in an Organization or Organizational Unit object.

BINDFIX

A NetWare BINDery FIX command-line utility in the SYS:SYSTEM directory that can be used to restore bindery data that has been corrupted. Such bindery data includes a user's name, password, rights, and error messages relating to the bindery and print spooling.

Binding

The process by which an object's type library is located.

Binding and unbinding

Binding assigns a communication protocol to network boards and LAN drivers. Unbinding removes the protocol. Each network board needs at least one communication protocol bound to its LAN driver to process packets. Multiple protocols can be bound to the same LAN driver and board. You can also bind the same protocol stack to more than one LAN driver on the server. Workstations with different protocols can be cabled on the same scheme.

BINDREST

Abbreviation for "BINDery RESTore." A NetWare 3.x command-line utility used to reconstruct the Bindery files if they become corrupted.

Biometric Access Control

Authentication based on measurable biological characteristics. Methods of biometric authentication include iris scan, keystroke dynamics, signature dynamics, voice pattern, facial recognition, fingerprints, palm scan, hand geometry, and retina pattern.

Bis

A suffix to CCITT v.xx standard numbers. Whenever a CCITT v.xx standard is followed by the bis extension, it indicates that modifications have been made to the original CCITT standard.

Bitmap

A group of bits (binary digits) representing an image stored in a computer's memory as a pattern of dots.

BITNET address

This is a mail address for the BITNET network made up of a user name and host name. BITNET hosts are accessed from the Internet by adding the suffix ".bitnet" to a BITNET address.

Bits per second (bps)

Usually the number of bits (binary digits) that can be transmitted or transferred each second.

Blind carbon copy

An electronic mail feature allowing users to send duplicate messages to other addresses without notifying the primary recipients.

Block

1. The smallest amount of disk space that can be allocated at one time from a disk partition or volume. Block size is determined by disk size, operating system, and file system type.

2. SQL Server statements enclosed between BEGIN and END.

Block suballocation

To better utilize disk space, NetWare's block suballocation allows part of several files to share one block on the disk. Any partially used disk block is divided into 512-byte sub blocks. These sub blocks can be used to store any leftover fragments of other files. This is set by default when NetWare 4 is installed.

Bomb

Macintosh term for a system crash generally accompanied by a dialog box informing the user of a system problem.

Bookmark

A flag that can be set to mark a particular row in the result set to enable the user to return to that row more easily.

Boolean expressions

Expressions that evaluate as "true" or "false" rather than return a specific value.

Boolean operators

The local operators AND, OR, NOT, and XOR (exclusive OR).

Boot

To start or restart your computer, loading the operating system from a disk drive.

Boot files

The files required to start the operating system, including drivers. Boot files are operating-system dependent.

Bootstrap Protocol (BootP)

The protocol in the TCP/IP suite that allows diskless workstations to boot over the network via RARP.

Border Gateway Protocol (BGP)

A routing information exchange protocol used to advertise efficient internal routes (routes within a site) to external sites.

Border network

A network that intercedes between internal networks and the Internet, whose purpose is analogous to the moat surrounding a castle. All traffic to and from the Internet must pass over the border network, which is configured to closely monitor traffic and deny access from unauthorized hosts. Also can function as a *jail* for an intruder who manages to gain access to the border network. The border network typically consists of Web servers, FTP servers, bastion hosts, and firewalls.

Bottleneck

Slowest-performing point in a process, causing overall performance degradation.

Bounds

The upper and lower limits of an array.

Break

An interruption in program execution or data transmission; a loss of communication between sender and receiver. Also a keyboard key that enables the interruption.

BRGCON

A NetWare 3.11 utility that allows the network manager to monitor Source Route Bridging on the MultiProtocol Router product.

Bridge

Bridges are network devices that are more intelligent than repeaters, in that they can read the specific physical address of devices on one network and filter information before passing it on to another network segment.

Bridges operate at the Data Link layer of the OSI Model or, more precisely, at the Media Access Control (MAC) sublayer. Bridges go beyond simply amplifying the signal and are able to regenerate the signal. This prevents the duplication and spread of line noise. Only a clean signal is sent. This allows bridges to expand a network beyond that which can be accomplished with only repeaters.

In general, bridges are transparent to higher-level protocols. Segments connected through a bridge remain part of the same logical network. Bridges can filter traffic based on addresses. This allows a bridge to reduce traffic between segments and can also be used to improve security by selecting the packets that can be passed between segments.

Briefcase

A specialized folder that allows synchronization of various files across multiple systems.

British Naval Connector (BNC)

A connector for coaxial cable.

Broadband

A technique for transmitting analog signals along a medium, such as a radio wave, also called wideband. Broadband signaling works the way radio and television work, by splitting up the available frequencies into different channels. The data is transmitted simultaneously and is represented by changes in amplitude, frequency, or phase of the signal.

Broadband transmission can be used to transmit different combinations of data, voice, and video information along one physical cable with multiple communication channels of different frequencies. In LAN technology, broadband is a system in which multiple channels access a medium, usually coaxial cable, that has a large bandwidth (50 Mbps is typical) using radio-frequency modems.

Broadcast

1. A transmission of a message intended for general reception rather than for a specific station.
2. In LAN technology, a transmission method used in bus topology networks that sends all messages to all stations even though the messages are addressed to specific stations.
3. A NetWare console command that transmits a message to all network nodes or list of nodes.

Broadcast storm

A situation in which multiple and recursive broadcasting causes a network to bog down from excessive traffic.

Browse mode

A capability provided by DB-Library that allows users to retrieve rows derived from several tables and selectively update columns within it a row at a time.

Browse right

A NetWare object right to view an object in the Directory tree.

Browser

1. This client program (software) is used to look at various Internet resources and retrieve information.
2. Windows service that collects and organizes shared network resources in a hierarchical manner.
3. A NetWare console command that transmits a message to all network nodes or list of nodes.

Browsing

1. Allows you to find objects in the NetWare Directory, which is arranged in hierarchical order.
2. Viewing and retrieving data from the Internet.
3. Viewing available network resources in hierarchical order.

Brute-force attack

An attack based on the simple exhaustion of possibilities to obtain passwords or decrypt a transmission.

BTW

An Internet shorthand for *By the way* in an online forum message. This accepted shorthand allows users to convey condensed messages.

Buffer

A memory area used by a program or device to store data temporarily before that data is used by the physical device or the program's logic.

Buffer Overrun Exploit

A type of attack on a computer system that exploits a fault in a critical system software component to gain unauthorized access to that system. By deliberately overflowing a buffer in a badly written program under proper conditions, the software component can be made to fail in such a way that administrative access is allowed to the system.

Built-in Domain users

User accounts created when Active Directory services are installed and the Active Directory is created.

Built-in group

Windows NT and Windows NT Server default groups. These are groups created during installation.

Built-in Local users

User accounts created when Windows 2000 is installed.

Bulk copy process (bcp)

In SQL Server, the bcp utility is used for transferring blocks of data into or out of the SQL Server. It is designed to be a flexible utility supporting features such as customized file format definitions and selection of individual columns.

Bcp is commonly used for transfers between SQL Server and other database management systems. It can also be used for transfers between SQL Server and other types of programs, such as spreadsheet programs.

When importing through bcp, set the select "into/bulkcopy" option to True on the destination database. You must have the INSERT permission on the destination table. Data is accepted in any ASCII or binary format as long as terminators (delimiters) can be described. The table structures do not need to match, and the data is appended to the destination table.

Terminators are the characters used to separate columns and rows. These are sometimes referred to as delimiters.

When transferring data out through bcp, you must have the SELECT permission on the source table, sysobjects, syscolumns, and sysindexes. You can select the output format.

For both importing and exporting, you need the database name, table name, view name, input or output file, and transfer direction.

BULK INSERT

Transact-SQL statement used for importing data into a table.

Bulletin Board System (BBS)

A popular PC network that allows users to dial into a central point and read group messages, copy public-domain information, and leave messages for other users.

Burst mode

A NetWare utility that allows a protocol window for higher performance.

Bursty

An adjective used to describe data transmission. Data sent in large packets requiring all available bandwidth, but which is quickly gone, is a *bursty transmission.*

Bus

1. A pathway data travels on. Examples of buses include the expansion bus (NuBus or PCI), Apple Desktop Bus (ADB), ISA bus, and SCSI bus.

2. LAN data pathway based on a single cable terminated at both ends.

Bus topology

A bus network topology consists of a linear transmission medium that is terminated at both ends. Nodes attach directly to the bus, making failures difficult to troubleshoot. Any break in the bus causes the entire network to become inoperable. Difficulty in troubleshooting is considered the biggest drawback for a bus topology.

Although a bus normally is drawn as a straight line in pictures and diagrams, most bus networks represent cables that snake, weave, and wrap their way through building's conduits and corridors. This can make the overall length of buses grow rapidly.

Bus topologies commonly use coaxial cable as their transmission medium. Traditionally, Ethernet has used a bus topology.

Business rule

An algorithm that governs how a particular service should be provided or that checks the data integrity against a coroporate rule. Business rules will differ from company to company. They are also subject to change over time due to changes in business processes, priorities, and culture.

Business service

An application serivcethat enforces a business rule. Business services are generally run in the middle-tier. However, those closely tied to data may be run on the database server and those closely tied to user input may be run on the client computer.

Byte

Short for "binary digit eight." A unit of information consisting of usually 8 bits. A file's size is measured in bytes or potential storage capacity is measured in bytes, but when dealing with very large numbers, the terms kilobyte, megabyte, or gigabyte are used.

Bytecode

Machine code created by compiling a Java language source file. Bytecodes are architecture-neutral and interpreted by the underlying Java Virtual Machine.

Bytes per second (Bps)

Usually the number of bytes that can be transmitted or transferred each second.

C

C

A popular programming language that originated concurrently with UNIX, developed by Bell Labs' Thompson and Ritchie. Successor to B. This high-level language is able to manipulate the computer at a low level, like assembly language. In the latter half of the 1980s, C became the language of choice for developing most commercial software and a general replacement for most assembly coding. In modern systems, especially RISC, part of the development strategy is to replace hand optimization of code with reliance on the ability of the compiler to optimize the code.

Cache

An area of computer memory set aside for frequently used data to speed operations. Some caches are general purpose, while others are for specific operations. A disk cache is an area of system memory reserved for caching disk reads and writes. A CPU cache is a dedicated, high-speed memory array used to cache pending instructions. A Web cache is used in proxy servers to serve frequently requested documents.

Cache buffer

Portable NetWare runs as a process program on the host and uses the host's cache, rather than having one of its own. Portable NetWare has a local or spot cache containing the file block that comes right after the block that is being used. Cache blocks have the same size as the host's block size and are assigned by the operating system on an as-needed basis from a cache buffer pool.

Cache memory

A dedicated area of RAM memory used for temporary storage of data. It provides faster access and typically improves overall performance. This is a function of most operating systems and many applications. The specific content of the cache memory is operating-system and application specific.

Caldera OpenLinux

A distribution of Linux aimed at businesses, featuring NetWare support.

Call stack

Contains all of the functions in the calling chain. These methods leave the stack on a Last-In-First-Out (LIFO) basis. For example, if GeneratePhoneList calls GetEmployeeName, which in turn calls GetFirstName, the call to GetFirstName would be at the top of the stack. Calls to asynchronous methods are not stored on the call stack.

Call waiting

The telephone service that allows customers to put a call on hold to answer a second incoming call on the same phone line.

Calling card

A card customers use to bill telephone calls.

CALLMGR

A NetWare 3.11 utility that allows the network manager to manually call other networks from the MultiProtocol Router product.

Captive thread

A thread that has been created by a dynlink package and that will stay within the dynlink code, never transferring back to the client process's code. Also, a thread that is used to call a service entry point and that will never return or will return only if some specific event occurs.

CAPTURE

A NetWare command-line utility that sends an application's print job to a network print queue in cases where the application can direct the job only to a station's LPT port. CAPTURE can also be used to send data to a file and print screen displays.

Carbon copy

This is an electronic mail feature that sends a duplicate copy of a message to all the addresses listed in the carbon copy field. It can also be called a courtesy copy.

Carnivore

A controversial program used by the FBI to scan e-mail before it is delivered or read by the intended recipient. Among other actions, the program looks for phrases that might be considered as indicative of criminal activity.

Carrier Sense Multiple Access (CSMA)

A contention method of operating a network, where multiple nodes *sense* the communications medium and transmit when the medium is free from transmissions. This technology greatly reduces the chance that two stations will try to use the channel at the same time. However, in networks with a large number of stations, another node will likely transmit at the same time and two messages will collide.

Carrier Sense Multiple Access/Collision Avoidance (CSMA/CA)

In a LAN (Local Area Network), when a single resource is to be used by multiple entities, some control method is required to regulate the use of the resources. There are several methods for each station to gain access to the LAN when it needs to send a message. The three main categories of LAN access methods are token passing, contention access, and time slot. CSMA/CA tries to avoid collisions by reserving specific time slots for each of the stations during which they may transmit without threat of collision. This works well for small networks with few stations. However, performance is quickly degraded as the network size and station number increase. A more widely used contention access method is CSMA/CD, where emphasis is on fast detection and recovery of collisions.

Carrier Sense Multiple Access/Collision Detection (CSMA/CD)

The most common implementation of contention access. It is Carrier Sensing in that it listens for systems to transmit. Multiple Access indicates that all systems have concurrent access to the network media. If two or more systems transmit at once, the systems realize the message didn't get through and repeat the messages at different time intervals, thus providing Collision Detection. Collisions slow cable throughput.

Transmission failures can be caused by collisions or bad cabling. It can happen due to improper termination or cable length.

At some point in its growth, an Ethernet network may encounter a reduction in performance. The time when this will occur depends on the amount of traffic generated by each workstation.

Cartesian product

All the possible combinations of rows from two joined tables. If table one contains *m* rows and table two contains *n* rows, the product will be *m* x *n* rows.

Cartridge fonts

A plug-in ROM cartridge that installs in a printer and supplies additional fonts for printing.

Cascade

Updates or Deletes that must be performed on related rows in one table as a result of updates or deletes in another table in order to maintain referential integrity. Implemented through triggers in SQL Server. Cascaded deletes, though not referenced by that term, are a feature of many operating systems.

Case sensitive

Linux allows both upper-case and lower-case characters in filenames and, therefore, requires that files be specified in their proper case. For example, unlike DOS, where the change directory command could be used in either upper case (CD) or lower case (cd), Linux requires that you use lower case as the program file is named using lower-case characters.

Cast

To convert an expression or variable from one data type to another.

CASTOFF

A NetWare 3.x and Portable NetWare command-line utility that prevents network messages from reaching the station. For example, CASTOFF could be used to disrupt an ongoing operation. Messages are displayed after the CASTON command-line utility is executed.

CASTON

NetWare 3.x and Portable NetWare command-line utility that allows a workstation to receive network messages. (In NetWare Lite, a station receives messages with the Receive Message command.)

Catalog stored procedures

A set of system procedures that provide a standard interface to information within the database catalog of any DBMS.

Catenet

A network in which hosts are connected to networks with varying characteristics, and the networks are interconnected by gateways (routers). The Internet is an example of a catenet.

Cathode Ray Tube (CRT)

An output device consisting of a television-like screen used for displaying the letters, numbers, or graphic output of a computer. Most personal computers use a monitor based on CRT technology.

CCITT (Comite Consultatif Internationale de Telegraphique et Telephonique)

An international consultative committee that sets international communications standards. It develops interface, modem, and data network recommendations. Membership includes PTT's scientific and trade associations, and private companies. CCITT is part of the International Telecommunications Union (a United Nations treaty organization in Geneva).

cd

The change directory command (cd) allows moving from one directory to another within the file system. Relative path names are then referenced from the new current directory.

Cdev

The name used to refer to Control Panels in Macintosh OS System 6.

Cell

1. This is a fixed length data element that can be transmitted in asynchronous transfer mode (ATM).
2. Cellular transmission boundary.

Central Processing Unit (CPU)

A highly complex set of electrical circuits that execute stored program instructions. The CPU consists of the control unit and the Arithmetic Logic Unit (ALU). In a personal computer, the CPU is typically a single, powerful microprocessor chip. CPUs can be measured by the amount of data they can read from memory in one access, the number of operations per second, the total amount of memory supported, and whether more than one job can be run at one time. Sophisticated computer systems can have more than one CPU operating within the same system.

Central site

The primary site that houses information about the entire SMS system. All other sites can be managed from the Central site. There can only be one Central site.

Channel

A route for electrical transmission between two or more points.

Channel capacity

The maximum bps (bits per second) a channel can accommodate.

Channel Definition Format (CDF)

An application of the Extensible Markup Language (XML) that provides additional tags that are used to describe channel information, such as the content included in the channel and how often the user should connect to the Web site for updates.

Channels

The technology that allows push updates from a Web site.

Character format

Text format for storing SQL Server data in an operating system text file.

Character set

A set of acceptable and recognizable characters used by a particular computer system or software package. Character sets are binary-coded and often follow a standard such as ASCII, ANSI, or EBCDIC.

Characters per second (cps)

Used as one measure of print speed.

Chart view

System Monitor view displaying real-time performance counter data as a line chart.

Checkbox

A toggle box that is either selected (marked with a checkmark) or unselected.

Checksum

1. A number created for a data set that provides assurance that the data has been delivered correctly.

2. Used in data communications to monitor the number of bits being transmitted between communication devices by means of a simple mathematical algorithm. The checksum is used to ensure that the full complement of bits is received successfully by the receiving device.

3. The checksum is recalculated on arrival or assembly and must match the checksum calculated before sending or fragmentation.

Child process

1. A process that is created by another process.

2. A dependent process; contrast with parent process.

Child site

A site that is directly below another site in the SMS hierarchy.

Child VLM

A Virtual Loadable Module (VLM) that handles a specific usage of a logical grouping of functions. For example, different uses of transport protocols and NetWare server types have their own child VLM: IPXNCP.VLM for IPX protocol services, BIND.VLM for NetWare 2 and 3 bindery servers, NDS.VLM for NetWare 4 NDS servers, and PNW.VLM for Personal NetWare servers.

CHKDIR

Abbreviation for CHecK DIRectory. NetWare 3.11 and Portable NetWare command-line utility that provides information about a specific directory and its volume, including maximum space, amount of space in use, and amount of space available.

CHKVOL

A NetWare command-line utility that provides detailed information about space use, including amount of space occupied by active and deleted files.

Choice list

A pop-up list of strings from which a single string can be selected.

Chooser

The Macintosh OS desk accessory (DA) that provides access to shared network drives and printers via AppleTalk.

chroot

In UNIX, a command that sets up a false root directory for subsequent commands. Often, vulnerable software such as mail and FTP servers will be executed in a *chrooted* environment so that any possible exploit will leave the attacker stranded in a noncritical area of the file system.

Cipher

A Windows 2000 command used for managing data encryption.

Circuit

1. In data communications, a circuit is a means of bidirectional communication between two points, consisting of transmit and receive channels.

2. In electronic design, a circuit is one or more components that act together to perform one or more functions.

Circuit switching

This describes the dedicated communication path (through a system of switches) between two hosts for the length of their exchange of information.

Claim Token

Used by a station to become the active monitor when no active monitor is present on a Token Ring network.

Class

In Visual Basic, the Properties window provides you information about any instance of any object in your application. In this window, one can view the Object name, Detail properties, and the object's Class.

The Class defines an object's characteristics, properties, supported events, and methods.

You can change the properties at design time and, in most cases, at run time. This changes characteristics for that particular instance of the object, but the object still retains its class. In other words, it stays the same kind of object. The object class cannot be changed. If the object class were changed, it would then be a different type of object.

Class library

A library that contains carefully written and tested classes. In Java, a class library is organized into packages.

Class module

Visual Basic object model not having a visual user interface. A class module defines an object class that is used to create an instance of the object.

Clean installation

Refers to a new installation of Windows 2000 as opposed to an upgrade.

Cleanup

SQL Server replication process-distributed updates and sync information are removed.

CLEAR STATION

A NetWare 3.x and 4.x console command used to sever the workstation's connection with the file server when a workstation crashes. The CLEAR STATION command closes files and breaks the workstation/file server communication link but does not break any links the workstation has to other file servers.

CLIB

A NetWare Loadable Module in 3.x or 4.x. It is an abbreviation for C LIBrary. CLIB is a library of C language routines used with several other NetWare Loadable Modules.

Client

1. A program that requests the services of another program, often on a separate computer, usually referred to as the server.

2. The portion of a client/server application providing the end-user interface (front-end).

3. In the case of the X Window System, the roles seem backward. The X server provides the local display, and the X client sends information to the display.

Client Access License (CAL)

Microsoft software license allowing one client connection for either per-server or per-seat licensing.

Client area

The area of a window where user interactions occur.

Client Network Utility

SQL Server utility used to manage client and server Network Library configurations and selections.

Client socket

The socket that requests connection to a server socket.

Client software

A software program used to contact and obtain data from a server software program on another computer, often across a great distance. Each client program is designed to work with one or more specific kinds of server programs, and each server requires a specific kind of client.

Client/server applications

Applications that have been designed to operate in a network environment. They usually consist of a front-end client application and a back-end server application.

Client/Server Model

The Client/Server Model concerns networking and provides for distributed computing. Applications and data files are stored on the file server. The files are downloaded to intelligent workstations (the clients) for processing. The results of the processing are uploaded to the server for storage. The server may provide additional services to the client such as printing, communications support, or relational database services.

Most high-level network operating systems use the client/server model. Novell's NetWare and Microsoft Windows NT Server operate in a client/server environment.

The terms client and server are also used when discussing interprocess communication. It is important to keep the term usage in this context separate from describing a network environment. In interprocess communications, the terms server and client refer only to the function of the process within the context of a transaction. When involved in a different transaction, the roles could be reversed.

In interprocess communications, the server is the process that provides information to another process or creates an object that is used by another process. For example, you may have a process that is responsible for gathering data from a spreadsheet and providing it to a presentation program. In this case, the data-gathering process would be referred to as the server.

The client is the process that accepts information from another process or uses an object that was created by another process. In the previous example, the data-gathering process would be the client of the spreadsheet and, at the same time, it is the server to the presentation program. The presentation program would be the client of the data-gathering process.

In the case of the X Window System, the roles seem backward. The X server provides the local display, and the X client sends information to the display.

Clipboard

In a software application, a temporary storage area or buffer for text and graphics that may have been cut or copied from a file. Information in the clipboard can be moved to another area or to another application. If not saved, the contents of the clipboard will be lost when the computer power is switched off.

Clipboard function

A function provided to enable the user or application to extract data from one window to another or from one application to another.

ClipBook

Collection of stored data that may be used as a source for data transfer. Provides nonvolatile storage of clipboard data.

Clipper Chip

A controversial electronic ROM component that allows specified U.S. government agencies to eavesdrop on encrypted communications occuring over the device containing the chip.

Clock speed

The speed (in megahertz) of a processor's primary clock oscillator.

Clock/Calendar

Used to identify the date and time of computer transactions. Certain software programs utilize the date and time functions more than others.

Closed-Circuit Television (CCTV)

One of the many services often found on broadband networks.

CLS

A DOS command to clear the screen in DOS. Supported at the command prompt for Windows NT and OS/2. It is also a NetWare 3.x and 4.x console command that serves the same function.

Cluster

1. A group of data stored together on one or more sectors of a floppy disk or hard disk. (A sector usually contains 512 bytes of data.) When DOS stores data on a disk, it usually breaks the data into smaller sections, which it writes to various places on the disk as appropriate.

2. A group of servers that perform the same service. A cluster of servers can be used to provide load balancing, fault tolerance, or parallel processing. The Beowulf project was begun to design a way to make use of clusters of Linux systems.

Cluster control unit

Also called cluster controller; a device that can control the input/output operations of more than one device connected to it. A cluster control unit may be controlled by a program stored and executed in the unit.

Clustered index

Indexing method where data is stored in index sort order.

Cmd.exe

The program that interprets and runs OS/2 commands.

CMIP Over TCP (CMOT)

An effort to use the OSI network management protocol to manage TCP/IP networks.

CMOS RAM

This memory stores system configuration data, for example, the number of drives, types of drives, and amount of memory. It is battery-powered, so it can retain the date, time, and other information that must be stored when the computer is turned off.

Coaxial cable

Coaxial cable is composed of two conductors that share the same axis. The center cable is insulated by plastic foam. The plastic foam is wrapped with a second conductor, usually foil. All is covered with an external plastic casing.

Common coaxial cable types include 10Base5 (Thick Ethernet), 10Base2 (Thin Ethernet), ARCnet, and Cable TV.

Coaxial cable is resistant to Electro-Magnetic Interference.

Transmissions over coax may be either baseband or broadband. With baseband, the cables carry a single high-speed signal. This is the transmission method used by Ethernet. Broadband coax carries multiple signals, each at a different frequency. Broadband transmission is sometimes used for backbone cables.

Code

A set of rules that specify the way data is represented, such as ASCII or EBCDIC. Code is also used to describe lines of instructions for the computer, as in program code.

Code page

A matrix that assigns graphic and control characters to specific hexadecimal values or code points.

Codec

1. An algorithm for compressing and decompressing files. The acronym was created from the terms COmpressor/DECompressor. This usage is common to multimedia environments.

2. An assembly comprising an encoder and a decoder in the same equipment. Also, a device that performs the dual function of encoding two-way analog data into digital data and two-way digital data into analog data. This usage is particularly relevant to telecommunications.

Coherence

The quality of being in sync with another object.

Collection

A set of similar objects. ActiveX servers use collections to organize and manage objects of the same class. Consumers can generally iterate through a collection or retrieve an object reference by passing an index or the object's name to the collection.

Collision

In some networking schemes, any station may transmit when it senses that the carrier is free. A collision occurs when two stations transmit simultaneously. If a collision is detected, each station will wait for a randomly determined interval before retransmitting the data.

Most network operating systems track retransmissions, which is a good indication of the number of collisions occurring on the network.

Color Graphics Adapter (CGA)

An older monitor technology, CGA was IBM's first attempt at a color monitor for the PC. The CGA had three wires representing the three primary colors (red, green, and blue) plus one wire for intensity. Together these four wires produced color on the display.

Color Manager

Software used to provide effective color matching between a Macintosh display monitor and color printer.

COLORPAL

NetWare COLOR PALette menu utility that specifies colors for five palettes.

Column

Vertical section of a table that stores one attribute for many entities.

Com

An extension for Internet addresses representing commercial enterprises. For example, galedsl@msen.com.

COM+

The latest implemenatation of the Component Object Model. It integrates COM libraries and Microsoft Transaction Server functionality within the operating system. It also provides serveral enhancements, such as Queued Components, In-Memory Databases, and Component Load Balancing.

COM port

A connection on the computer where the cable for a serial device is attached. The serial device could be a printer, network interface card, modem, or other device. COM ports are often called serial ports. COM ports are numbered, and generally COM1 through COM4 are supported on most personal computers. It is possible to have more or less than four COM ports.

Command

Any executable statements.

Command processor

Sometimes shown as COMPROC or CP, a program executed to perform an operation specified by a command. Also, the portion of an operating system that executes commands.

Command prompt

1. A displayed symbol, such as C:>, that informs the user that a DOS system is idle. It represents that the command-line interface is ready to receive input.

2. A displayed symbol, such as $ or #, that informs the user that the command-line interface is ready to receive input. If the command prompt is displaying the # symbol, you can usually assume that the root user is currently logged in. The $ symbol is traditionally used for all other users.

Command subtree

A process and all its descendants.

Command.com

The program that interprets and runs DOS commands.

Command-Line Interface (CLI)

Similar to DOS, Linux allows the manipulation of files and execution of programs from a text prompt. Many experienced users and old-fashioned users prefer the speed of a command-line interface over a graphical user interface (GUI).

Commercial Internet Exchange (CIX)

A consortium of companies formed in 1992 to promote commercial use of the Internet.

Commit

To specify that a transaction should be completed at once.

Comite Consultatif International de Telegraphique et Telephonique (CCITT)

An international consultative committee that sets international communications standards. It develops interface, modem, and data network recommendations. Membership includes PTT's scientific and trade associations, and private companies. CCITT is part of the International Telecommunications Union (a United Nations treaty organization in Geneva).

Commitment, Concurrency, and Recovery (CCR)

An OSI application service element used to create atomic operations across distributed systems. Used primarily to implement two-phase commit for transactions and nonstop operations.

Committed Information Rate (CIR)

When an ISP gives you a CIR, it is a guarantee that your bandwidth will never be below that rate.

Committed memory

Memory that is backed by physical memory.

Common carrier

In the U.S., a private business or corporation that offers general communication services to the public such as telephone, teletype, or intercomputer communications. All common carriers operate under FCC guidelines, and all services offered are subject to tariff schedules filed with and approved by the FCC.

Common Command Language (CCL)

The National Information Standards Organization (NISO) Z39.50 protocol for specifying a command system that can be used to search bibliographic information retrieval systems, such as online library catalogs. The protocol assists in information retrieval across systems.

Common Gateway Interface (CGI)

A set of conventions that allows developers to create programs that run on a Web server. CGI programs are launched by the Web server and receive their input from environmental variables passed over HTTP. Their output is usually HTML. CGI applications are multiplatform and can be developed with Perl, C, C++, C Shell, and Korn Shell. CGI is often used to construct and validate forms, perform database lookups, authenticate a client, or perform other dynamic, customized functions.

Common Management Information Protocol (CMIP)

The OSI network management protocol.

Common Name (CN)

Refers to a leaf object in the NDS tree. This could be a user's login name, a printer object, or a server object.

Any name that points to a leaf object, usually seen as CN=leafobject.

Communication buffer

An area set aside in memory to temporarily hold data packets arriving from other stations. In NetWare, it was formerly referred to as packet receive buffer.

Communication protocols

Rules used by a program or operating system to communicate between two or more points. They allow information to be packaged, sent, and delivered.

Communications rate

Also called the transfer rate or the transmission rate. The communications rate cannot exceed the maximum rate that both devices can handle.

Communications software

To communicate with the modem, communications software is required. The software helps control the modem and specifies what data should be sent where. Communications software is required at both the sending and receiving computers.

Community Antenna Television (CATV)

CATV cable is used for broadband local networks and broadcast TV distribution.

Compact

Windows 2000 command-line command for managing data compression.

Compact Disc Read-Only Memory (CD-ROM)

A read-only optical disc commonly used to distribute applications software or archive data.

Compare right

A NetWare property right that allows users to compare a stated value to an object's property value.

Comparison operators

Operators used for comparing one expression to another. In SQL, they are commonly used in WHERE or HAVING clauses. Operators are = (equal to), > (greater than), < (less than), >= (greater than or equal to), <= (less than or equal to), and != or <> (not equal to).

Compile error

Error occurring while program statements are being typed in the code editor.

Compiler

A program that translates language-specific source code to machine-readable code.

One of the many reasons that Linux became popular in the educational community is the fact that Linux is distributed with an Open Source C compiler. This allowed programming students to write C code, compile it, and test it for free rather than paying for an expensive commercial compiler.

Complementary Metal Oxide Semiconductor (CMOS)

A specialized memory chip, powered by a small battery, that stores basic system configuration information.

Complete Trust Model

In Microsoft Windows NT's complete trust model, each domain can act as both a master domain and a resource domain. In most cases, each domain is managed separately, with access to other domains granted through two-way trust relationships.

The complete trust model is a mix of independence and interdependence—independent in that each domain has its own users and groups. Each domain sets its own access, rights, and permission policies. Each domain administrator is responsible for his or her domain and must be trusted to manage that domain properly.

The model is interdependent because, unless there is a need to share resources between domains, there would be no reason for setting up a complete trust model. Domain administrators must work together to provide resource access while ensuring that security is not compromised.

This model is most appropriate to organizations that do not have a central MIS department available to manage master domains. It often fits well into organizations made up of somewhat independent departments or divisions. Companies must be ready, however, to accept the potential risks inherent in a noncentralized management structure.

Component

Hardware or software that is part of a functional unit.

Component Load Balancing

Allows middle-tier components to run on a cluster of servers. This provides fault tolerance and scalability.

Component Object Model (COM)

A binary specification that allows unrelated objects to communicate with each other. Also known as COM, the Component Object Model is the foundation of the OLE and ActiveX technologies.

Composite indexes

Indexes based on more than one column in a table.

Compressed attribute

The NetWare status flag (Co) indicating a file is compressed.

Compulsory tunnel

A tunnel created by an intermediary system or device that a client can communicate through with the target server.

Computer Emergency Response Team (CERT)

This organization was formed by DARPA in November 1988 to work with the Internet community to improve its response to computer security events for Internet hosts, to raise awareness of computer security issues, and to improve the security of existing systems. CERT products and services include 24-hour technical assistance for computer security incidents, product vulnerability assistance, technical documents, and tutorials. In addition, the team has a number of mailing lists (including one for CERT Advisories at Carnegie Mellon University) and has an anonymous FTP server at cert.org, where security-related documents and tools are archived. The CERT may be reached by e-mail at cert@cert.org and by telephone at +1-412-268-7090 (24-hour hotline).

Computer object

A leaf object representing a computer on the network. Its properties can store data, such as the name of the person the computer is assigned to or the computer's serial number.

Computer Science Network (CSNET)

CSNET was a large computer network located mostly in the United States but with some international connections. CSNET sites included universities, research labs, and some commercial companies. It was merged with BITNET to form CREN.

COMSPEC

NetWare login script command that enters the drive letter and path of the DOS command interpreter (command processor), usually Command.com.

Concatenate

The process of appending the contents of one file or text string to the end of another.

Concentration

Collection of data at an intermediate point from several low- and medium-speed lines for transmission across one high-speed line.

Concentrator

A small programmable device that acts as a communications control unit used to maintain control over a communications network by handling a variety of functions, such as converting code. Concentrators are also used for combining signals from many terminals and then retransmitting these signals over a single channel; also for directing communications traffic, buffering, multiplexing, and polling.

Conceptual design

The design that describes the features and requirements of an application.

Concurrency

The quality of being sure that modifications made by one user are not inadvertently overwritten by changes made by another user. For example, if Jane and Joe are both accessing their joint bank account from different branches of the bank, Jane's withdrawal should not be canceled when Joe withdraws money.

Conditional operators

Statements used to make decisions and set paths of execution based on those decisions.

CONFIG

NetWare 3.x and 4.x console command that displays configuration information about the file server or bridge/router.

Config.nt

The replacement for Config.sys for DOS programs running under Windows NT.

Config.sys

The DOS environment is set up and configured by loading device drivers. This is done through two system configuration files: Autoexec.bat and Config.sys. When DOS is booted, these two files are executed.

Config.sys is a text file. It must be located at the root directory of the boot drive. The Config.sys is called by the Io.sys file and contains commands to configure hardware and load device drivers.

It is always a good idea to make a backup of this file prior to installing a new application. Many applications will automatically make changes to this file during the installation process. It is wise to make note of these changes in case of system errors. Applications that alter this file typically make a backup copy. Refer to the application's documentation for details.

Changes to the Config.sys file will not take effect until the system is rebooted.

Mistakes in the Config.sys file may cause system startup errors. You can bypass the execution of Config.sys by pressing the *F5* key when you see the "Starting DOS" message. Using *F8* instead of *F5* will allow you to selectively bypass commands in the Config.sys file. This can help isolate problem lines within the configuration file.

Config.sys is still supported with Windows 95 to provide backward compatibility.

Configuration Manager

The component of a Plug-and-Play system that manages the software configuration associated with a particular hardware configuration.

Conflict

Two or more devices or programs attempting to use the same system resources at the same time. Conflicts are not uncommon among ISA hardware, as many do not correctly make use of the Plug and Play specification and, therefore, attempt to use interrupts or addresses already in use.

Conflict Catcher

A popular third-party Extensions and Control Panels management utility for the Macintosh.

conf.modules

An alternate naming convention for the kernel module configuration file, now deprecated.

Connecting column

In SQL usage, a column that participates in a join, allowing one table to link with another or with itself. Connecting columns are columns from one or more tables that contain similar values.

Connection

A successful user login to SQL Server.

Connectionless

The model of interconnection in which communication takes place without first establishing a connection. Sometimes called datagram. Examples: LANs, Internet IP and OSI CLNP, UDP, ordinary postcards.

Connectionless Network Protocol (CLNP)

The layer 3 (routed) connectionless protocol used between host nodes in an OSI network.

Connectionless Transport Protocol (CLTP)

Provides for end-to-end Transport data addressing (via Transport selector) and error control (via checksum) but cannot guarantee delivery or provide flow control. The OSI equivalent of UDP.

Connection-oriented

The model of interconnection in which communication proceeds through three well-defined phases: connection establishment, data transfer, and connection release. Examples include X.25, Internet TCP and OSI TP4, and ordinary telephone calls.

Connection-Oriented Network Protocol (CONP)

The layer 3 (routed) connection-oriented protocol used between host nodes in an OSI network.

Console

1. A keyboard and display device directly connected to a system. From the console, an operator sends commands to the system and performs other operations. Also, any UNIX terminal session.

2. In NetWare, a console is a terminal directly connected to a file server or connected by way of the RCONSOLE or ACONSOLE menu utilities. From the console, an operator sends console commands to the file server and performs other server operations. Console commands, issued only from a console, are used to monitor and control the file server and its use by stations.

Consortium for Research and Educational Network (CREN)

CREN, which was founded in 1989 from a merger of BITNET and Computer Science Network (CSNET), operates the BITNET electronic mail and file transfer network for its academic members.

Constant

A name used to refer to a value that does not change during application execution.

Constraints

Under SQL Server, these are applied definitions that help enforce entity integrity, referential integrity, and business rules.

Constructor

A special method that initializes an object when it is first created. A constructor has the same name as its class.

Consumer

The application or component that uses the services provided by another component. For example, if an application uses the Spell Search functionality exposed by Microsoft Word, that application is a consumer of Microsoft Word.

Container login script

This script sets a general environment for all users in a container, for example, an Organizational Unit. These scripts execute before other types of login scripts.

Container object

1. The type of object in NetWare's NDS used to organize other objects on the network into groups, such as work groups, departments, or divisions. A container object will contain other objects.

2. Visual Basic object defining a set of objects as a group.

3. Special type of object within Windows 2000 Active Directory that is used to hold other objects.

Contention

The state that occurs when multiple applications or instances of an application need access to the same resource.

Context

The context points to where you are located in the NDS tree. This serves as a logical pointer to an object such as a user, printer, or server.

Context switch

The immediate switching from one program to another without first closing the files, allowing users to operate several programs concurrently, such as a graphics program and a word processing program. With context switching, unlike multitasking, when one program is being used, the other halts. Advantages of context switching are rapid switching, exchange of clipboard files, and fast data transfer. In a multiple loading operating system such as Macintosh, the programs are held in random access memory.

Control

Visible Visual Basic object used to generate an event or display on-screen information.

Control character

Any one of 32 special hardware control characters and symbols available in ASCII that are used to control a communication process or a peripheral device such as a printer. Control characters may be used to instruct the printer to advance paper or move one line; also can be used to signify the start and finish of a data transmission.

Control Panel

1. On a Macintosh, the Control Panel is a system software utility stored in the Control Panels folder (found in the System Folder). Panels are used to configure various services such as AppleTalk and user preferences such as desktop patterns and wallpaper.

2. Windows-family utility containing management tools.

Control statements

Statements that control the execution flow of a program.

Control Strip

A tool palette included with Macintosh System 7.5 (and later) that allows fast access to commonly used applications.

Control Unit (CU)

In the processor, the CU is the part that retrieves instructions in proper sequence, interprets each instruction, and applies the proper signals to the arithmetic logic unit and other parts in accordance with this interpretation.

Also, one of two parts of the Central Processing Unit (CPU) containing circuits that, with electrical signals, direct and coordinate the entire computer system.

Control-of-flow language

Statements that provide constructs to control the execution flow of statements. These are provided in programming languages, batch languages, and many applications. Examples include IF...THEN...ELSE, GOTO, WHILE, and so on.

Controller

An application that can be used to build solutions using ActiveX objects. Visual Basic is a controller.

Controller board

A device, also called a Host Bus Adapter (HBA), that allows a computer to communicate with another device, such as a hard disk or tape drive. It manages input/output and regulates the operating of the other device.

Conventional memory

The first 640 KB of memory in a PC is called conventional or base memory. It is used to load the DOS command processor, device drivers, and Terminate and Stay Resident (TSR) programs. It is also used by DOS applications.

Cooked mode

A mode established by programs for keyboard input. In cooked mode, OS/2 handles the line-editing characters such as the back space.

Cookie

A data file placed by a remote Web site on a local computer with the help of the local Web browser. It is intended to record information about the user for reuse the next time the site is visited.

Cooperation for Open Systems Interconnection Networking in Europe (COSINE)

A program sponsored by the European Commission, aimed at using OSI to tie together European research networks.

Cooperative multitasking

A multitasking method where an application must release the processor before the next application may be given processor time.

Coprocessor

An auxiliary processor designed to relieve the demand on the main processor by performing a few specific tasks such as floating-point math or graphics calculations. In general, coprocessors handle tasks that would be performed more slowly by the main processor.

COPS

A program for UNIX workstations that evaluates the workstation for security vulnerabilities.

Copy Inhibit attribute

A NetWare file attribute (Ci) that prevents users from copying the file. It is valid only for Macintosh computers.

Copyleft

A copyright notice that both protects the author and his original work as well as giving the ability of a person to use and modify that work so long as credit is given to the original author and the terms of the copyleft agreement are used in all derivitive works.

Core dump

A copy of memory contents saved when a program terminates abnormally (aborts).

Core gateway

One of a set of gateways (routers) operated by the Internet Network Operations Center (NOC) at BBN. The core gateway system forms a central part of Internet routing in that all groups must advertise paths to their networks from a core gateway using the Exterior Gateway Protocol (EGP).

Corporation for Open Systems (COS)

A vendor and user group for conformance testing, certification, and promotion of OSI products.

Correlated subqueries

A SQL subquery that refers to a table in the outer query and hence cannot be processed independently of the outer query. A correlated subquery is evaluated once for each row in the referenced outer table.

Counter log

A log used for collecting performance counter data over time.

Countermeasure

A response to an attack consisting, at least in part, of measures to attack the attacker, disable his attack, and deter him from conducting further attacks.

Country object

A container object that represents a country where your network is located. It organizes other Directory objects. The two-letter standard must be followed in naming a country object.

Cracker

This refers to an individual who attempts to illegally break into a computer system. It is often confused with hacker, an expert at solving problems with computers.

Cracking program

A program designed to obtain passwords or decrypt transmissions, often by *brute force*.

Crash

A system failure or *bomb*. A system crash requires that the user perform a reboot to restart the computer.

Create right

A NetWare file system right that allows the creation of new files or subdirectories and the salvaging of a file after it has been deleted. It is also a container object right allowing creation of a new object in that container.

Crop

Cut the edges off an object so that it can fit in a particular area. Typcally used in reference to graphics.

Crosstalk

The disturbance caused in a circuit by an unwanted transfer of energy from another circuit. Also, interference that occurs when cables are too close to each other, resulting in loss or corruption of data.

Cross-thread marshaling

The process by which arguments are packaged so that they can be used by a different thread.

crypt

In UNIX, a program used to encrypt passwords using DES 56-bit encryption.

Cryptographic key

A string of characters used to encrypt a plaintext message or data stream or decrypt an encrypted message or data stream.

Cryptographic Service Provider (CSP)

A dynamic-link library that is responsible for performing cryptographic services for applications. Microsoft provides the Microsoft Base Cryptographic Service Provider and the Microsoft Enhanced Cryptographic Service Provider (in North America only). Applications use the CryptoAPI to access these services. Third-party developers can build additional CSPs using the CryptoSPI.

Cryptography

The science of creating and decoding encrypted messages.

Current Activity Window

SQL Server Enterprise Manager component that allows viewing and management of current processes and lock activities.

Current loop

1. (Single-current signaling, used in U.S.A.) Methods of interconnecting Teletype terminals and transmitting signals that represent a mark by current on the line and a space by the absence of current.

2. (Double-current signaling, used everywhere else.) A mark is represented by current in one direction and a space by current in the other direction.

Current site

The site you logged in to with the SMS Administrator. The current site is identified by a globe in the Sites window of the SMS Administrator.

Cursor

1. An indicator that keeps track of the current position in the result set.

2. Visual cue provided for data input or user interaction.

Custom control

Nonstandard Visual Basic control implemented as a .VBX or .OCX file.

Customer Information Control System (CICS)

An IBM program and mainframe operating environment designed to enable transactions entered at remote terminals to be processed concurrently by user-written application programs. CICS includes facilities for building and maintaining databases.

Cyberspace

This is a term popularly used to indicate the meeting place of ideas and people using telecommunication technology. It describes the whole range of information resources available through computer networks. Science fiction writer William Gibson coined the term in his novel *Neuromancer.* He also called cyberspace the fourth dimension, created out of information.

Cyclic Redundancy Check (CRC)

A redundancy check in which the check key is generated by a cyclic algorithm. Also, a system checking or error checking performed at both the sending and receiving station after a block check character has been accumulated.

Cylinder

On a disk drive, a cylinder is the data area that can be accessed by all of the drive's read/write heads while they are lined up in a single position. When the *gang-mounted* read/write heads move to a position on one platter, they all move to the same position on every platter. Gang-mounted means that they are moved in unison.

D

Daemon

In UNIX, a program that operates in the background, disconnected from any particular console and often owned by a special noninteractive user as a security measure.

Data

1. In a database, facts about places, individuals, objects, events, concepts, and so on.

2. Used to refer to any stored information.

Data communication

The transfer of data from one device to another via direct cabling; telecommunication links involving modems, a telephone network, or other connection methods. Transfer of information between functional units by means of data transmission, according to a protocol.

Data compression

This refers to the technique that eliminates gaps and redundancies in data files. It is beneficial for users since smaller files take less time to transmit through a network.

A process by which a sampling algorithm is used to reduce the size of a data file. Windows 2000 supports data compression on NTFS volumes only.

Data definition

The process of determining the objects required by a database and their structure.

Data Definition Language (DDL)

The component of a database language that allows for definition of the database and its objects. For example, statements that create, modify, and remove databases and objects.

Data dictionary

The system tables that contain descriptions of the database objects and how they are structured.

Data Encryption Standard (DES)

A widely used and fairly secure encrypting technology based on 56-bit encryption keys.

Data file

1. A collection of related data records, such as a payroll file or an inventory file, organized in a specific manner.

2. An operating system file used to store all or part of a SQL Server database and database objects.

Data Fork

The portion of a Macintosh file that contains the data.

Data integrity

The data quality that exists as long as accidental or malicious destruction, alteration, or loss of data does not occur.

Data Link Control (DLC)

Windows NT, Windows 95, or Windows 98 protocol used for communication with mainframe systems and printers directly attached to a network.

Data Link layer

OSI Layer 2, the OSI layer that is responsible for data transfer across a single physical connection, or series of bridged connections, between two Network entities.

Data manipulation

The process of retrieving and modifying data.

Data Manipulation Language (DML)

The component of the database language that allows data manipulation.

Data modification

Changing data. Under SQL Server, this is through the SQL Statements INSERT, DELETE, and UPDATE.

Data retrieval

Finding and displaying data in the database via queries (SELECT statements).

Data service

An application service that is closely tied to the data or the database structure. Data services are usually run on either the middle-tier server or on the database server.

Data set (DS)

The major unit of data storage and retrieval, consisting of a collection of data in one of several prescribed arrangements and described by control information to which the system has access.

Data stream

All data transmitted through a data channel in a single read or write operation. Also, a continuous stream of data elements being transmitted, or intended for transmission, in character or binary-digit form, using a defined format.

Data structure

A custom variable that can contain multiple variables of various types.

Data structure diagram

A diagram that shows how the objects in a database fit together. It is also called an *entity-relationship (E-R) diagram.*

Data Terminal Equipment (DTE)

In general, devices such as terminals or computers that connect to data communications equipment.

Data Terminal Ready (DTR)

The signal that indicates to a serial device when the data terminal equipment is ready to begin communications.

Data transfer rate

Determines how fast a drive or other peripheral can transfer data with its controller. The data transfer rate is a key measurement in drive performance.

Data Transformation Services (DTS)

SQL Server utility for transferring data into and out of SQL Server. Also performs data mapping and data manipulation.

Data type

1. In SQL Server, identifies the type of data stored in a column and allows for calculating the amount of storage required to hold such a column value.

2. In Visual Basic and other programming languages, defines the type of data that can be stored in a variable.

Database

A collection of interrelated data stored together that is fundamental to a system or enterprise. A data structure for accepting, storing, and providing on-demand data for multiple independent users.

Database Consistency Checker

SQL Server statement used to verify database and database object integrity and consistency.Database device

Database device

SQL Server storage allocation. Supported for SQL Server 6.5 and below. Not used on SQL Server 7.0.

Unlike some other relational database management systems, SQL databases and their transaction logs are not stored as discreet files but in one or more preallocated files, known as database devices. A database device can contain multiple databases. A database can span multiple database devices.

When you install SQL Server, the MASTER (MASTER.DAT) database device is created to store the master, model, tempdb, and pubs databases. The MSDBDATA (MSDB.DAT) and MSDBLOG (MSDBLOG.DAT) database devices are also created. These store the msdb database and its transaction log respectively. The msdb database is SQL Server's scheduling database.

These devices all default to installing under the same path, each with a unique filename. For SQL Server 6.0, the path is d:\SQL60\DATA\. For SQL Server 6.5, the default location is d:\MSSQL\DATA\.

Drive d: defaults to the drive on which the SQL Server program was installed. A different path may be specified during installation.

SQL Server can have up to 256 database and dump devices. Each database device may be up to 32 GB in size.

One or more of the database devices will be the default database devices. Unless otherwise specified, commands default to using this device.

Database Management System (DBMS)

The software that manages the storage and access to the data in the databases.

Database object

A database component such as a table, view, index, stored procedure, etc.

Database Object Owner (DBOO)

The creator or owner of a database object. The DBOO has responsibility for that object only in a database.

Database Owner (DBO)

The creator or owner of a database. The DBO has responsibility for all of the objects in his or her databases.

Database server

1. A server running database management system software.

2. The Microsoft SQL Server that houses the SMS site database.

Data-driven attack

A type of attack that relies on exchanging data in some form with the target computer, typically via an exploit or network SYN flood.

Datagram

A raw network packet containing sufficient information to be routed from source to destination without reliance on previous exchanges.

Datagram Delivery Protocol (DDP)

A layer 3 (routed) protocol used by Apple between Apple-brand computers. DDP is a *connectionless* protocol, which means that it does not require an acknowledgment of delivery.

DataInputStream class

A class used to read primitive Java data types from an input stream.

Data-over-voice

An FDM technique that combines data and voice on the same line by assigning a portion of the unused bandwidth to the data; usually implemented on the twisted-pair cables used for in-house telephone system wiring.

DB-Library

The call-level client API for SQL Server. It is available for a variety of PC, Macintosh, and mainframe platforms.

DCONFIG

NetWare Driver CONFIGuration command-line utility (3.x, 4.x, Portable NetWare) used to change LAN driver information in the IPX.COM shell file (all versions) or NET$OS.EXE. Information includes network address, shell node address and configuration, controller type, and number of buffers.

Deadlock

A condition where two SQL transactions' locks are in direct conflict and neither transaction can continue.

Debian/GNU Linux

Debian is one of the older and stronger Linux distributions on the market today. Debian's most recent release contains more than 2,000 software packages. Like other distributions, Debian is available for free over the Internet.

Debugger

An application that allows a programmer to see the statement that is being executed and the contents of variables or registers to facilitate the location of programming errors.

Declaration

Statement defining a variable or reference to an external procedure in a DLL.

DECnet

Trademark for DEC's communications network architecture that permits interconnection of DEC computers using DDCMP.

Dedicated line

This term indicates a communications line reserved for the use of one customer only.

Default

1. One of a set of operating conditions that is automatically used when a device such as a printer or computer is turned on or reset. Pertaining to an attribute, value, or option when none is explicitly specified.

2. An access modifier that limits access to a class's variables and methods to other classes in the same package.

Default database

The database a SQL Server user is connected to immediately after successful login.

Default drive

The drive the workstation is currently using. It is identified by a drive prompt, such as A:> or F:>.

Default profile

User profile called when a user account does not have an assigned profile or the user's personal profile is not available from the server.

Default server

The server that a workstation attaches to when the NetWare Requester is loaded. The default is the server specified in the NET.CFG file.

Default Sort Order

Selected set of rules governing collation and presentation of data by SQL Server during queries.

Default zone

Usually the first defined zone within a zone list.

Defense Advanced Research Projects Agency (DARPA)

The U.S. government agency that funded the ARPANET.

Defense Communications Agency (DCA)

The government agency responsible for the Defense Data Network (DDN).

Defense Data Network (DDN)

A collection of networks, including MILNET, portions of the Internet, and classified networks used for military purposes. DDN is managed by the Defense Information Systems Agency (DISA).

Defense Information Systems Agency (DISA)

The U.S. government agency that manages the DDN portion of the Internet, including the MILNET. Currently, DISA administers the DDN and supports the users assistance services of the DDN NIC. It was known as the Defense Communications Agency (DCA).

Delegation event model

An event model that separates objects that generate events from objects that receive them. These objects are called event sources and event listeners, respectively.

DELETE

Transact-SQL statement used to remove rows from tables.

Delete Inhibit attribute

A NetWare file system attribute (Di) that safeguards the directory or file from being erased.

Delete right

A NetWare object right that allows users to delete an object from the Directory tree.

DELETED.SAV

A hidden directory in NetWare 3.x, 4.x, and Portable NetWare containing files from deleted directories. DELETED.SAV is automatically created in each volume.

Demilitarized Zone (DMZ)

Named after the buffer region established by the United Nations between North and South Korea at the end of the Korean War.

Demodulation

The decoding of modulated analog signals after being received from a carrier wave so they can be converted back to digital signals. For example, the demodulation or extraction in a television receiver of a video signal from a UHF carrier.

Demultiplexing

Dividing one or more information streams into a larger number of streams.

Denial of Service (DoS) attack

Any attack on a computer system designed to incapacitate the target system by exhaustion of some kind of resource. The system resource, usually network connection bandwidth but also possibly e-mail storms, disk capacity exhaustion, or RAM, is targeted with excessive amounts of a particular kind of traffic, effectively disabling the service.

Denormalization

The process by which decisions are made to violate one or more normal forms in order to improve the performance of the database.

Deny

To remove a permission from a user and block the user from gaining that permission through other permission assignments.

Dependent service

A service that will not run unless a prerequisite service is loaded.

depmod

A command that determines kernel loadable module dependencies.

Design time

The point in an ActiveX control's lifetime during which developers can change property values and have their settings stored persistently. Some controllers, like Internet Explorer, do not support design-time editing of controls. Others, like Visual Basic, do.

Designations

One-to-many relationships among data.

Desk Accessory (DA)

Macintosh system accessories such as the Calculator, Find File, AppleCD Audio Player, Note Pad, and Scrapbook. NetWare for Macintosh provides a desk accessory called the NetWare Desk Accessory (NetWare DA).

Desktop

Most Graphical User Interfaces (GUIs) refer to the work area on the computer screen as the desktop. All window items appear and are moved around on this desktop area.

Desktop file

A file stored on each Macintosh disk containing information about the disk and its contents. This file is not normally visible and may be rebuilt by holding down the Command and Option keys during the system boot process.

Destroy ()

A method that is called just before an applet terminates execution.

Device

Any computer peripheral or hardware component (such as printer, mouse, monitor, or disk drive) capable of receiving and/or sending data, generally through the use of a device driver.

Device driver

Hardware-specific software that acts as an interface between the operating system and the hardware attached to a computer. Device drivers allow applications to communicate with hardware in a controlled and orderly fashion. A device driver is installed when the system is initialized, either by the operating system or through an installable device driver. Some examples of installable device drivers are mouse, graphical/video monitor, communications port, printer, and network interface card.

Device Driver Interface (DDI)

A set of functions a driver provides to allow communication between the device driver and the operating system.

Device independence

The quality of being identical, regardless of the type of monitor or other device that is used to display or print the graphic.

Device Manager snap-in

MMC snap-in that lets you view and manage hardware devices.

Device mirroring

A process whereby data on one SQL Server database device is duplicated on another device.

Device virtualization

A technique used by Windows 95 and Windows 98 to replicate the hardware characteristics of a device in a software interface. This allows more than one application to manipulate a single hardware device at the same time.

Dfs link

Dfs association with an existing network share.

Dfs link replica

Copy of a Dfs link hosted on a different server. It provides redundancy for failover and load balancing and is only supported under domain Dfs roots.

Dfs root

Top-most point (root) of a Dfs hierarchy.

Dfs root replica

Copy of a Dfs root hosted on a different server. It provides redundancy for failover and load balancing and is only supported for domain Dfs roots.

DHCPAck

DHCP server response verifying a DHCP client's acceptance of an IP address and containing a valid lease. The broadcast may include client configuration parameters.

DHCPDiscover

DHCP client broadcast used to locate a DHCP server and request an IP address.

DHCPNAck

DHCP server response for an unsuccessful lease attempt.

DHCPOffer

DHCP server broadcast used to offer an IP address and lease to a DHCP client.

DHCPRequest

DHCP client broadcast used to accept an offered IP address and lease.

Dial network

Synonymous with public telephone network.

Dial-in router

Windows 2000 RRAS configuration that supports IP and IPX WAN connections over dial-up or persistent links.

Dialog box

An on-screen window used to display information. Generally used when user intervention is required, such as clicking on the OK or Cancel buttons.

Dial-up connection

A connection between computers that has been established over standard telephone lines.

Differential database backup

A backup method where only data that has changed since the last full database backup is backed up.

Digital

Devices that represent data in the form of digits, based on the binary system where the binary digits (bits) are zero or one. Also, pertaining to data that consists of digits.

Digital, Intel, and Xerox (DIX)

A type of Ethernet connector.

Digital adapter

The digital display adapter inside the PC transmits digitized color and intensity information to the monitor. The monitor must then decode the digitized data to create the displayed image. Most MDA, CGA, and EGA adapters transmit digital code.

Digital Audio Video

The expansion slot included in Macintosh and Power Macintosh AV models that provides access to the computer's Digital Signal Processing (DSP) hardware.

Digital Certificate

An attachment to an electronic message serving as a means of authenticating the recipient of the message and also to provide a key for use by the recipient to encode any reply.

Digital data

Data represented by digits, perhaps together with special characters and the space character.

Digital envelope

Encrypts a package for transfer across a network or across the Internet. It is encrypted with a public key and decrypted using the corresponding private key. A digital envelope ensures that only the appropriate recipient can decrypt the package.

Digital Multiplexed Interface

One of two voice/data PABX standards for using T1 transmission that involves T1-to-64 Kbps conversion prior to connection to the computer bus; represents a move toward an open architecture. Compare with CPI.

Digital signature

Verifies that the sender of a package is who he claims to be. A digital signature is encrypted with the private key and verified using the corresponding public key.

Digital switch

A star topology local network. Usually refers to a system that handles only data, not voice.

Digital-to-Analog Converter (DAC)

DAC chips are found on analog adapters. Because the PC operates digitally, it sends digitized information to the adapter. If the device accepts analog input only, the DAC on the adapter must convert the digital data into analog instructions for the device.

Digital transmission

The transfer of encoded information using on and off pulses; unlike analog transmission, which uses a continuous wave form and carries more than one channel at a time.

Digital Video Disc (DVD)

An optical storage device that can store up to 17 GB of data. It is typically used for storing video and other types of multimedia. A DVD player can read standard CD-ROMs.

Direct device name

A defined SQL Server dump device.

Direct inward dial

A telephone line that can accept incoming calls for various numbers but cannot make outgoing calls.

Direct Memory Access (DMA)

Direct Memory Access (DMA) channels allow devices to communicate directly with memory. This is generally used with add-in boards or devices that transfer large amounts of data. Examples include network interface cards, CD-ROMs, and sound cards.

IBM XT-style systems have four available DMA channels (0 through 3). ISA/AT, MCA, and EISA systems have eight DMA channels (0 through 7).

Each device that uses DMA must have its own unique DMA channel. Channel 0 is available in ISA/AT-type systems and above. Channel 1 is used for the disk controller in XT systems but is available for AT-style systems and above. DMA channel 2 is used for the floppy disk controller. Channels 3 through 7 are available for use.

For some devices, use of a DMA channel may be optional but will normally result in improved performance.

DirectDraw

A DirectX media service that allows programmers to create high performance graphics by providing an optimal device-independent interface to the hardware.

DirectInput

A DirectX media service that provides optimized access to input devices.

Directory

1. Part of a structure for organizing files on a disk. A directory can contain files and subdirectories. The structure of directories and subdirectories on a disk is called a directory tree. The top-level directory in a directory tree is the root directory. In Windows 2000, the Active Directory provides the methods for storing directory data and making this data available to network users and administrators.

2. In NetWare, the highest organizational level is the file server. Each server's main directory is called a VOLUME, and subdirectories are called directories.

Directory and file permissions

These permissions, assigned to users and groups, set user access level.

Directory and file rights

These rights control what a NetWare trustee can do with a directory or file.

Directory caching

A way to decrease the time it takes to find a file's location on a disk.

Directory entry

Information on directories and files, such as file or directory name, owner, date and time of the last update (for files), and location of the first block of data on the network hard disk.

Directory entries are located in a directory table on a network hard disk and list information about all files on the volume. The server uses this information to track file location, changes made to the file, and other related properties.

Directory Entry Table (DET)

A table containing information about files, directories, directory trustees, or other items on the volume.

Directory Map object

A leaf object that refers to a directory on a volume.

Directory path

Information including the server name, volume name, and name of each directory connected to the file system directory you need to access.

Directory permissions

A list of permissions given to a particular directory. They can include, but are not limited to, read, write, and execute permissions. Permissions are assigned on a user or group basis.

Directory rights

Rights that specify what a trustee can do with a directory in the file system.

Directory Server Postoffice

Primary postoffice Microsoft Mail directory synchronization containing the global address list.

Directory services

Services utilized within Active Directory or NetWare 4.x and later that store information about network resources in one centralized location in order to simplify administrative management of the domain.

Directory structure

Most computers use a tree or filing system to organize volumes, directories, files, and data on their hard disks.

Directory Synchronization

A process for automatically transferring user list changes and updates between Microsoft Mail postoffices.

Directory System Agent (DSA)

The software that provides the X.500 Directory Service for a portion of the directory information base. Generally, each DSA is responsible for the directory information for a single organization or organizational unit.

Directory tree

A hierarchical structure of objects, based on a logical or physical organization of objects, in the Directory database.

Directory User Agent (DUA)

The software that accesses the X.500 Directory Service on behalf of the directory user. The directory user may be a person or another software element.

DirectShow

A DirectX media service that provides video capture, playback, and media streaming.

DirectX

A set of APIs designed to provide developers of multimedia applications with the tools they need to access hardware accelerators and provide streaming and animation.

DISABLE LOGIN

A NetWare console command that prevents users from logging in to the file server, as when hardware or file maintenance needs to be done. The ENABLE LOGIN console command restores use.

DISABLE TTS

A NetWare console command that temporarily turns off the Transaction Tracking System (TTS). The purpose of the DISABLE TTS command is to permit testing of applications that might conflict with TTS.

Discrete access

An access method used in star LANs; each station has a separate (discrete) connection through which it makes use of the LAN's switching capability. Contrast with shared access.

Disjoining LDT space

The LDT selectors reserved for memory objects that are shared or that may be shared among processes.

Disk

A circular object with a magnetic surface used to store files (programs and documents) on a computer. For example, a floppy or hard disk.

Disk Cleanup

Utility that can be used to locate and remove temporary and other unused or unneeded files.

Disk Defragmenter

Utility used to analyze and defragment disk partitions, logical drives, and volumes.

Disk drive

A magnetic or optical device used to store files and folders. Types of disk drives include fixed (hard) disks, floppy disks, and removable media such as Syquest, Jaz, Zip, and magneto-optical (MO) disks.

Disk driver

1. Software device driver allowing the operating system to communicate with a hard disk controller.

2. NetWare NLM (with a DSK extension) that interfaces between the NetWare server operating system and the hard disk controller. The disk driver communicates with an adapter connected to the disk drives. Depending on the type, one or more disk drives can be connected. Drivers are loaded into the operating system during installation or at the command line.

Disk Druid

Disk partitioning software more convenient and helpful than fdisk.

Disk duplexing

Disk duplexing is an implementation of Redundant Array of Independent Disks (RAID) Level 1 and is similar to disk mirroring. It uses two disk drives that are configured to have the same logical size. Both drives are connected to separate disk controllers. During each data write, the same data is written to both disks.

Disk I/O performance is generally better than when using disk striping with parity. Performance is better during data reads than with disk mirroring.

The boot partition (active system partition) can be duplexed.

Disk duplexing is designed to keep a network going in spite of disk errors or the loss of a hard disk. If a read error occurs, data from the other disk is used.

If one drive or controller fails, the server will continue running by using the other drive and controller. Users can continue to work without interruption.

Disk duplexing is normally used on peer-to-peer networks and smaller LANs for the protection of critical data files. Due to the amount of storage lost through redundancy, it is not commonly used on larger LANs.

Disk fragmentation

A phenomenon that occurs during normal system usage. As files are copied to, moved, and deleted from a disk drive, the disk blocks used to store data become fragmented (split to different areas of the disk). Fragmented files require more time to retrieve and can result in a condition known as *disk thrashing*–a significant amount of head movement required to read or write all of the blocks of a file. Disk optimization utilities such as Norton Speed Disk can be used to place files into contiguous disk blocks, which allow data to be efficiently stored and retrieved.

Disk Management

MMC snap-in used for managing hard disks, disk partitions, and disk volumes.

Disk mirroring

Disk mirroring is an implementation of Redundant Array of Independent Disks (RAID) Level 1. It uses two disk drives configured with equal-sized partitions and connected to the same disk controller. During each data write, the same data is written to both disk partitions.

With disk mirroring, disk utilization is 50% of the dedicated storage space. I/O performance generally is better than when using disk striping with parity. A mirrored pair can be split without loss of data.

Disk mirroring is designed to keep the computer operational in spite of disk errors or loss of a hard disk. If a read error occurs, data from the other disk is used. If one drive fails, the server will continue running by using the other drive.

Use disk mirroring when data must be protected against drive failures, and hard disk resources are and will be plentiful as system requirements grow.

Disk mirroring is normally used on peer-to-peer networks and smaller LANs to protect critical data files. Due to the amount of storage lost through redundancy, it is not commonly used on larger LANs.

Disk Operating System (DOS)

The software programs that control the operation of the computer and the movement of information throughout the computer system.

DOS is the medium by which the user communicates with the computer system and manipulates data.

Disk partitioning

Hard disk initialization takes care of the physical preparation of the hard disk. The logical disk preparation must also be completed. This involves partitioning the hard disk.

When a hard disk is partitioned, logical divisions are created on the hard disk. This makes the disk storage areas available to the system. Multiple partitions may be created on the same hard disk, including partitions for different operating systems. For example, a hard disk may be set up as an OS/2 dual boot system with both DOS and OS/2 disk partitions.

Partitioning creates a partition table for each partition. The partition table contains information such as the partition type (operating system), size, and any logical drives configured within the partition.

When the disk is partitioned, the active partition must be identified. This is the partition that is read by the system during system startup. The active partition is also referred to as the boot (bootable) partition.

Disk partitions may be changed at any time, but extreme care must be taken. Creating, deleting, or modifying the size of disk partitions will cause all of the information in the affected partitions to be lost.

Linux usually requires a minimum of two partitions, one for the file system and one for swap space. It is possible to run Linux without a swap partition, but it is not recommended. It is also possible to install Linux on a FAT partition, as used by DOS, however, it is preferable to let Linux have its own partition.

Linux uses partition type 83 for its file system and partition type 82 for swap partitions.

Disk quota

Windows 2000 feature allowing limits to be set on users' available disk space. Disk quotas are set by volume and by user. Disk quotas are only supported on NTFS volumes.

Disk striping

A method of spreading data evenly across multiple physical hard disks.

Disk striping with parity

Disk striping is an implementation of Redundant Array of Independent Disks (RAID) Level 5. Microsoft Windows NT Server does the same thing as commercial RAID drive arrays but through software rather than hardware.

Between 3 and 32 disk drives may be included in an NT Server stripe set. The disk space used on each drive will be approximately the same. NT Server will match the space selected to the smallest single partition when the stripe set is created.

Disk striping provides improved performance on disk reads. Disk utilization is reduced by the size of one disk drive.

Data and parity is spread across all of the drives in a stripe set. As data is written, it passes through an algorithm to generate the information for the parity stripe.

The way data clusters are organized, large data files tend to get written across multiple drives. There is a loss in write performance; however, this is made up by splitting read requests, giving excellent read performance and improved data security.

Possibly more important is the data security aspect. If a drive is lost, the system can recover any missing data by going through its calculations on the remaining data and parity stripes. When this happens, read performance suffers. All of the data can be re-created when the drive is replaced.

When implementing disk striping without parity, data is written to the drives in much the same manner. The major difference is that the stripe used here for parity is instead used for additional data storage.

One thing to remember is that the boot partition (active system partition) cannot be a stripe set.

Disk striping with parity is normally used on large networks where data integrity and minimized down time are critical concerns. While the amount of storage space lost can be significant, as more drives are added, the percentage of space lost to parity becomes less.

Use disk striping with parity when multiple hard disks are available, optimal read performance is desired, and data integrity is a critical concern. You are protected against the failure of any one drive. A failing drive should be replaced as soon as possible, even though the users can continue working after the failure. Performance will be the same on disk writes but will degrade on disk reads.

When performance is the overriding concern and budget constraints allow, you should install a RAID disk subsystem rather than configuring discrete hard disks through disk striping with parity. A RAID disk subsystem, though more expensive, will provide significantly better performance.

Diskperf

Command-line command that is used to activate and deactivate disk performance counters.

DISKSET

A NetWare utility that identifies an external hard disk drive for a Disk Coprocessor Board (DCB) and enables hard disk drive/file server communication. The identifying information is stored in a programmable chip on the board and includes disk type, controller address or number, and channel number. Each external drive must be defined for each DCB. DISKSET can also be used to back up or restore external drive information or to change previously entered information. In 3.x and 4.x, it can also be used to format an external drive.

DISMOUNT

A NetWare 3.x and 4.x console command that prevents users from accessing any volume that has been made available using the MOUNT console command. DISMOUNT allows for completion of maintenance of the volume without closing down the file server on which it resides. Dismounting unused volumes frees cache memory for other uses.

Dispatch program

Microsoft Mail program controlling directory synchronization.

Dispinterface

The dispatch interface that is used by the IDispatch method in OLE Automation.

DISPLAY

A NetWare login command that provides for display of an ASCII text file when the user logs in to the server.

Display adapter

The circuitry used to drive a video display monitor. Some computers include the video adapter circuitry on the system board while others require an expansion card. There are two formats with which data may be sent from the adapter to the display: analog or digital.

DISPLAY NETWORKS

A NetWare 3.x and 4.x console command that displays a list of networks known to the router. Each network is identified by the network address, the number of networks that must be crossed to reach it (hops), and the time required to transmit a packet in eighteenths of a second (ticks) to that network.

DISPLAY SERVERS

A NetWare 3.x and 4.x console command that displays a list of file servers and other service devices such as print servers known to the bridge/router. Each server is identified by a server name and the number of networks that must be crossed to reach the server (hops).

Distance education

Using computers and networks, such as the Internet, to provide teachers/resources to students.

Distributed architecture

A LAN that uses a shared communications medium. Uses shared access methods; used on bus or ring LANs.

Distributed Component Object Model (DCOM)

DCOM is an extension to the Component Object Model that allows components to be run across machines. It is more optimal than its predecessor, Remote Automation, because it only marshals arguments once. DCOM is only available for 32-bit operating systems.

Distributed computing

The name of the trend to move computing resources such as minicomputers, microcomputers, or personal computers closer to individual workstations.

Distributed Computing Environment (DCE)

An architecture of standard programming interfaces, conventions, and server functionalities (e.g., naming, distributed file system, remote procedure call) for distributing applications transparently across networks of heterogeneous computers. Promoted and controlled by the Open Software Foundation (OSF), a consortium led by HP, DEC, and IBM.

Distributed Data Management (DDM)

Allows transparent record-level access to files on remote machines.

Distributed database

This collection of information files or databases resides at different sites yet appears to the user to be a single database.

Distributed File System (Dfs)

Technology that allows file system resources across the entire network to be browsed and accessed within a hierarchial display. The physical location of the files is transparent to the user. Windows, NFS, and Samba all provide Dfs services.

Distributed Internet Application Architecture (DNA)

An *n*-tier architecture that divides an application into user services, presentation services, and data services. This is also called Windows DNA.

Distributed processing

A technique for implementing a set of information processing functions within multiple, physically separate physical devices.

Distributed query

A single query accessing data from multiple data sources (multiple servers or databases).

Distributed transaction

An SQL Server transaction affecting multiple servers.

Distributed Transaction Coordinator

The SQL Server 7.0 service that coordinates transactions that cross machine boundaries. DTC guarantees that if all servers involved in the transaction are happpy, the transaction will be committed. If any one server in the distributed transaction is unhappy, the transaction will be rolled back.

Distribution agent

The SQL Server replication component responsible for updating Subscribers with the contents of the distribution database transaction log and scheduled Snapshot jobs.

Distribution database

Database holding transactions waiting distribution to Subscribers as well as status information about replication activities.

Distribution folder

Shared folder used as the installation source during Windows NT and Windows 2000 over-the-network installations.

Distribution group

Active Directory domain group used for distribution management, typically e-mail distribution.

Distribution List object

A leaf object that represents a list of mail recipients, including users, other Distribution List objects, Group objects, or Organizational Role objects.

Distribution server

A server that contains a distributed copy of a package's source directory.

Distribution statistics

Selectivity and distribution information maintained by SQL Server for index key values.

Distributor

The SQL Server responsible for Subscriber updates. A Distributor can support multiple Publishers and multiple Subscribers.

dmesg

A command to list messages (error and other) that had been displayed to the operating console, which are stored in the file /var/log/dmesg.

Document-centric design

A technique used by Windows 95 that allows users to focus on documents instead of their associated applications.

DOMAIN

In NetWare, used as a console command that will create a protected operating system domain for running untested NLMs in Ring 3. This prevents a module from interfering with the core operating system.

Domain

In the Internet, a domain is a part of the naming hierarchy. The domain name is a sequence of names (separated by periods) that identify host sites. For example: galenp@mail.msen.com.

Domain controller

Server within a domain and storage point for domainwide security information. This also refers to a partition of the Active Directory the Windows NT Server holds.

Domain Dfs root

Dfs root hosted by a server but stored in Active Directory services. Root and link replicas are supported.

Domain Information Groper (DIG)

A tool for interactively gathering information from DNS servers.

Domain integrity

Integrity that enforces column values to adhere to the underlying domain definitions.

Domain Local group

Active Directory domain group scope. In mixed mode, members can include user accounts from any domain in the forest or Global groups from any domain in the forest. In addition, Domain Local groups from the same domain and Universal groups from any domain in the forest are supported in native mode.

Domain model

A method of organizing Windows NT Server domains for security and management.

Domain name

A unique domain name designates a location on the Internet. Domain names always have two or more parts separated by periods. The leftmost part is the most specific, and the part on the right is the most general. A given machine may have more than one domain name, but a given domain name points to only one machine.

Domain Name System (DNS)

A hierarchical, distributed method of organizing systems and network names on the Internet. DNS administratively groups hosts (systems) into a hierarchy of authority that allows addressing and other information to be widely distributed and maintained. A big advantage of DNS is that using it eliminates dependence on a centrally maintained file that maps host names to addresses.

The diagram above shows the hierarchical organization of domain names. The bottom level of the tree structure contains the names of companies or even machines within a company. For example, consider wuarchive.wustl.edu. The bottom of the tree is wuarchive. This is the name of a particular piece of equipment within the wustl domain, which is under the edu domain.

The name of a particular domain is read from the bottom of the tree up to the root. The root is unnamed and is represented with just a period. For example, wavetech.com is a particular domain. If we were to give the Fully Qualified Domain Name (FQDN), we would include the unnamed root, so it would be written as "mycompany.com." The final period at the end of the name specifies the root of the tree. The root must always be specified for the host equipment. To make it easy, most software will convert a domain name to an FQDN for the user by appending any missing domain names all the way to the root.

The top of the tree lists the top-level domains. These are reserved names. Every domain will have a top-level domain by type or country.

Domain SID

Unique value embedded in the SID for all domain servers, workstations, users, and groups. The Domain SID identifies domain ownership of objects.

Domain user account

A user account created as an Active Directory object and used for domain logon and resource access verification.

Don't Compress attribute

A NetWare file system attribute (Dc) that protects files from compression.

Don't Migrate attribute

A NetWare file system attribute (Dm) that protects files from migration to a secondary storage device, for example, a tape drive or optical disc.

Don't Suballocate attribute

A NetWare file system attribute (Ds) that prevents individual files from being suballocated, even if suballocation is enabled for the system. It is most often used for files that are often enlarged or appended, for example, database files.

DOS client

A workstation that boots with DOS and accesses the network through the NetWare DOS Requester software (for NetWare 4) or a NetWare shell (for NetWare 3, and NetWare 4 with bindery services). While on the network, users can map drives, capture printer ports, and send messages with DOS software. Users can also change contexts using the NetWare Requester in NetWare 4.

DOS Open Data-link Interface (ODI)

Novell ODI software that allows various network protocols to be used on a single network board and forms a logical network board that emulates various protocol configurations on the installed board. The logical network board operates as if physical boards were being used.

DOS prompt

The character or characters that appear at the beginning of the DOS command line. This indicates that the computer is ready to receive input.

DOS Requester

Software that enables a DOS workstation to communicate on a network.

Dot pitch

On color monitors, the dot pitch is the mask through which the electron beam is focused for each set of red, green, and blue phosphors. The dot pitch is the spacing between the holes. The smaller the spacing, the more dots and phosphors; therefore, a finer (i.e., smaller) dot pitch provides a sharper image.

Dots per inch (dpi)

A measurement (dpi) of the resolution of a video display monitor, printer, or other output device.

Dotted-decimal notation

The syntactic representation for a 32-bit integer that consists of four 8-bit numbers written in base 10 with periods (dots) separating them. Used to represent IP addresses in the Internet, as in 192.67.67.20.

Double Density (DD)

Density refers to how tightly data can be recorded on the media. The name, "Double Density (DD)," came from recording improvements over the original method. The capacity of the diskette was effectively doubled.

Double Sided (DS)

For diskettes, the ability to write to both sides of the diskette medium is called double sided (DS).

Double Sided, Double Density (DSDD)

Can refer to both the medium being used, a DSDD floppy diskette, for example, and the drive's mechanical recording capabilities, a DSDD floppy diskette drive.

Double Sided, High Density (DSHD)

Can refer to both the medium being used, a DSHD floppy diskette, for example, and the drive's mechanical recording capabilities, a DSHD floppy diskette drive.

DOWN

A NetWare console command that automatically performs file and network functions in preparation for turning off the file server. DOWN saves file updates from the buffer, closes files, updates system records, and closes the operating system.

Download

A process where a file is transferred from a host computer to a user's computer. Download is the opposite of upload.

Downloadable font

Also known as soft font, an electronically represented printer font (a graphic design of characters and symbols) that must be installed on the computer and sent to a printer before it can be printed.

Downloading

Downloading is the transfer of a file from a remote computer to the user's computer.

Drawing Interchange Format

A file format commonly used by 3D Illustration and CAD/CAM applications.

DRIVE

A NetWare login script command that specifies the drive that will be presented to the user after the login script is completed. This is the default drive.

Drive mapping

A letter assigned to a directory path on a network drive. To locate a file, users follow a path that includes the drive letter and any subdirectories leading to the file.

Drive type

The drive type number is placed in a table stored in the computer's CMOS memory. The table identifies the drive and its characteristics (number of read/write heads, storage capacity, number of cylinders, number of sectors per track, etc.) so that the operating system knows how to access the drive.

Driver

Software used to allow the operating system to communicate with an add-on hardware device such as a disk controller or display adapter.

Drop

Individual connections (sometimes called nodes) on a multipoint (also called multidrop) circuit.

DSPACE

A NetWare 3.x menu utility that allows the administrator to restrict the size in kilobytes of the disk space assigned to a directory or restrict disk space on a given volume available to a user.

Dual, In-Line Memory Module (DIMM)

A high-density, 168-pin module used to package RAM.

Dumb terminal

A workstation consisting of keyboard and monitor. A dumb terminal is used to put data into the computer or receive information from the computer. Dumb terminals were originally developed to be connected to computers running a multiuser operating system so that users could communicate directly with them. All processing is done at and by the computer, not the dumb terminal.

In contrast, a smart terminal contains processing circuits that can receive data from the host computer and later carry out independent processing operations.

Dump

Backup of a database or transaction log onto another device whether it be the same or different media. Dumps are used for regularly scheduled backups or to recover from media failures. The term is used less often with SQL Server 7.0, where the term "backup" is preferred.

Dump devices

SQL Server devices defined to receive data during a dynamic dump.

Duplex transmission

A method of transmitting information over a communications channel in which signals may be sent in both directions. Other methods of transmission include half duplex, full duplex, and simplex.

Duplexing

A method of protecting data by duplicating it onto two hard disks, each on a separate disk channel.

Dynamic

Pertaining to a priority of a process that is varied by the operating system. Contrasts with absolute priority.

Dynamic Data Exchange (DDE)

A process that allows two applications to exchange information.

Dynamic disk

A Windows 2000 disk configuration that supports disk volumes rather than industry-standard disk partitions. Basic disk is an industry-standard disk partitioning scheme.

Dynamic Domain Name System (DDNS)

A newer standard of DNS where client hosts can automatically register A (host) and PTR (pointer) resource records. DDNS allows clients with a dynamically assigned address to register directly with the Windows 2000 DNS server and update the DNS table dynamically.

Dynamic drive

Dynamic attach and release of network drives under Microsoft Mail.

Dynamic dump

Also called a Dynamic Backup. Process of backing up active databases and logs.

Dynamic heap

A block of memory set aside to allocate memory as it is needed.

Dynamic Host Configuration Protocol (DHCP)

A TCP/IP application-layer protocol that provides for dynamic address assignment on a network.

Dynamic HTML (DHTML)

An extension to HTML that provides Web developers with an object model they can use to create interactive Web pages. DHTML is interpreted by the browser.

Dynamic linking

Using an update command to ensure that all data changed in one program is automatically changed in another program, thereby keeping the data consistent. Dynamic linking is particularly useful in database management.

Dynamic priority

The priority assigned to a thread in response to how the user interacts with it.

Dynamic Random Access Memory (DRAM)

The most commonly used memory type for personal computers. Because of its passive componentry design, DRAM requires a periodic refresh signal to maintain valid data.

Dynamic-Link Library (DLL)

A module that is linked at load time or run time.

E

ECHELON

A controversial secret spying network reputed to have been created during the Cold War under the aegis of the NSA, shared by English-speaking Western block countries. Little is known about its operation or architecture. Its existence is routinely denied by member governments.

Echo

The reflection of transmitted data back to its source. Also a phenomenon in voice circuits.

Echoplex

An asynchronous communications protocol in which the information sent to the receiving station is echoed to the sender, or transmitter, to acknowledge correct receipt of data. Also, low-speed data transmission usually used between a keyboard unit and the computer. When a key is struck on the keyboard, a character is sent over the line and echoed back to the sending unit, where it is shown on a screen or printed.

EDIT

A utility program for creating or editing ASCII text files such as batch or CONFIG.SYS files. This DOS utility was introduced with DOS 5.0. In NetWare 3.x and 4.x, a similar utility is available as a loadable module.

Edu

The Internet address suffix that identifies educational institutions. For example, xxx@stanford.edu.

Effective rights

The rights that allow an object to see or modify a particular directory, file, or object. NetWare determines an object's rights to a directory, file, or object each time an action is attempted. Effective rights to a file or directory are set by the trustee assignments of the object to the directory, file, or other object. Effective rights can also be inherited rights from an object's trustee assignments to parent directories. Trustee assignments of Group objects to which a User object belongs and trustee assignments of objects listed in a User object's "Security Equal To" list.

Electron gun

Enclosed in the CRT, the electron gun produces a beam that fires at the phosphor elements on the screen, causing them to produce a single pixel of light on the display. The electron gun is controlled by the incoming digitized or analog data sent from the adapter.

Electronic Data Interchange (EDI)

A specialized application of electronic mail referring to the transfer of customized business forms such as invoices, purchase orders, and shipping notices. EDI usually requires special protocol conversions and a prearranged business agreement between trading partners. In a general electronic mail environment, by contrast, each user receives a mailbox that can accept unstructured mail from anyone on the system. EDI systems are also capable of verifying authorization on orders and connecting orders with invoices.

Electronic Frontier Foundation (EFF)

A foundation established to address social and legal issues arising from the increasingly pervasive use of computers as a means of communication and information distribution.

Electronic mail (e-mail)

The most popular Internet application and the driving force behind the Internet's rapid growth. While controlling another computer remotely or transferring files from one computer to another may be useful, neither is as exciting as being able to communicate with millions of Internet users around the globe. Many users join the Internet just for e-mail access.

Fortunately, it is possible to exchange e-mail with people that are not directly part of the Internet. For example, by using gateways to other public e-mail networks, Internet e-mail can reach users with commercial service provider accounts such as CompuServe, BITNET, America Online, Prodigy, and the Microsoft Network. E-mail can also reach users who work at companies that get their mail access from corporate network providers such as MCImail, Applelink, and uuNet.

E-mail is popular because it works very quickly, while traditional mail can take a day or two to cross town or weeks to reach an international destination. E-mail can travel from sender to receiver within hours (sometimes minutes) despite the distance between them. If the network is extremely busy or if an administrator configures a user's system to send e-mail once a day (as opposed to every few minutes), the e-mail may take a little longer to arrive. In general, however, e-mail moves around the world at a rapid pace. It is possible for a person in the U.S. to send a message to West Africa, receive a response, and send another message, all in the space of an hour.

E-mail is also very flexible. Users can attach different types of files to their e-mail messages. Marketing can embed audio and video clips within text messages, co-workers can transfer spreadsheets or project updates, families can share pictures and birthday messages.

Electronic mail address

Designation given to an individual or domain that directs messages or other information over computers in general to a specific person or destination.

EMACS

A UNIX text editor (Editor MACroS) developed at MIT that includes a number of distinctive features including multiple windows and an internal programming language based on LISP. Common alternative to vi.

Embedded object

Information created in one document and inserted into another document. The two documents usually were created in different applications.

Emoticon

An ASCII art symbol used to indicate *inflection* or emotion in an e-mail text message. The most common emoticon is a smiling face turned sideways.

Empty variable

A variable not assigned a value, returning either 0, zero-length string, or null.

EMSNETx.COM

NetWare expanded memory shell file that places most of the NetWare shell in a workstation's expanded memory. The x represents the station's version of DOS. For example, EMSNET5.COM is used for DOS 5.x, EMSNET3.COM for DOS 3.x. Novell has also released a "universal" version of this program called EMSNETX.COM. (In this case, the X is the character "X," not representative of a number.) This version of the program works with DOS versions 3.x through 5.x. The file is automatically executed when the filename is included in the Autoexec.bat file.

Emulation

The imitation of all or part of one system by another. This can be accomplised either in hardware or software. The imitating system accepts the same data, executes the same programs, and achieves the same results as the imitated system.

Products such as SoftWindows and Virtual PC allow Macintosh computers to emulate the Windows or Windows 95 operating system and an Intel-based PC.

Apple designed the "68K" emulator for the PowerPC processor in order to allow Power Macintosh computers to run older 680x0-specific software.

ENABLE LOGIN

NetWare 3.x and 4.x console command that allows the user to log in to a file server after access has been prevented with the DISABLE LOGIN command.

ENABLE TTS

NetWare 3.x and 4.x console command that restores the Transaction Tracking System (TTS) after it has been disabled automatically by the file server due to memory limitations or disabled manually with the DISABLE TTS console command.

Encapsulated PostScript (EPS)

A file format used by graphics and publishing applications.

Encapsulation

In Object-Oriented Programming (OOP), encapsulation defines a data structure of attributes and a group of member functions as a single unit called an object. In networking, encapsulation is the process of enclosing packets of one type of protocol by another.

Encrypting File System (EFS)

Windows 2000 data encryption service based on a user's public and private keys. Data encryption is only supported on NTFS volumes.

Encryption

The process of encoding information so that it is difficult for others to read or modify it. The two main types of encryption are symmetric and asymmetric, which is also known as public key encryption. The Data Encryption Standard (DES) is a popular symmetric encryption algorithm. RSA is a popular public key algorithm.

End system

An OSI system that contains application processes capable of communicating through all seven layers of OSI protocols. Equivalent to Internet host.

End System-Intermediate System (ES-IS)

The routing protocol used between routers and end nodes to assist in finding each other.

ENDCAP

Abbreviation for END CAPture. A NetWare command-line utility that reverses the effect of the CAPTURE utility. The CAPTURE utility takes data from an LPT port intended for a local printer and reroutes it to a remote printer. ENDCAP, when issued without options, ends the capture of LPT1.

End-to-end process

Governs the interaction from the source computer to the destination device and vice versa; i.e., a program in the source machine exchanges messages with a similar program in the destination machine. The Transport layer (fourth layer) of the International Organization for Standardization (ISO) reference model of Open Systems Interconnection (OSI) is an end-to-end process, as are Layers 5 to 7. In contrast, Layers 1 to 3 of the ISO model specify intermediate, or subnetwork, interactions between a device and its immediate neighbor. Layers 1 to 3 are referred to as chained.

English query

A feature of SQL Server 7.0 that developers can use to create an application that can translate a question asked in English into SQL syntax.

Enhanced Capabilities Port (ECP)

A printer port that allows for high-speed printing.

Enhanced Connectivity Facilities (ECF)

A set of micro-to-mainframe programs used for file transfer, printer sharing, virtual disk, and virtual file services.

Enhanced Graphics Adapter (EGA)

Introduced as an enhancement to the first color display for PCs (CGA). The EGA was equipped with two more wires providing intensity for each of the three primary colors and the ability to produce more color combinations. Also, the horizontal scanning frequency was synchronized for a much clearer output display.

Enhanced Metafile (EMF)

A print job rendering that is device-independent. An EMF is generated more quickly than a rendering that is device-dependent.

Enhanced mode

One of two modes of operation for Windows 3.1. If a computer has the minimum configuration, Windows automatically runs in the Enhanced mode.

Enhanced Small Device Interface (ESDI)

Introduced in 1988, ESDI is a 32-bit bus designed for x86-based computers.

Enlightenment

A window manager that runs under X, programmable in perl.

ENQ/ACK protocol

A Hewlett-Packard communications protocol. The HP3000 computer follows each transmission block with ENQ to determine if the destination terminal is ready to receive more data; the destination terminal indicates its readiness by responding with ACK.

Entity

1. OSI terminology for a layer protocol machine. An entity within a layer performs the functions of the layer within a single computer system, accessing the layer entity below and providing services to the layer entity above at local service access points.

2. A definable object during database definition.

Entity integrity

The process by which each database entity is identified as unique within a database.

Entity-Relationship Modeling

Identifying the important subjects about which information will be stored, their attributes, and the relationships among these entities. Also known as entity modeling.

Envelope

An envelope is the destination point of an electronic mail message. In other words, the electronic mail message recipient's address.

Environmental variables

Environmental information such as drive, path, or filename that is associated with a symbolic name that can be used by an operating system.

Equijoin

Joining columns on the basis of equality, where values match exactly. Also called a "Natural Join."

Erase right

A NetWare file system right that allows the user to delete directories, subdirectories, or files.

Error control

An arrangement that combines error detection and error correction.

Error correction

A method used to correct erroneous data produced during data transmission, transfer, or storage.

Error handling routine

Program code that executes when an error occurs, determining what steps to take to recover from the error or end execution.

Error log

A data set or file in a product or system where error information is stored for later access.

Error rate

The ratio of the total number of errors detected to the total amount of data transmitted or transferred.

Error trap

Statement that enables the error handler.

Error-detecting code

A code in which each coded representation conforms to specific rules of construction so that their violation indicates the presence of errors.

Errors

A term used to refer to errors or messages generated by DB-Library, the OS, or the network software.

Ethernet

A Carrier Sense Multiple Access/Collision Detection (CSMA/CD) specification.

Ethernet was originally developed by Xerox, Intel, and Digital Equipment Corporation in the late 1970s, with specifications first released in 1980. The standard defines the cabling, connectors, and other characteristics for the transmission of data, voice, and video over local area networks at 10 Mbps. Recent improvements have increased the speed to 100 Mbps.

There are four types of Ethernet frames defined: 802.2, 802.3, Ethernet_SNAP, and Ethernet II. These are similar but incompatible.

The types of Ethernet cables are Thin Ethernet (Thinnet), Thick Ethernet (Thicknet), twisted pair, and fiber optic.

Ethernet meltdown

A condition where the traffic on an Ethernet network nearly saturates the available capacity.

EtherTalk

A name used to describe the AppleTalk protocol suite running over an Ethernet network.

European Academic and Research Network (EARN)

A network begun in 1983 as a backbone connecting European academic and research institutions with electronic mail and file transfer services.

European Workshop for Open Systems (EWOS)

The OSI Implementors Workshop for Europe.

Event

An action that results in a message being sent or activity in a program. An event can be generated by a user, an application, or the operating system.

Event forwarding

The process of forwarding reports of selected events or errors to a centralized server.

Event handlers

Open Data Services events requested by clients on a regular basis.

Event procedure

A procedure that runs in response to an event.

Event sinks

A request to be notified when a particular event occurs.

Event-driven programs

In Visual Basic programming, events are actions that are recognized by an object. An object will only recognize those events defined by its class. For example, a command button recognizes a click event but not a double-click event.

One of the key concepts to Visual Basic programming is that it is designed to create event-driven programs. Programs are written to react to things happening within and around it. Visual Basic can react to three types of events: user-generated, program-generated, and system events.

User-generated events, as the name implies, are events resulting from the user's action or interaction with the interface. These actions can include clicking a mouse button, pressing a key, moving the mouse, etc.

A Visual Basic program can generate events and react to the events it has generated. These are program-generated events. One area where this is normally implemented is in custom error recovery. A program generates an event due to an error, then reacts to the event to recover from it.

System events are generated by the computer.

Exeception handler

A procedure that enables programs to catch and handle errors.

Exceptions

An event that indicates that something unexpected occurred. An exception can be generated by hardware, by the operating system, or by an application.

Exclusive lock

A lock set command at the start of a read operation preventing read or write access.

Execute Only attribute

A file system attribute (X) that protects a file from being copied.

EXIT

1. A NetWare login script command that ends execution of the script.

2. In NetWare 3.x and 4.x, EXIT is a console command that returns a file server to DOS after the NetWare files have been closed with the DOWN console command.

Expanded Memory Specification (EMS)

Created when PC processors were limited to 1 MB of Random Access Memory (RAM). Spreadsheet users needed a way to create extremely large spreadsheets and could not do this in the 640 KB available in PCs of that era. A way to work around this memory limitation was needed.

To answer this need, Lotus, Intel, and Microsoft (LIM) developed the Expanded Memory Specification.

This specification utilized a special EMS adapter board to store additional memory where data could be stored for later use. When needed, data is moved from the EMS board to system memory by *paging* the data through a 64-KB page frame in the Upper Memory Area (UMA). The page frame is made up of four 16-KB pages. An expanded memory manager, such as EMM386.EXE, is used to control the paging of data between the EMS board and system memory.

Eventually, the special EMS board was entirely emulated in software, making the special hardware requirement obsolete.

EMS is typically only used by older DOS applications.

Expansion slots

Electrical connectors on the system board that allow additional hardware to be added to the computer. PCs can include 8- or 16-bit ISA, EISA, MCA, Vesa LocalBus, or PCI slots, or a mixture of ISA and any other slot type. Macintosh computers provide either NuBus or PCI slots.

Explicit variable

A declared variable.

Exploit

The generic word for a type of computer attack that triggers vulnerabilities in improperly coded systems software in order to gain unauthorized access to the system hosting it.

export

1. In Linux shell, the export command flags a variable for use by other shells spawned by the current shell, i.e., export PATH=$PATH:$HOME/bin:.

2. The transportation of software executable code across national boundaries, subject to government restriction by the Department of Commerce. Export restrictions have been primarily applied to software products implementing strong encryption. A reduction in export restrictions took place in early January 2000 after years of dispute.

Exporter

System acting as a replication source.

exports

In NFS, the file on a system that instructs the NFS server daemon which directories to advertise as remotely mountable.

Expression

In SQL Server, a query instruction consisting of an attribute, an operator, and a value that is used to search for particular database objects.

Extended Binary-Coded Decimal Interchange Code (EBCDIC)

A coding scheme established by IBM providing 256 letters, numbers, and symbols, using eight bits per character. EBCDIC is used mainly on IBM mainframes and minicomputers, whereas ASCII is used in a desktop microcomputer environment.

Extended memory manager

A program that prevents different applications from using the same part of extended memory at the same time.

Extended Memory Specification (XMS)

All memory above 1 MB (1,024 KB). Intel 80286 processors were limited to 16 MB of extended memory. This was increased to 4 GB in the 80386 and later processors.

DOS systems must have an extended memory manager, such as HIMEM.SYS, loaded to access this area of memory. XMS memory can be used for applications, disk caching, and Expanded Memory Specification (EMS) emulation.

The official XMS specification, "Extended Memory Specification Version 3.0," is available from Microsoft at ftp.microsoft.com/softlib/mslfiles.

Extended partition

A basic disk partition. An extended partition can have multiple logical drives. An extended partition is not bootable. A basic disk can have one extended partition.

Extended stored procedure

Procedure installed with SQL Server that runs a .DLL function.

Extension

1. The period and up to three characters at the end of a DOS format filename. The File Allocation Table (FAT) file system is used by DOS and some other operating systems. Many applications use the extension to designate a particular type of information or data contained in the file.

2. A system software utility that adds functionality to the operating system.

Extension snap-in

A snap-in designed to add additional administrative features to another snap-in. Also referred to as an extension.

Extensions Manager

A Macintosh utility that allows users to manage Control Panels and Extensions without the need for editing configuration files.

Extent

A set of eight contiguous SQL Server pages, or 16 KB of storage.

Exterior Gateway Protocol (EGP)

A reachability routing protocol used by gateways in a two-level Internet. EGP is used as part of the Internet's core system.

External Data Representation (XDR)

A standard for machine-independent data structures developed by Sun Microsystems. Similar to ASN.1.

External Entity object

A leaf object representing a non-native NDS object that has been imported into NDS or registered in NDS. NetWare Message Handling Service (NetWare MHS) uses External Entity objects to represent users from non-NDS environments and provides an integrated address book for sending mail.

External procedures

Procedures that SQL Server loads and executes from inside a DLL.

External program

Microsoft Mail MTA element.

External Viewer

A program used by Mosaic when it cannot handle a particular file type internally. For example, .ps or postscript files. When Mosaic retrieves a .ps file, it will pass the file to a postscript viewer and the viewer will display the file to the user.

The bulk of the expense that characterizes fiber optic cabling systems can be attributed to the interface devices that convert computer signals to and from light pulses. The light pulses are generated by Light Emitting Diodes (LEDs) or Injection Laser Diodes (ILDs). Photo diodes reconvert the light pulses to electrical signals.

Data transfer rates from 100 Mbps to over 2 Gbps are supported at distances from 2 to 25 Km.

Because it doesn't carry electric signals, fiber-optic cabling is ideal for use in hazardous, high-voltage, or secure environments.

Common fiber-optic cables are classified based on the diameter of the light-conducting core. Thicker cores allow the signal to reflect from side-to-side and are thus referred to as multimode, while narrow core fiber cable is referred to as single-mode.

Most LAN fiber networks use 62.5 micron fiber cable.

There are advantages to using fiber-optic cables. It supports extremely high bandwidth, is immune to Electromagnetic Interference (EMI), has extremely low attenuation, and is reliable and secure.

There are also disadvantages to this cabling scheme. It is fragile and requires careful handling. Installation is complex, tedious, and expensive. Also, the component parts are relatively expensive.

F

Failover support

Fault tolerance method implementing clustering to allow one server to take over automatically should a second server fail.

Fail-safe operator

The operator who is paged if none of the designated operators are available to be paged.

Failure handling

An SFT III process that prevents system downtime from a single hardware failure in a NetWare server. With SFT III, the mirrored partner of a NetWare Server takes over if the other server fails. This is instantaneous, automatic, and transparent to NetWare workstations.

Family Applications Program Interface

A standard environment under MS-DOS versions 2.x and 3.x, and OS/2. The programmer can use the Family API to create an application that uses a subset of OS/2 functions (but a superset of MS-DOS 3.x functions) and that runs in a binary-compatible fashion under MS-DOS versions 2.x and 3.x, and OS/2.

Fat binary

A Macintosh application that contains both 680x0 and PowerPC-specific code. The application determines the hardware platform and executes the appropriate instructions.

Fat Mac

An original, Motorola 68000 microprocessor-based Macintosh computer that has been upgraded from 128 KB to 512 KB of RAM.

Fault tolerance

Operating-system features designed to accommodate failures, therefore improving disk reliability and application accessibility. Related terms are "Disk Mirroring," "Disk Duplexing," "Disk Striping with Parity," "Clustering," and "Load Balancing."

Fault-tolerant Dfs root

Windows 2000 Active Directory implementation of Distributed File System (Dfs), where the Dfs structure is integrated into the Active Directory and file replication services allow multiple computers to host the Dfs, providing fault tolerance.

FCONSOLE

A NetWare 3.x menu utility that allows users to change file servers and view the current version of NetWare and its user connections. FCONSOLE also allows for the file server to be shut down, allowing the operator to alter the file server's status, disable the Transaction Tracking System (TTS), and broadcast messages.

fdisk

A disk partitioning utility available on every Linux distribution, similar in function, but more flexible than the DOS FDISK utility.

FDISPLAY

An abbreviation for File DISPLAY. FDISPLAY is a NetWare login script command that sends a file, excluding all but ASCII characters, to network workstations and displays the file when users log in.

Federal Communications Commission (FCC)

A U.S. government board of seven presidential appointees (established by the Communications Act of 1934) that has the power to regulate all U.S. interstate communications systems as well as all international communications systems that originate or terminate in the U.S.

Federal Information Processing Standards (FIPS)

A publication (FIPS PUB) issued by the U.S. National Bureau of Standards that serves as the official source of information in the U.S. federal government regarding standards issued by NBS.

Federal Networking Council (FNC)

The body responsible for coordinating networking needs among U.S. federal agencies.

Federal Research Internet Coordinating Committee (FRICC)

Now replaced by the FNC.

Fiber Distributed Data Interface (FDDI)

A LAN (Local Area Network) specification from ANSI X3T9.5 committee on computer input/ output interface standards. FDDI uses fiber optic cables with token-passing access in a ring topology and transmits at 100 megabits per second across a cable length of up to 62.1 miles with up to 1.24 miles between nodes.

Fiber optic cable

Fiber optic networking cable is comprised of light-conducting glass or plastic fibers that are surrounded by a protective cladding and a durable outer sheath.

The bulk of the expense that characterizes fiber optic cabling systems can be attributed to the interface devices that convert computer signals to and from light pulses. The light pulses are generated by Light Emitting Diodes (LEDs) or Injection Laser Diodes (ILDs). Photo diodes reconvert the light pulses to electrical signals.

Data transfer rates from 100 Mbps to over 2 Gbps are supported at distances from 2 to 25 km.

Because it doesn't carry electric signals, fiber optic cabling is ideal for use in hazardous, high-voltage, or secure environments.

Common fiber optic cables are classified based on the diameter of the light-conducting core. Thicker cores allow the signal to reflect from side-to-side and are thus referred to as multimode, while narrow core fiber cable is referred to as single-mode.

Most LAN fiber networks use 62.5-micron fiber cable.

There are advantages to using fiber optic cables. It supports extremely high bandwidth, is immune to Electromagnetic Interference (EMI), has extremely low attenuation, and is reliable and secure.

There are also disadvantages to this cabling scheme. It is fragile and requires careful handling. Installation is complex, tedious, and expensive. Also, the component parts are relatively expensive.

Fiber optics

Transmission of data in the form of light pulses produced by a laser or Light Emitting Diode (LED) through glass fiber, plastic, or other electrically nonconductive material. Fiber optics provide high-speed, long-distance transmission at low power.

File

1. A sequence of bytes stored on a secondary storage medium such as a floppy disk or hard disk. Generally, a computer file contains either a program or data.

Program files contain instructions or commands that are to be executed by the computer. Data files that contain only ASCII characters are text files, while files containing binary data, i.e., data other than ASCII characters, are called binary files. Bytes that comprise a file are not necessarily stored on contiguous disk blocks and may be scattered across a disk due to fragmentation.

Macintosh files generally consist of a Data Fork (the file contents) and a Resource Fork (a pointer to the application that created the file).

2. The file command, from the GNU commands, used to show file type, e.g., ELF 32-bit LSB executable, C program text, gzip compressed data, ASCII text, etc.

File Allocation Table (FAT)

The file system used by DOS machines. Some other operating systems also support the FAT system.

In order to organize your disk, DOS divides it into two parts. The first part is a small system area that DOS uses to keep track of key information about the disk. This system area uses approximately 2% of a floppy diskette and approximately several tenths of a percent of a hard disk. The second part is the data storage area, which represents the bulk of the disk area.

The system area is divided into three parts called the boot record, FAT, and root directory.

The boot record holds a very short program that performs the job of beginning the loading of the operating system into the computer's memory.

The next part of the system portion of a disk is called the File Allocation Table (FAT). The operating system divides the disk storage area into logical units called clusters. The FAT contains an entry for each data cluster on the disk. A file's FAT entry points to the first cluster for the file. Each cluster points to the next cluster assigned to the file. The final cluster contains a delimiter of FFF (hex), which signals the end of the file.

File caching

This improves file access time by using the RAM memory to store recently accessed files.

File compression

More data can be stored on server hard disks by compressing files that are not being used. NetWare and Windows NT support identifying files and directories to be compressed. With DOS, Windows, and Windows 95, disk partitions are identified for compression.

File Control Block (FCB)

A record that contains all of the information about a file. For example, its structure, length, and name in a FAT file system.

File format

The arrangement of information in a file. There are many standard and nonstandard file formats used on various computing platforms. The use of standard formats for information such as vector graphics, bitmapped graphics, audio, word processing, and spreadsheets allows information to be accessed by applications from multiple vendors.

File Format API (FFAPI)

API sets supporting message transfer between Microsoft Mail and foreign mail systems.

File indexing

Allows faster access to large files by the indexing of FAT entries.

File lock

A file lock prevents more than one user from using a file at the same time. Locks can be put into place for security purposes or to prevent users from making changes to a file simultaneously. A lock can be placed on part of a file if it is supported in the application being used.

File rights

Rights that specify what a trustee can do with a file.

File Scan right

A NetWare file system right that allows the user to *see* a directory or file.

File server

A computer that stores files and provides access to them from workstations. File servers generally contain large hard disks and high amounts of memory.

If a computer is used exclusively as a file server, it is a dedicated file server. If a computer is used as a workstation and a file server simultaneously, it is a nondedicated file server.

The Network Operating System (NOS) runs on the file server and controls access to files, printers, and other network resources.

In Linux, the NFS daemon allows sharing of files, the lp daemon allows sharing of printers, and the Samba suite provides both.

File server protocol

A communications protocol that allows application programs to share files.

File sharing

1. The ability for more than one person to use the same file at the same time.
2. The process of making a file or directory available for network client access.

File system

A file system is composed of files and directories, organized in a tree-like structure. The file system can be made up of multiple partitions and/or devices, all accessed seamlessly under a single tree without the end user knowing the difference.

File System Hierarchy Standard (FHS)

An attempt to standardize path name usage for commonly used directories.

File system namespace

Names that have the format of filenames. All such names will eventually represent data or special disk files.

File system type

There are a number of different standard file system types; Linux uses the ext2 file system, DOS uses the FAT file system, and CD-ROMs use the ISO 9660 file system. There are also distributed file systems supported by Linux, including the Network File System (NFS).

File transfer

The process of copying a file from one computer to another over a network. FTP is a popular program used to copy files over the Internet.

File Transfer Protocol (FTP)

A part of the TCP/IP suite that is used to transfer files between any two computers, provided they support FTP. The two computers do not have to be running the same operating system.

In general, people use FTP to move files from one account or machine to another or to perform what is called an "anonymous FTP." For example, if storage space on a particular machine is low, the user can free up storage space by using FTP to move the files to a machine with more space. Another reason to move a file to a different account is to print a file to a particular printer. If the file is on a machine that cannot access the desired printer, it must be moved to a machine that does have access.

Whatever the reason for the transfer, FTP requires the user to know the proper login name and the password for both computers to move files between them.

While an anonymous FTP also moves from one computer to another, it has two main differences. An anonymous FTP session usually involves gathering files that a user does not have. Anonymous FTP does not require the user to know a login name and password to access the remote computer.

The Internet has many anonymous FTP sites. Each site consists of an FTP server, a large number of files, and guest login names such as "anonymous" or "FTP." This allows any user to visit these systems and copy files from the FTP site to their personal computer. With the appropriate authority, users can copy files from their system to an anonymous FTP site.

Despite the variety of FTP servers and clients on the Internet and the different operating systems they use, FTP servers and clients generally support the same basic commands. This standard command set allows users to accomplish tasks such as looking at a list of files in the current directory of the remote system, regardless of the operating system in use. Other common commands allow users to change directories, get specific file information, copy files to a local machine, and change parameters.

Graphical Web browsers transform the traditional character-based, command-line FTP interface into a point-and-click environment. The only way a user may know that they are in the middle of an FTP session is that the Uniform Resource Locator (URL) box in the browser will change from an address that begins with "http://..." to "ftp://...".

File Transfer, Access, and Management (FTAM)

The OSI remote file service and protocol.

File/filegroup backup

A backup method that backs up the contents of a specified file or filegroup.

Filegroup

Named set of SQL Server data files for database object storage.

FILER

A NetWare menu utility used to view directory information, such as owner, creation date and time, effective rights, directory attributes, rights in the Inherited Rights Mask (3.x and Portable NetWare), or Inherited Rights Filter in 4.x, and user or group trustees and rights. FILER can be used to modify directory information, including rights and attributes, user or group trustees, and trustee rights. Rights under the Mask can also be revoked or restored.

Fill pattern

In a Token-Ring network, a specified bit pattern that a transmitting data station sends before or after frames, tokens, or abort sequences to avoid what would otherwise be interpreted as an inactive or indeterminate transmitter state.

Filter

A device or program that separates data, signals, or material in accordance with specified criteria.

find

The find command allows searching of a file system or part of a file system for a particular string. It searches recursively, checking each subdirectory below the starting point. Depending on the search and the size of the file system specified, a search can take anywhere from seconds to an hour or more, depending on the speed of the storage medium, the amount of available memory, and the speed and current load of the processor.

Finder

The system software that controls the Macintosh Desktop and is used for file and application management tasks.

Finger

An Internet software program that retrieves information and allows users to locate a particular user on the local or remote system. It typically shows the full name, last login time, idle time, terminal line, and terminal location (where applicable). In addition, it may display plan and project files defined by the user.

Finger is also sometimes used to give access to nonpersonal information, but the most common use is to see if a person has an account at a particular Internet site. Many sites do not allow incoming Finger requests.

FIPS

A DOS program used to resize DOS partitions.

FIRE PHASERS

A NetWare login script command used to specify the number of times the phaser sound will be activated at the user's workstation.

Firewall

Used as a security measure between a company's Local Area Network (LAN) and the Internet. The firewall prevents users from accessing certain address Web sites. A firewall also helps to prevent hackers from accessing internal resources on the network. A combination of hardware and software that separates a LAN into two or more parts for security purposes. Today, firewalls are commonly used to prevent unauthorized access to a network from the Internet.

Linux distributions and the Linux kernel contain the software and code necessary to set up an effective packet-level firewall.

FireWire

A high-speed serial interface designed by Apple Computer to allow communications between a Macintosh computer and peripherals such as scanners, disk drives, printers, digital cameras, etc.

First Normal Form

First of the five normal forms. It requires that tables have a fixed number of columns and that there be no repeating groups (one-to-many relationships).

Flag

A variable indicating that a certain condition holds.

FLAGDIR

An abbreviation for FLAG DIRectories. A NetWare command-line utility used to change subdirectory attributes in a given volume or directory.

In NetWare 3.x and Portable NetWare, subdirectory attributes are Delete Inhibit, Hidden, Normal, Purge, Rename Inhibit, and System.

Flame

Originally, flame meant to carry forth in a passionate manner in the spirit of honorable disagreement. It most often involves the use of flowery language.

More recently, flame has come to refer to any kind of electronic mail message with a derogatory comment. A flame may be used to tell the recipient in strong words (*shouted in all capital letters)* that there has been a breach of netiquette (Internet etiquette).

FLeX/IP

A Novell NetWare Loadable Module that adds FTP server capability to a NetWare file server.

Flicker

The noticeable flashes seen while viewing a screen display. The rate at which the screen is scanned and refreshed as well as the persistence of the phosphor coating on the monitor to hold the light. Monitors are designed to operate at different refresh rates; slower rates produce a significant flicker. The flicker is a result of too much time elapsing before the image is refreshed; therefore, the image begins to decay.

Floating-point processor

A microprocessor that has been optimized to perform floating-point math operations such as trigonometric functions.

Floating-point unit

Another term used to describe a floating-point processor.

Floppy disk

A magnetically sensitive, flexible disk used as a secondary storage medium. The two most common sizes are the 3-1/2-in. disk that is fully enclosed in a rigid plastic casing and the 5-1/4-in. floppy disk.

Floppy drive

A device that stores data externally on small portable devices called "floppies." Floppies come in different sizes and hold different amounts of data. The two most common sizes are the 5-1/4-in. and the 3-1/2-in..

Fnode

HPFS entry describing the location of a file on the hard disk.

Focus

Term used to refer to the active screen object or control.

Folder

A directory. The Macintosh operating system uses folders as an analogy for directories. Folders may contain files and other folders.

Folder Redirection

A process whereby a user's local folders, such as My Documents, are redirected to a network share location.

Font

In typography, a complete set of characters of one particular size, style, and weight, including punctuation marks, symbols, and numbers. The term "font" is often confused with typeface, which refers to a particular style of character or type family the font belongs to.

For Your Information (FYI)

FYI notes accompany RFCs (Request For Comments). FYIs contain information about the Internet, including information useful to new Internet users.

Foreground category

A classification of processes that consists of those associated with the currently active screen group.

Foreground process

A process that can receive user input. You can move a suspended process or a process in the backgound to the foreground using the fg command.

Foreground task

A task that is able to receive interactive input from a user.

Foreign address book provider

An address book provider for a foreign messaging system.

Foreign e-mail address

This address specifies a mailbox in a foreign (non-MHS) e-mail system. An object is allowed only one foreign e-mail address.

Foreign e-mail alias

This lists an object's aliases as known in a foreign (non-MHS) messaging system. A foreign e-mail alias is the return address value that is used when the NetWare MHS user sends e-mail to an X.400 user. An object can have one alias for each type of foreign e-mail system.

Foreign key

A key used to establish a link between two tables, with the foreign key in one table referencing values in the primary key of the second.

Foreign Mail System

Under Microsoft Mail usage, any electronic mail system other than Microsoft Mail.

Forest

A collection of two or more trees. They do not share a common namespace but do share a Global Catalog and a common schema.

Form

In NetWare, a screen window that includes fields containing information that can be entered or changed. A form can also contain menu items to select. Forms can also be the type of paper specified for printing a document.

Form module

Fundamental Visual Basic user interface module.

Forward

A feature of electronic mail transmission that enables a message recipient to re-address the mail and send it to a third party.

Forward lookup zone

DNS zone used for host name-to-IP address resolution.

Fragment

Part of an IP message.

Fragmentation

The process in which an IP datagram is broken into smaller pieces to fit the requirements of a given physical network. The reverse process is termed reassembly.

Frame

In Institute of Electrical and Electronics Engineers (IEEE) terminology, the unit of data transferred at the Open Systems Interconnection (OSI) Data Link layer.

Frame Check Sequence (FCS)

The error check portion of a LAN data frame.

Frame Relay

Commonly referred to as "bandwidth on demand." Unlike other transmission protocols or processes, frame relay offers users significant benefits over other transmission services, such as T1, by eliminating the processing overhead associated with packets of data moving between packet-forwarding devices.

Free software

Free software refers to the rights a user has in regards to using the software; it does not necessarily mean free as in cost. The Free Software Foundation defines the free software principle as:

- Freedom to run the software.
- Freedom to look at the internal workings of a software.
- Freedom to give away copies of the software.
- Freedom to make changes to the software and distribute your changes to the community.

Free Software Foundation (FSF)

The Free Software Foundation is a nonprofit organization dedicated to promoting the use of free software and helping in the development of the GNU operating system.

Freenet

A network of bulletin board systems offering services such as electronic mail and information services. Freenets are generally community-based systems.

Freeware

Software that is publicly available for downloading. There are no charges for downloading. Users may copy and distribute the software freely.

Frequency

The number of times one complete incident or function occurs. In electronics, frequency usually refers to the number of waveforms that are repeated per second, measured in Hertz.

Frequency Modulation (FM)

The modification of the frequency of a carrier wave so that it carries information. A frequency is the number of waveforms that are repeated per second and is measured in Hertz.

Frequently Asked Questions (FAQ)

A file posted for many usergroups, newsgroups, and other services containing questions and answers of general interest or which are commonly asked by new users on the Internet. Such lists have come to be known as FAQs (pronounced *faks*).

There are hundreds of FAQs on subjects as diverse as pet groooming and cryptography. Subject FAQs are usually written by people who have tired of answering the same question over and over. Internet users are encouraged to read FAQ files before asking questions.

Most Linux distributions provide a selection of FAQs in the /usr/doc/FAQ directory. The Linux Documentation Project Web site, http://www.linuxdoc.org/, is a good place to find new and updated FAQs.

From

The field in an electronic mail header that contains the return address of the message originator.

Front end

As in processor (IBM FEP), which is a stand-alone intelligent device that executes the transfer of data or the protocols for the host machine.

Front-End Processor (FEP)

Usually a minicomputer that is connected to a larger host computer in order to handle all of the communications requirements independently, thereby leaving the host computer free to concentrate on internal data processing.

fstab

In Linux, a file located in the /etc directory containing a list of frequently used file systems, where they are located, what type of file system they are, what permissions to set on them, whether to check them when mounting, and if they are to be mounted automatically during the initialization process.

Full database backup

Backup method where all database and transaction log data is backed up.

Full-duplex transmission

A method of transmitting information over an asynchronous communications channel in which signals may be sent in both directions simultaneously. This technique makes the best use of line time but substantially increases the amount of logic required in the primary and secondary stations.

Full-height

Full-height describes the size, in height, of the drive. Full-height drives originated in the IBM PC and XT models. They are roughly 3 inches in height.

Full-text database

A computer file that holds the complete text of original sources, such as newspaper or periodical articles, books, court decisions, and directories.

Full-text search

The SQL Server 7.0 feature that allows you to create a catalog of the text contained in particular fields. A column with full-text search enabled and the catalog populated allows users to search for records based on a field containing certain words.

Fully Qualified Domain Name (FQDN)

The name of a host, including its domain hierarchy. For example, a host named HR inside the MyCo.com domain would have a fully qualified domain name of HR.MyCo.com.

Function key

"Extra" keys on a computer keyboard. PCs and Macintosh keyboards generally have 12 function keys. Other types of computers have more.

Function keys are used for various purposes by the operating system and applications software.

Function procedure

A procedure that does return a value to the calling procedure.

fvwm

In Linux, a common window manager for use under X.

G

Garbage collection

A process that de-allocates memory not required by an object. The freed memory space is then allocated to another object.

Gated Gatedaemon

A software program that allows for multiple routing protocols and protocol families. The software is available for free via anonymous FTP from gated.cornell.edu.

Gateway

A router, or other host, that serves as a middleman between two networks. The primary linkage between mixed environments such as PC-based LANs and host environments such as SNA.

Gateways generally operate at all seven layers of the OSI Reference Model. They may provide full content conversion between two environments, such as ASCII to EBCDIC, as well as other application and presentation layer conversions.

Other types of gateways include fax gateways, which allow users to send and receive faxes from their workstations. These may also be integrated with mail service gateways, which allow communications between users of different mail systems.

Gateway list

List of Microsoft Mail gateways available to a local postoffice.

General priority category

The OS/2 classification of threads that consists of three subcategories: background, foreground, and interactive.

GeoPort

An Apple-designed architecture found in most Power Macintosh computers. It provides inexpensive telephony solutions when a product such as Apple's Geoport Telecom Adapter is connected to the modem or printer port.

Giveaway shared memory

A shared memory mechanism in which a process that already has access to the segment can grant access to another process. Processes cannot obtain access for themselves; access must be granted by another process that already has access.

Global account

A Windows NT Server user account-authorized interactive logon in its own and trusting domains.

Global address list

Combined user list including users from all postoffices taking part in directory synchronization.

Global Catalog (GC)

A database containing scaled-down attributes of every Active Directory object from every domain in a tree or forest. The GC replies to queries so that users in one domain can locate resources in another domain.

Global Catalog server

The first domain controller created in a tree that, by default, stores the Global Catalog.

Global data segment

A data segment that is shared among all instances of a dynlink routine. In other words, a single segment that is accessible to all processes that call a particular dynlink routine.

Global Descriptor Table (GDT)

An element of the 80286/80386 memory management hardware. The GDT holds the descriptions of as many as 4,095 global segments. A global segment is accessible to all processes.

Global group

A group definition in Windows NT allowing permission assignments to local machines or other domains through Local group membership of the Global group.

Active Directory domain group scope. In mixed mode, members can include user accounts from the same domain. In addition, Global groups from the same domain are supported in native mode.

Global naming

A naming convention that allows users to view and access resources anywhere on a network. The users do not need to become concerned with the physical location of a resource because they can simply browse and choose a resource from a list.

Global variable

Predefined, system-supplied SQL Server variable that is used to store global server information. Some global variables are maintained by the server on an ongoing basis; others can be set by the user to affect server operation. They have names beginning with two @@ characters, for example, @@error.

GNOME

The GNU Network Object Model Environment. With a window manager, part of a GUI user environment under Linux.

GNU Public License (GPL)

The GPL is a license that protects a software while maintaining and ensuring freedom. According to the GPL license, anyone has the "freedom to distribute copies of free software (and charge for this service if you wish), that you receive the source code or can get it if you want it, that you can change the software or use pieces of it in new free programs, and that you know you can do these things."

GNU's Not UNIX (GNU)

The GNU project's purpose is to create a free UNIX-like operating system with all of the tools commonly found on a UNIX system.

Gopher

A hierarchical, menu-based information service developed at the University of Minnesota. It provides access to information collections across the Internet by taking file directories and turning them into easily navigable menus. Gopher also makes file transfer convenient.

Gopher functions as a client server that connects the user to the menu item(s) selected from the gopher server menu. The user must have a Gopher Client program.

Although Gopher spread rapidly across the globe in only a couple of years, it is being largely supplanted by Hypertext, also known as WWW (World Wide Web). There are thousands of Gopher Servers on the Internet and they will remain for a while.

GOTO

1. In DOS, GOTO is used in batch files to execute a script line or sequence of lines out of order.

2. In NetWare, GOTO is a login script command used to execute a script line or sequence out of order.

3. In SQL Server, GOTO is used to start execution at a defined label.

Gov

A governmental organization is identified by this Internet address suffix. For example, whitehouse.gov.

Government OSI Profile (GOSIP)

A U.S. government procurement specification for OSI protocols.

Grant

1. A SQL Server command used to allocate users' various levels of read/write access to database objects.

2. A NetWare command-line utility that grants file or directory access rights (trustee rights) to a user or group.

Graphical Identification and Authentication (GINA)

Windows 2000 component that collects logon information that it packages and sends to the Local Security Authority.

Graphical User Interface (GUI)

A program that executes commands given by the user to the computer. A GUI uses graphic representations of commands and/or a menu format to display commands that the user may execute with a mouse or similar device.

The graphical user interface makes using a computer easier, especially for the beginner. Mosaic is a Graphical User Interface for the Internet. Microsoft Windows, OS/2, and the Macintosh operating system are examples of graphical user interfaces for personal computers.

Graphics Device Interface (GDI)

The component of Windows-family products that is responsible for implementing the graphical instructions provided to the operating system.

Graphics Interchange Format (GIF)

Established by Compuserve, GIF is a format for graphics files. In Web documents, IMG links often point to GIF files.

Graphics mode

The mode enabling applications to display graphics in addition to text. GUI-based applications always run in a graphics mode. DOS applications can run either in graphics or text mode.

Group

A collection of users used for security management or distrubtion management. All members get, as implicit rights, any rights assigned to the group. Each group has a name and a group ID. Under UNIX, groups may be local to the machine or distributed among several machines via *NIS*. Under Windows NT, groups are characterized by being local to a given machine or as domain-level groups, which are defined for anyone authenticated against the Windows NT domain. Windows 2000 groups can contain other objects such as computers.

Group ID (GID)

The unique numerical ID of a group under Linux.

Group object

A leaf object that represents several User objects. It provides collective, rather than individual, network administration. Group objects are created based on the use of applications, printers, or print queues. Group objects may also be created based on users who perform similar tasks or need similar information, or to simplify trustee assignments.

Group Policy (GP)

Windows 2000 feature that allows administrators to assign security settings and additional properties to domain members based on their personal accounts or group memberships.

Group Policy Object (GPO)

An Active Directory object that contains configuration information on desktop environments, servers, users, and other objects. GPOs can be applied to domains, sites, or OUs for the purpose of simplifying administrative control over AD objects.

Group reply

An electronic mail tool used to respond to a number of individuals simultaneously. Sometimes improperly used in a type of attack known as an *e-mail bomb.*

Grouped view

A view with a GROUP BY clause in its definition.

Guard band

The unused bandwidth separating channels to prevent crosstalk in an FDM system.

Guest

1. A network device controlled by another network device, or a host device, during data transmission.

2. GUEST, in NetWare 3.x, is a temporary user of the network, assigned to the default group EVERYONE and granted group rights.

3. Default SQL Server database user.

H

Hacker

A person who is an expert at solving problems with computers. The term is often confused with cracker, which is the name given to a person who illegally attempts to access computer systems or has destructive intentions.

Half-duplex (HDX)

Transmission link that allows two-way communication, although transmission is possible only one way at a time. When the communications device at one end has completed its transmission, it must advise the device at the other end that it has finished and is ready to receive. Half-duplex transmission is analogous to a single-lane bridge on a two-way road.

Half-height

Half-height describes the size, in height, of the drive. Drives that are half-height are half the height of full-height drives. Half-height drives are about 1-1/2 inches in height. Two half-height drives can fit in a full-height drive bay.

Handle

1. In draw programs and similar object-oriented graphics programs, handles are the small black squares that appear around a selected object so the object can be resized, moved, copied, or scaled by using a mouse or similar pointing device.

2. An operating system object that contains a reference to an object like a window or printer.

Handshake

Used in communications technology to define the exchange of data when connection is achieved.

Handshaking

Before data is transmitted serially, certain communications conditions, or protocols, must be met. Handshaking allows both the sending and receiving computers to understand the required signals, i.e., the method of transmission.

Hard disk

A peripheral mass-storage device that uses sealed, rotating, nonflexible, magnetically coated disks to store data and program files. Hard disk types include SCSI, IDE, and EIDE.

Hard Disk Controller

The board that communicates with and controls the hard (fixed) disk drive.

Hard Disk Encoding

A method of compression of data within the hard disk drive. An example is MFM or RLL. Hard disk encoding is mostly used in older devices.

Hard Disk Interface

The communication device that allows the hard disk drive to interact with the hard disk controller. There are many different types that will affect the speed of data transfers. Examples of hard disk interfaces are ST506, SCSI, ESDI, and IDE.

Hardcopy

Sending computer data out to the printer and printing the information on paper is referred to as producing hardcopy, or a copy on paper that can be physically handled.

Hardware

All electronic components of a computer system, including peripherals, circuit boards, and input and output devices. Hardware is the physical equipment, as opposed to software consisting of programs, data procedures, rules, and associated documentation.

Hardware Abstraction Layer (HAL)

Windows NT module that isolates the operating system kernel from the hardware platform.

Hardware Compatibility List (HCL)

A list of systems and adapters maintained by Microsoft. The HCL is a list of systems tested and verified as compatible with a specific operating system version.

Hayes

The company, Hayes Microcomputer Products, developed a special synchronizing compression technique that allows fast line turnaround, making a half-duplex modem simulate full-duplex transmission speeds. Hayes patented its method and allows other vendors to utilize the method through licensing fees and royalties. Hayes and Hayes-compatible modems are the de facto standard for PC communications.

Head crash

The read/write heads fly across the surface of the disk drive's platters, traveling on a cushion of air. If the head comes in contact with the platter, a head crash occurs. Head crashes damage the platter and corrupt the data. Often the data is rendered inaccessible.

Header

1. The portion of an electronic message (e-mail, network packet, etc.) that contains information about the structure, ownership, and possibly origin and destination of the message.

2. Electronic mail message headers contain the message originator's name and address, receiver, subject, date, etc.

A packet header carries the source and destination addresses along with other information.

Heads

The read/write head on a hard disk drive is similar to the read/write head on a tape recorder. Data is stored as changes in magnetic flux on the disk platters. The read/write heads sweep across the surface, traveling on a cushion of air. Read/write heads can perform both the reading and writing of data. The drive will usually have an additional read-only, servo head that is used for disk positioning.

Heap

1. A block of memory that is set aside for dynamic allocation.

2. SQL Server term for the collection of all pages containing all rows in a table.

HELP

A NetWare 3.x, 4.x, and Portable NetWare menu utility that provides online information about NetWare utilities, commands, and operations.

Help

1. Generally, any online assistance/documentation.

2. SQL Server menu utility that provides online information about utilities, commands, and operations.

3. The Macintosh operating system includes *Balloon Help* (sometimes referred to as Rollover Help), which may be activated through the Finder Help menu.

Helper servers

Logon servers that contain SMS components that have been moved from the site server to lessen the load on the site server.

Hertz (Hz)

The International System of Units measure of frequency. Hertz was named for German physicist Heinrich Hertz and was often abbreviated as Hz. One Hertz is one complete cycle per second. A cycle may relate to light, heat, radio waves, or other vibrations.

Heterogeneous data

Data coming from a mix of data sources.

Hexadecimal

A base-16 numeric notation system that specifies addresses in computer memory. In hexadecimal notation, the decimal numbers 0 through 15 are represented by the decimal digits 0 through 9 and the characters A through F (A=decimal 10, B=decimal 11, and so on).

Hidden attribute

A file system attribute (H) that hides a directory or file and protects it from being deleted or copied by users.

Hidden file

A file that is not visible in a normal directory listing. By placing a period (.) at the beginning of a UNIX filename, it is possible to make a file hidden from normal view. By using the **ls -a** command to get a directory listing, you can see the hidden files. In Windows, one sets the H attribute with Windows Explorer or from the command line with the **attrib** command to hide a file. Although the files are hidden from directory listings, most commands will still operate on them if the name is explicitly referenced as an argument to the command, under both UNIX and Windows. This is the absolute minimum level of file-based security.

Hierarchical File System (HFS)

The file system architecture used by the Macintosh operating system.

Hierarchical Model

A database model where entities and relationships are organized into hierarchies, where some entities are subordinate to others.

Hierarchical routing

Designed to simplify routing on large networks, hierarchical routing considers a network as a series of levels, where each level handles its own routing. The Internet operates as three levels: the backbone level that carries data (packets) at high speed and knows how to route between the next level (mid-level); the mid-level that knows how to route between the sites; and sites (or local or stub networks) that know internal routing.

Hierarchy manager

Monitors the site database for any changes to the site configuration.

High Capacity Storage System (HCSS)

A component of NetWare, it is a data storage system that extends the storage capacity of a NetWare server by allowing an optical disk library, or jukebox, to become a part of the NetWare file system.

High Density (HD)

The density refers to how tightly data can be recorded on the media. This is usually used to describe floppy diskettes. Using a magnetic medium that has much finer (smaller) magnetic particles, more data can be recorded on the media. HD diskettes require high-density drives.

High Memory Area (HMA)

HMA is the first 64 KB of extended memory and is located in the address range of 1,024 KB to 1,088 KB. An Extended Memory Specification (XMS) driver such as Himem.sys is required for use of the HMA.

Only one program may reside in the HMA.

High Performance File System (HPFS)

This is the native file system for OS/2.

High-level Data Link Control (HDLC)

A data link control protocol developed by ISO (International Organization for Standardization) in response to IBM's SDLC (Synchronous Data Link Control), which is a subset of HDLC.

High-level Format

Once the partition(s) have been created on a hard disk, another format is required before the disk can be used. This is called a high-level format and is operating-system-dependent. With limited exceptions, a disk formatted under one operating system cannot be used by another. The steps performed in the formatting process include creating the boot record and file allocation tables (or other file tracking system), initializing the disk directory, verifying the disk surface, and, if needed, transferring the system files.

The boot record contains the *bootstrap* program that allows the computer to load (or boot) the operating system from the disk.

For DOS, File Allocation Tables (FATs) are created. These tables keep track of the sectors assigned to a particular file, as well as the available (empty) sectors on the disk. Other operating systems have their own equivalent to the FAT system.

Most operating systems use a hierarchical, tree-like directory system to keep track of directories, subdirectories, and files on the disk. Formatting initializes the directory tables by clearing the root (top-most) directory.

During the formatting process, each disk sector is examined to verify that there are no bad sectors on the disk. Bad sectors are locked out and flagged in the file allocation table (or equivalent) so the computer will not attempt to write to these disk areas.

The next step of the formatting process allows the user to have the operating system's startup files transferred to the disk.

For DOS versions 4.01 and below, the FORMAT process is a destructive one. The FAT is erased. Even though none of the data on the disk is erased, the data cannot be recovered without the FAT and directory table information.

DOS 5.00 and newer versions support a *safe* format. The FAT and directory information is backed up to a new location on the disk, allowing the user to unformat the disk, if necessary.

Always approach formatting a hard disk as if it is a destructive procedure. Unformat or safe format utilities do not always guarantee the ability to recover all of the disk information.

Himem.sys

An extended memory manager. It coordinates the use of the computer's extended memory. This prevents two applications from using the same block of memory at the same time.

Histogram view

System Monitor view displaying average performance counter data as a bar chart.

History list

1. A list of Document Titles and URLs a browser keeps in memory that represents the visited URLs during a given Internet session.

2. A list of previous steps or processes completed by a program. The bash shell has a history function so that you can see previous commands issued; the list is normally stored in the ~/.bash_history file.

Hit count

The number of objects found in the site database that match the query criteria.

Hive files

Component files making up the Windows NT Registry.

Home directory

1. The top-most (root) directory for Web sites using IIS. Serves as the default location for a Web site's content pages.

2. On Local Area Networks, a directory that belongs to a single user for storage of data. Normally, the user is the only person with access to this directory. On most networks, the supervisor, administrator, or root account can also access any user's home directory.

Home folder

The NetWare for Macintosh's equivalent of a Home directory.

Home page

A document coded in Hypertext Markup Language (HTML) that acts as a top-level document for an Internet site or a topic. A home page contains hypertext links to related documents.

Honey pot

A system deliberately left in an insecure state with the hope that it will deflect attacks from the actual production host or cause the attacker to reveal information about his/her site and intentions.

Hookswitch

The switch that activates to connect a device to a phone line.

Hop

Describes routing through a network. A single hop is a data packet moving through a single router, from the point of origination to the destination. After a predefined maximum number of hops, the packet is discarded.

Hop count

The number of individual networks a packet crosses. In UNIX, the count begins at 0. In Windows it begins at 1.

Horizontal filtering

Limiting replication by identifying the rows to be published from an article (published table).

Host

A computer that is remotely accessible and provides information or services for users on a network. It is quite common to have one host machine provide several services, such as WWW and USENET. A host computer on the Internet can be accessed by using an application program such as electronic mail, telnet, or FTP. A host computer may also be a bulletin board.

Host name

The name given to a computer that identifies it on a LAN or the Internet. Also, the part of a Fully Qualified Domain Name (FQDN) referring to the host itself.

hosts

A file listing IP addresses and associated names; generally supplanted by DNS. In Linux, it is located in the /etc directory; in Windows NT, it is located in the C:Winnt\System32\Drivers\etc directory.

hosts.allow

File listing hosts that are allowed to access specified network services on the local machine, commonly located in the /etc directory.

hosts.deny

File listing hosts that are denied access to specified network services on the local machine, commonly located in the /etc directory.

hosts.equiv

A file located in /etc that grants or denies password-free access to the "r" network services (rlogin, rsh, rcp) on the local machine.

Hot Fix redirection

In NetWare, a method to prevent data from being written to bad data blocks on a hard disk. When data is saved to the hard disk, the NetWare operating system verifies the save's accuracy by comparing the disk and RAM versions. If the two versions aren't identical, the disk version is moved to a disk address known as the Hot Fix redirection area.

Hot Fix redirection area

This is the hard disk space set aside to hold data redirected from faulty disk blocks.

HotJava

A Web browser developed by Sun Microsystems.

Hotlist

A user-defined list of preferred URLs to a given World Wide Web document.

Hotspot

A region of the screen that is associated with some action.

HOWTO

Similar to README, but less common, this file contains tips on using or on installing software in the including directory.

Href

In a link tag, href denotes the address of the target of the link.

HTML editor

A tool that automates and simplifies HTML document preparation.

Hub

1. In disk drives, the hub is the central mechanism within the drive that causes the disk to rotate and keeps it centered during the rotation. On floppy diskettes, the hub fits into the hole in the center of the diskette to keep it level and balanced during rotation.

2. In networking, a central connecting point for network wiring.

Hue

A value between 0 and 239 that indicates whether a color is more red, yellow, or blue. Both 0 and 239 are shades of red, with numbers greater than 0 becoming increasingly yellow and numbers less than 239 becoming increasingly blue. Cyan has a hue of approximately 120.

Huge segments

A software technique that allows the creation and use of pseudo segments larger than 65 KB.

Human Interface Device (HID)

The firmware specification developed by the USB Implementers Forum. This specification defines a standard for self-describing input devices that connect through a Universal Serial Bus (USB).

HyperCard

A multimedia authoring application introduced by Apple Computer.

Hyperlink

Words, phrases, images, or characters highlighted in bold indicate connections in a given document to information within another document. The user also has the option to underline these hyperlinks.

Hypermedia

The name for richly formatted documents containing a variety of information types such as textual, image, movie, and audio. These information types are easily found through hyperlinks.

Hypertext

Allows users to move from one site or place in a document to another. Hypertext links in World Wide Web documents link the user from terms in one document to the site referenced in the original document.

Hypertext Markup Language (HTML)

Standard Generalized Markup Language (SGML) is a worldwide method of representing document formatting. It is also a broad language that is used to define particular markup languages for particular purposes.

The language that the Web uses is a specific application of SGML called Hypertext Markup Language (HTML). As HTML has evolved, it has moved away from the SGML conventions. With newer versions of HTML, there has been some effort to rebuild the relationship between the two languages. Because of the worldwide investment in SGML, future versions of HTML will most likely comply with SGML even more closely.

HTML is the standard language that the Web uses for creating and recognizing hypermedia documents. Web documents are most often written in HTML and normally have an .html or .htm extension.

Languages such as HTML follow the SGML format and allow document creators to separate document content from document presentation. As a markup language, HTML is more concerned with the structure of a document than with the appearance.

HTML documents are standard 7-bit ASCII files with formatting codes that contain information about layout (document titles, paragraphs, breaks, lists) and hyperlinks. Although most browsers will display any document that is written in plain text, by creating documents using HTML, writers can include links to other files, graphics, and various types of media.

HTML specifies a document's logical organization. While a formatting language, such as Rich Text Format (RTF), indicates typeface, font size, and style of the text in a document, HTML uses tags to mark the headings, normal paragraphs, and lists (and whether or not they are numbered).

While the HTML standard supports simple hypermedia document creation and layout, it is not capable of supporting some of the complex layout techniques found in traditional document publishing. As the Web and HTML gain additional momentum and are used by more people for more purposes, it will most likely gain some of the functionality used in desktop publishing.

HTML has been added to most major Internet browsers. Examples include Netscape Navigator and Microsoft Internet Explorer.

HTML is an evolving language. Different Web browsers recognize slightly different HTML tags. Some Web document creators attempt to get around formatting limitations in HTML by using graphics and browser-specific HTML tags. The creators do this in an attempt to make their documents look a certain way in a particular browser. Though approximately 80% of all users view Web documents with Netscape or Microsoft browsers, browser-specific documents look bad or can be inaccessible with the other browser.

Even with comprehensive capabilities, HTML is still an easy-to-use language and is simple enough to type directly into a word-processing application without the use of an HTML editor.

Hypertext Transfer Protocol (HTTP)

A set of directions for Web servers that tells them how to respond to various events initiated by users. HTTP is the most important protocol used in the World Wide Web (WWW).

The simplest example is clicking on a link to another part of the same file. The server receives the information that the link has been activated and sends back the designated part of the file for display.

An HTTP client program is required on one end and an HTTP server program on the other. Most Linux distributions come with both clients and a server. Apache is currently the Web's most popular Web server software and is Open Source Software that is included in most Linux distributions. Netscape and Lynx, two clients, are also available with most distributions.

HTTP should be distinguished from *HTML*, the markup language for formatting Web pages.

Hyplus

An online guide that provides examples of types of library systems and companion resources, identifies directories and other sources for locating currently available systems, and relates strategies used by experienced searchers to make the most of exploring new resources.

Hytelnet

Hytelnet identifies, through hypertext links, Internet sites and services accessible through telnet.

I

IBM PC network

A CSMA/CD network introduced by IBM in 1984 that uses a star or bus topology. It was originally a broadband network using coaxial cable, but lower-cost twisted-pair wire was subsequently introduced by IBM.

IBM Token Ring network

A baseband star-wired ring network developed by IBM, using the token-passing access method and running at 4 or 16 megabits per second (Mbps).

Icon

A graphical picture used to represent an application, folder, file, disk drive, or printer.

Identifier

The name of a database or database object.

ifconfig

A command used in Linux to configure kernel-level network interfaces, including TCP/IP.

IF...THEN...ELSE

1. A programming convention providing conditional execution.

2. A NetWare 3.x, 4.x, and Portable NetWare login script command for writing conditional statements that define conditions under which other commands will be executed.

Image Color Management (ICM)

Microsoft's technology for accurately displaying and printing color images on a variety of devices.

IMG

In HTML, IMG is an abbreviation for "image" and denotes a link to a graphic file.

If using a text Internet browser, you will see this abbreviation in place of the images that a graphical browser would display.

Graphical browsers will let you turn off the downloading of images if doing so becomes too time-consuming.

Immediate Compress attribute

A NetWare file system attribute (IC) that causes files to be compressed as soon as compression is enabled. A specific event, such as a time delay, is not needed before compression begins.

Implicit variable

A variable defined by use rather than by declaration.

Importer

System receiving data during replication.

In My Humble Opinion (IMHO)

A shorthand appended to a comment written in an online forum, IMHO indicates that the writer is aware that they are expressing a debatable view, probably on a subject already under discussion.

INCLUDE

NetWare login script command that allows text files or other login scripts to be included in a user's login process.

Inclusive range

The BETWEEN keyword is a range operator where values are searched in between the lower and higher limits specified, including the values themselves.

Index

A database object that provides efficient access to rows in a table, based on key values.

Index hole

In the past, a 5-1/4-inch floppy drive had to identify the starting position of a 5-1/4-inch floppy diskette. The drive had to sense when that starting position reappeared, thus indicating completion of one full rotation of the diskette. Most drives have a light sensor that reads the index hole rotations and sees the index hole in the floppy diskette when it lines up with the hole in the floppy diskette's outer jacket.

Indexed attribute

A status flag (I) that is set automatically when a file exceeds a set size. It indicates the file is indexed for fast access.

Indirect device name

Used when executing a SQL Server database dump to a destination that has not been defined as a dump device.

INETCFG

A NetWare utility that allows the network manager to control the MultiProtocol Router product.

inetd

In UNIX/Linux, the Internet metadaemon; waits for requests on several IP ports and launches programs to service those requests as required. Services such as *telnet, FTP,* and *rexec* often are executed under the aegis of the inetd metadaemon.

inetd.conf

In Linux, the configuration file for inetd, which consists of a list of services, the protocols they are allowed to service, and the port numbers required to connect those services. It is commonly located in the /etc directory.

Infopop

An extensive online guide to using the Internet and a variety of other online information systems. While hytelnet is concerned with only telnet accessible sites, Infopop gives information on many types of online information and includes background material.

Infrared

Light waves in the 100-GHz to 1,000-THz range.

Infrared Data Association (IrDA)

An organization founded in 1993 to establish standards for infrared communication.

Inheritance

The means by which a child object can get information from its parent.

Inheritance chain

The path from a particular class to its superclasses in the class hierarchy.

Inheritance hierarchy

The collection of all subclasses that extend from a common parent class. Each subclass inherits the properties of its parent class.

Inherited Rights Filter (IRF)

In NetWare 4, the Inherited Rights Filter (IRF) restricts access privileges to a particular object. The IRF blocks rights that would normally flow down from a parent object.

An object's Access Control List (ACL) property contains the IRF. To change the ACL, the user needs the Supervisor or Write Property Rights to the ACL property.

The IRF rights are the same as the trustee assignments.

The IRF affects only rights that have *trickled down* from a parent object and will not override trustee assignments made at the same level (explicit) or lower levels.

Specific rights given to a user object for a property do not flow down. The only time property rights flow down is when a trustee has rights to all properties for that container object.

If the Supervisor object or Property right has been granted, it can be blocked by the IRF. The system has a built-in safety net. Before removing the Supervisor right through the IRF, the utilities will alert you if no other object has the Supervisor right.

In NetWare 3, the IRF restricts access privileges to a particular subdirectory or file. The IRF blocks rights that would normally be assigned as part of the user's cumulative rights.

Subdirectories and files allow all assigned rights by default. Any rights removed from the Inherited Rights Filter are not allowed to the user.

As in NetWare 4, the IRF in NetWare 3 affects only rights that have *trickled down* from a higher-level directory. It will not override trustee assignments made at the same or lower levels. Unlike NetWare 4, the supervisory right cannot be removed by the IRF.

Inherited Rights Mask (IRM)

NetWare 3.x set of rights that apply to a file or directory when it is created. These rights are Access Control, Create, Erase, File Scan, Modify, Read, Supervisory, and Write. Rights in the IRM automatically apply unless revoked by a user with Supervisory or Access Control rights.

INI files in Windows for Workgroups

Win.ini contains environmental information, while System.ini contains system configuration information. The settings for the desktop, color schemes, and multimedia information are located in Control.ini. Progman.ini contains Program Manager appearance and configuration information, and Winfile.ini contains the settings for File Manager's appearance and operation. The network drivers and protocol information is found in Protocol.ini. Msmail.ini contains information for the Mail program. Efaxpump.ini is only present if the fax is installed and contains information about fax modems, security, and received faxes. Schdplus.ini contains information about Schedule+'s appearance and behavior. Finally, there is Shared.ini, which contains settings that allow users in the same workgroup to share custom commands and messages for Mail.

Many Windows applications create their own INI files during installation. Others will add entries to the Win.ini file.

The contents of the INI files are read during Windows for Workgroups startup. After editing the files, restart Windows for Workgroups to activate the changes.

INIT

Macintosh Operating System 6 term for an operating system extension.

init

The first process that starts on a Linux system.

Initial ramdisk image (initrd)

A special device initialized by the boot loader as a RAM disk before the Linux kernel is started.

Initialization files

Files with the .ini extension that contain information that define your setup and various other parameters that are needed by a program. This is used extensively in Microsoft Windows and OS/2 for storing environmental or other device information.

inittab

In Linux, the table read by init to determine how to start the system, commonly located in the /etc directory.

In-line image

A graphic image displayed within an HTML document.

Inner class

A class that is defined within other classes.

Insert

SQL Server command to add a row to a table.

insmod

The command to load Linux kernel modules; does not handle dependencies.

INSTALL

1. Common software installation filename.

2. A NetWare 3.x and 4.x loadable module used to install, modify, or update the NetWare operating system. The module is contained in the INSTALL.NLM file and is loaded with the LOAD console command. NetWare 3.12 and 4.x also have DOS INSTALL programs that are used to initialize the original install process.

Installable File System (IFS)

A body of code that loads at boot time. The code provides the software to manage a file system on a storage device, the ability to create and maintain directories, allocate disk space, and so on.

Installation script

A file containing a group of commands used to automate a setup program.

Instance

An occurrence of an object in memory.

Institute of Electrical and Electronics Engineers (IEEE)

A professional ANSI-accredited body of scientists and engineers based in the U.S. IEEE promotes standardization and consults to the American National Standards Institute on matters relating to electrical and electronic development. The IEEE 802 Standards Committee is the leading official standard organization for Local Area Networks (LANs).

Integrated Drive Electronics (IDE)

The standard interface for a hard disk drive. Controller electronics are integrated into the drive. The controller connects to a paddleboard that may be external to, or on, the system board. The paddleboard then interfaces with the bus to the CPU. An IDE bus can be identified by its 40-pin connector, as opposed to the 50-pin connector of a SCSI bus.

Integrated Login Security

Validation method where members of a Windows NT domain are automatically logged in for SQL Server access.

Integrated Services Digital Network (ISDN)

A special kind of telecommunications network designed to handle more than just data. Digital network operating over PSTN local loop wiring. Multiple services, including video, text, voice, data, facsimile images, and graphics, are supported over 64-Kbps channels. Standard configurations combine multiple channels to provide higher transfer rates.

Integrity

Data consistency and accuracy, especially in the context of security. In a general sense, the level of confidence that can be placed in a system. For example, a system may have been invaded in such a way that no obvious damage has occured, but which can no longer be trusted in a secure environment–it has suffered a reduction of integrity in the attack.

Integrity constraint

A constraint that needs to be enforced to ensure the integrity of the data in the database.

IntelliMirror

The Microsoft technology that stores a mirror image of a client computer on a server. In Microsoft 2000, the umbrella term for a collection of technologies designed to reduce the cost of network ownership.

Interactive

The exchange of information and control between the user and a computer process.

Interactive also refers to time-dependent (real-time) data communications. Typically communications in which a user enters data and then waits for a response message from the destination before continuing.

Interface

1. A shared boundary between two functional units, defined by functional characteristics, signal characteristics, and other characteristics, as appropriate. Also, any of the electrical and logical devices that permit computers and peripherals to be interconnected.

2. A contract between an object and its users.

3. Any of the electrical and logical devices that permit computers and peripherals to be interconnected. A network interface is the most common example.

Interfaces

A set of methods that can be implemented by Java classes.

Interior Gateway Protocol (IGP)

The protocol used to exchange routing information between collaborating routers in the Internet. Routing Information Protocol (RIP) and Open Shortest Path First (OSPF) are examples of IGPs.

Interlaced

In monitors, interlacing is often implemented because it is less expensive. Interlaced monitors allow lower-cost circuitry to be used to display higher resolutions (scan rate) than it would otherwise be capable of producing.

Interleave

A method of arranging disk sectors to compensate for relatively slow computers. It attempts to minimize the amount of time required to read consecutive sectors from a single track on the fixed disk. By numbering every other sector it encounters as though it were the next consecutive sector, the controller is effectively able to slow the spin rate of the fixed disk drive so that it can issue a command to read the next consecutively numbered sector.

An interleave ratio that is set to read every other sector as consecutive is said to run at a 2-to-1 rate. For example, it would start with Sector 1, skip a sector, number the next sector 2, skip a sector, number the next sector 3, skip a sector, etc. If set to read every third sector, the interleave is 3-to-1. Ideally, interleave should be set to the lowest number that the computer, the disk drive, and the disk controller can support. Virtually all new computers and disk controllers support a 1-to-1 interleave rate.

Intermediate system

An OSI system that is not an end system but which serves instead to relay communications between end systems.

Intermediate System to Intermediate System (IS-IS)

The routing protocol used by routers to share network information in an OSI network.

Internal Organization of the Network Layer (IONL)

The OSI standard for the detailed architecture of the Network layer. Basically, it partitions the Network layer into subnetworks interconnected by convergence protocols (equivalent to internetworking protocols), creating what Internet calls a catenet or internet.

International Data Encryption Algorithm (IDEA)

A more recent form of data encryption, similar in form to DES but using more elaborate encryption schemes. It is meant to be more secure and more internationalized than DES.

International Organization for Standardization (ISO)

Founded in 1946, ISO promotes the development of international standards for the computer, communications, and other fields. ISO members are the standards organizations of 89 countries. The United States representative is the American National Standards Institute (ANSI).

Note that ISO is not an acronym in this instance. The word *iso* is derived from the Greek word *isos*, which means equal.

Internet

An international computer network of networks that connect government, academic, and business institutions. Networks on the Internet include MILNET, NSFNET, and other backbone networks, as well as mid-level networks and stub (local) networks.

Internet networks communicate using TCP/IP (Transmission Control Protocol/Internet Protocol). The Internet connects colleges, universities, military organizations and contractors, corporations, government research laboratories, and individuals.

Although parts of the Internet operate under single administrative domains, the Internet as a whole reaches around the globe, connects computers (from personal computers to supercomputers), and is not administered by any single authority. The Internet in July 1995 roughly connected 60,000 independent networks into a vast global Internet.

Used as a descriptive term, an internet is a collection of interconnected packet-switching networks. Any time you connect two or more networks together, you have an internet—as in *inter*national or *inter*state.

Internet address

A 32-bit value written or displayed in numbers that specify a particular network and node on that network.

Internet Architecture Board (IAB)

The IAB is the technical body that oversees the development of the Internet suite of protocols commonly referred to as "TCP/IP." It has two task forces, the IRTF and the IETF, each charged with investigating a particular area.

Internet Connection Server (ICS)

RRAS configuration within Windows 2000 Server that enables you to share a single Internet connection with other computers on the network.

Internet Control Message Protocol (ICMP)

Used for error reporting and recovery, and is a required component of any IP implementation.

Internet Engineering Steering Group (IESG)

The executive committee of the Internet Engineering Task Force (IETF).

Internet Engineering Task Force (IETF)

One of the task forces of the IAB, the IETF is responsible for solving short-term engineering needs of the Internet. It has more than 40 Working Groups.

Internet Gateway Routing Protocol (IGRP)

A proprietary IGP used by Cisco System's routers.

Internet Group Management Protocol (IGMP)

Part of the TCP/IP protocol suite. Provides multicasting broadcasts for communications and passing management information in a multicasting group.

Internet Information Server (IIS)

Microsoft Internet Information Server is a network file and application server that transmits information in Hypertext Markup Language.

Internet Network Information Center (InterNIC)

Developed in 1993 by General Atomics, AT&T, and NSI to provide information services to Internet users, it offers a reference desk that provides networking information, referrals to other resources, and associate users with their local NICs. InterNIC also provides coordination to share information and activities with U.S. and international organizations, as well as education services to train mid-level and campus NICs, and to end users to promote Internet use.

Internet Protocol (IP)

The OSI layer 3 routed protocol used to transmit packetized information on a TCP/IP network.

Internet Relay Chat (IRC)

An Internet protocol that supports real-time conversations between Internet users worldwide.

Internet Research Task Force (IRTF)

One of the task forces of the Internet Architecture Board (IAB), it is responsible for research and development of the Internet protocol suite.

Internet Server Application Programming Interface (ISAPI)

An API that is used to build server-side filters and extensions. When IIS starts, it loads each ISAPI component into memory. This is the copy of the component that IIS will use each time a user causes the component to run. This is more optimal than CGI applications that load a new copy every time they are used.

Internet Service Provider (ISP)

Companies that provide an Internet connection for educational institutions, individuals, companies, and organizations.

Internetwork

Two or more networks connected by a router.

Internetwork Packet Exchange (IPX)

Used with SPX as the resident protocol in NetWare. A router with IPX routing can interconnect Local Area Networks (LANs) so that Novell NetWare clients and servers can communicate.

In NetWare 3.x, IPX is the name of the command-line utility used to see the versions and options of IPX.COM. This was used prior to the introduction of ODI drivers.

Internetwork Packet Exchange Open Data-link Interface (IPXODI)

This is a module that takes the workstation requests determined to be for the network by the NetWare DOS Requester and packages them with transmission information (such as their destination), then transfers them to the Link Support Layer (LSL). IPXODI requires that each packet have an initialized header specifying information targeting network delivery and announcing from where the packet came, where it is going, and what happens after delivery.

Interoperability

The ability to use products from different vendors in the same system. Communication protocols, such as IP or AFP, can be used in ODI to process information from the network. The user does not have to know each protocol's required method of packet transmission. Interoperability also means an application can share files, even when running on different platforms, such as Macintosh or UNIX.

Interoperability Technology Association for Information Processing (INTAP)

The technical organization which has the official charter to develop Japanese OSI profiles and conformance tests.

Interprocess communication

The exchange of information between processes by means of messages.

Interrupt

A request for attention by a subsystem. Depending on conditions and the type of interrupt, an interrupt may be handled immediately or deferred either until the current interrupt has been handled or until all higher priority interrupts have been handled. An interrupt is usually fairly important and should not be kept waiting for very long.

Interrupt Request (IRQ) lines

Interrupt Request lines are normally referred to as IRQ lines, and each line requires a separate IRQ number. Many PC add-in boards and devices require a unique dedicated IRQ line. Some IRQs are assigned to system devices.

The original IBM PC was an 8-bit system with eight available IRQ lines numbered 0 through 7. These lines support the system timer, keyboard, COM and LPT ports, and the floppy disk controller.

With the 16-bit IBM AT came eight additional IRQ lines that *cascade* through IRQ 2. These IRQ lines support the Real Time Clock, hard disk controller, math coprocessor, and other devices. Examples of devices that use these IRQ lines are VGA and network adapters, CD-ROM drives, and SCSI controllers.

Some COM ports share IRQ lines. All odd-numbered COM ports (COM1, COM3, etc.) share IRQ 4, while all even numbered COM ports share IRQ 3.

Intranet

A private internet, usually within a company, for facilitating information sharing. It looks and acts just like the public Internet.

Intrinsic function

A function for which the compiler can generate inline code rather than calling the external function.

Introspection APIs

APIs that provide the functionality necessary to allow development tools to query a component for its internal state.

Intrusion detection

The process of establishing monitoring software and personnel to maintain vigilant watch over traffic to and from a secure site, and to provide some degree of automated alarm capability in case of suspicious transmissions directed at a site. The software tools rely on signatures to identify particular attacks, much as antivirus software looks for byte patterns in files.

Inventory

The hardware and software information of every SMS client that is collected by SMS.

Inventory agent

An SMS component that scans for inventory information and reports it to the SMS system.

Inventory frequency

Determines how often the Inventory Agent will scan for inventory.

I/O

I/O (Input/Output) refers to the sending and receiving of data from the Central Processing Unit (CPU) to other peripheral devices such as disk drives. The input/output channel carries out all transfer of data so as to free up the CPU. The keyboard is the most common input device, and the monitor is the most common output device.

I/O address

Space used to access I/O hardware such as I/O adapters, buses, and special registers used by I/O devices known as Control and Status Register (CSR). I/O address space is one of two equal parts of primary memory, or addressable memory. The other equal part is memory address space.

I/O privilege mechanism

A facility that allows a process to ask a device driver for direct access to the device's I/O ports and any dedicated or mapped memory locations it has. The I/O privilege mechanism can be used directly by an application or indirectly by a dynamic link package.

IP address

Each host in the network is assigned a unique IP address for each network connection (installed network adapter). The IP address is used to identify packet source and destination hosts.

An IP address is a 32-bit address, written as 4 octets (bytes) separated by periods. For example, 195.143.67.2.

This way of representing an IP address is also known as dotted decimal notation. Each address will also have an associated subnet mask, dividing the address into its network prefix and host suffix. For example, you might have the following defined as a subnet mask: 255.255.255.0. The subnet mask is used to identify the network and host portions of the address.

The network portion identifies where the host is located, and the host portion identifies the device connected to that network.

When dealing with a network the size of the Internet, address assignments must be carefully coordinated. With millions of hosts operating on thousands of networks, the potential for duplicate addresses is significant. The job of coordinating Internet IP addresses is given to the Network Information Center.

An assigned address is only required if your network is connected to the Internet. If connected to the Internet, your network address will be assigned through the Internetwork Network Information Center, or InterNIC.

To get an Internet address, contact the InterNIC at InterNIC Registration Services, c/o Network Solutions, Inc., 505 Huntmar Park Drive, Herndon, Virginia 22070, (703) 742-4777, or at hostmaster@internic.net.

An organization is assigned a network address. The organization can further divide this into its own subnets and assign the host addresses.

Rather than going to the InterNIC, it is more likely that an organization will work through a local provider for address assignment. The organization will then subdivide the address, if necessary, and assign host addresses.

IP datagram

The fundamental unit of information passed across the Internet. It contains source and destination addresses along with data and a number of fields that define the length of the datagram, the header checksum, and flags to indicate whether the datagram can be (or has been) fragmented.

IP hijacking

A form of spoofing in which one host is disabled, usually by a Denial of Service attack, and the transmissions of another are modified to masquerade as the disabled host. The most famous such attack, and a model of the process, was that of legendary hacker Kevin Mitnick on the systems of Tsutomu Shimomura. Also known as *IP splicing*.

IP number

Sometimes called a *dotted quad*, it is a unique number consisting of four parts separated by periods. For example, 109.123.251.2. Each value in the dotted quad ranges from 0 to 255, representing the decimal form of an 8-bit binary number.

Every machine that is on the Internet has a unique IP number. If a machine does not have an IP number, it is not really *on* the Internet. Most machines also have one or more Domain Names so that they are easier for people to remember.

ipchains

In Linux, a program that can act as a packet-filtering firewall. Similar functionality has existed historically in the ipfwadm tool and is undergoing a revision in the new tool, *netfilter*.

IPX external network number

A network number that uniquely identifies a network cable segment. An IPX external network number is a hexadecimal number, one to eight digits (1 to FFFFFFFE). When the IPX protocol is bound to a network board in the server, the number is assigned. IPX can be bound with multiple frame types or protocols to the same network board. Network number and network address are two terms used to refer to the IPX external network number.

IPX internal network number

A logical network number that identifies an individual NetWare server. During installation, the service is assigned an IPX internal network number. It is a hexadecimal number, 1 to 8 digits (1 to FFFFFFFE), that is unique to each server on a network. The IPX internal network number must also be different from any IPX external network number on the internetwork.

IPX internetwork address

A 12-byte number (represented by 24 hexadecimal characters) divided into three parts: the 4-byte (8-character) IPX external network number, the 6-byte (12-character) node number, and the 2-byte (4-character) socket number.

IPXODI.COM

A NetWare file containing the IPX and SPX protocol stacks for use with the Open Data Link Interface. It allows workstations to communicate with NetWare file servers.

IPXS

NetWare 3.x and 4.x loadable module for use with other modules, such as CLIB, that require the STREAMS IPX module services.

isapnptools

In Linux, a set of utilities for probing and configuring PnP (Plug and Play) devices.

ISO Development Environment (ISODE)

A popular implementation of the upper layers of OSI. Pronounced eye-so-dee-eee.

Isochronous

Dependent on proper timing. The term isochronous is frequently used to refer to media that requires audio and visual synchronization.

ISOCON

A NetWare 3.11 utility that allows the network manager to monitor and control OSI routing on the MultiProtocol Router product.

isql

A SQL Server text-based command-line interface.

isql/w

isql/w (listed as ISQL_w in the Windows NT 4.0 Start menu) provides a graphic environment for working with SQL Server. You can compose and execute Transact-SQL statements, generically referred to as queries, review the results, see I/O statistics, and the plan of execution for your statement.

Not only does isql/w run queries, it also provides an easy way of viewing and executing SQL scripts. Scripts are similar to operating system batch files and contain a series of commands to be executed on your server. SQL Server provides a number of scripts for various purposes, such as preparing a server to support data replication.

J

Java

A programming language with a colorful history and a meteoric rise. Java was not designed for the Internet or World Wide Web. It was developed by a team at Sun Microsystems that was developing software for consumer electronics.

Existing languages like C and C++ were inadequate for the purposes of the software the team was developing. C and C++ programs need to be compiled for particular computer chips. When a new chip is released, C and C++ programs must be recompiled to run on the new chip. These programs are not flexible enough to be moved to new software libraries.

In the consumer electronics market, pricing of components is crucial, and chips are often replaced with newer, more cost-effective chips at a rapid rate. This swapping of chips is not the ideal environment for C and C++ programs.

Backward compatibility is an issue in consumer electronics because it is not uncommon for somebody to have a TV that is 5 or 10 years old. Reliability is another issue because consumer electronics normally have to be replaced if a component goes bad.

Java was originally named Oak by James Gosling, who was the team leader for the original development project. The name was inspired by a large oak tree outside of Gosling's office. It was discovered that there was another programming language called Oak, and a new name had to be coined for the language. The name Java was an inspiration after some of the team members visited a coffee shop near their office.

The Java market is rapidly expanding with many companies licensing Java technology for integration into their products. For browsers, Netscape Communications Corporation added Java support to their Netscape Navigator 2.0 browser giving Netscape Navigator users the opportunity to view Java-enhanced Web pages. Other browser vendors, like Microsoft, are adding Java support in their browsers. Microsoft has also licensed Java for inclusion in future versions of Windows.

Sun Microsystems has started a new business unit called Javasoft and has announced the release of new Java development tools. Java WorkShop is a set of Java development tools designed to work within a Java-capable browser. With Java WorkShop, developers have the ability to design, test, and deploy Java applications for the Web. Another new product is Internet WorkShop, which includes Java WorkShop, Visual WorkShop for C++, and a Network Object Environment (NOE) for development of powerful Web applications.

From a security perspective, Java is a real boon since it has tight security controls built into all levels of its application programming interfaces (APIs), unlike C and C++ which must rely on the native security mechanisms of the host operating system. Java also implements its own memory management and *garbage collection* (reclaiming unused memory) independently of the underlying operating system, eliminating one of the worst sources of exploits–C and C++ programs with faulty memory allocation code.

Java Beans

Platform-independent component technology based on the Java platform.

Java compiler (javac)

Compiles Java source code files into executable Java bytecode.

Java Database Connectivity (JDBC)

A structured interface to SQL databases.

Java Development Kit (JDK)

Software that has a compiler, basic debugging tools, and common class libraries.

Job

Contains instructions for actions that will be performed. This replaces the SQL Server 6.5 term task.

Job schedule

Schedule identifying when a job will execute.

Job step

Individual executable action within a job.

jobs

In Linux, a command to list currently running or stopped background processes associated with the current session. Also, the set of background processes associated with the current session.

Join

1. In database terminology, a relational operator that produces a single table from two tables, based on a comparison of particular column values (join columns) in each of the tables. The result is a table containing rows formed by the concatenation of the rows in the two tables. The values of the join columns compare or, if specified, include nonmatching rows.

2. A command in GNU/Linux (and UNIX) to join sorted files.

Join column

In database terminology, a column used to set conditions for a join. A join column is usually a primary key or foreign key column.

Join-compatible columns

In database terminology, key columns or columns of similar data type and values.

Joint Academic Network (JANET)

A university network in the U.K.

Joint Photographic Experts Group (JPEG)

JPEG is a format for storing a graphics file in digital format and is similar to GIF. It is a standard for images on the Web.

The names of jpeg-formatted files often end in .jpg. The main differences between gif and jpeg are the manner in which data is compressed. Gif uses lossless compression, while jpeg uses lossy compression. The bit depth is 8-bit for gif and up to 24-bit for jpeg. More information is available in the JPEG FAQs on the Internet.

Jughead

A server that maintains a database of menu items at a gopher site. It allows users to search the site. Jughead is an acronym for Jonzy's Universal Gopher Hierarchy Excavation and Display.

K

K Desktop Environment (KDE)

An Open Source collection of X Window applications.

KA9Q

A popular implementation of TCP/IP and associated protocols for amateur packet radio systems.

Kerberos

A comprehensive approach to distributed system security developed for UNIX platforms based on message encryption and tightly enforced authentication semantics, but now existing on others. It is the default authentication protocol for Windows 2000 clients and services. A drawback of Kerberos is that often it is difficult to incorporate into legacy networks because, by design, passwords are never transmitted over the network even in encrypted form. Rather, all authentication requests are referred to a *key server*, which is the centerpiece of a Kerberos protected network.

Kermit

A popular file transfer and terminal emulation program.

Kernel

A set of essential operating routines used by the operating system (usually hidden from the user) to perform important system tasks such as managing the system memory or controlling disk operations.

Kernel mode

Lower-level Windows NT or Windows 95 operating system functions.

Kernel panic

An unpredictable termination of a process being controlled by the kernel.

Key Distribution Center (KDC)

Kerberos protocol authentication server and ticket-granting service.

Keyboard

The device that allows the user to input data into the computer or to execute commands. Most keyboards resemble a typewriter. The standard is a 101-key keyboard.

Keys

1. Attribute columns that show a unique value for each entity.

2. The fields in a record (line) used by the Linux **sort** command to sort a file when the **keys** option is used.

Kickstart

A Red Hat utility for installing Linux locally or remotely, used to automate an installation and minimize local keyboard input.

kill

In Linux, a command to send interrupt signals and completion instructions to end, suspend, or otherwise modify the status of a running job or process.

Kilobit (Kb)

In computing, it refers to 1,024 bits. (A bit is the basic unit for storing data in primary storage.) Kilobit is used mainly to express the speed of data transmission.

Kilobits per second (Kbps)

Thousands of bits per second.

Kilobyte (KB)

In computing, it refers to 1,024 bytes. (A byte is a unit of information consisting of 8 bits.) Kilobyte is mainly used to express the capacity of primary storage.

Kilobytes per second (KBps)

Thousands of bytes per second.

Knowbot

A computer program that automates the searching and gathering of data from distributed databases. The general term is sometimes shortened to bot.

Knowledge Consistency Checker (KCC)

A Windows 2000 service that uses site and subnet information, provided by domain administrators, for the purpose of generating a replication topology. The KCC uses its topology information to calculate the best connections for Active Directory replication.

L

Label

1. The Macintosh operating system allows users to identify files and folders by assigning a category name and corresponding color. Labels are visible in the Finder, as well as application Open and Save dialog boxes, and may be used as a sort criteria for file management tasks.

2. Linux TK built-in command to create and manipulate label widgets.

Laboratoire Europeen pour la Physique des Particules (CERN)

This is the network for the European Laboratory for Particle Physics in Switzerland that developed the World Wide Web software and the concepts behind HTTP and HTML. CERN stands for the previous network name "Conseil Europeen pour la Recherche Nucleaire."

Lamp

A light on a phone device that provides information about the state of a particular call.

LAN Adapter and Protocol Support (LAPS)

The program that provides LAN adapter and protocol device drivers for OS/2.

LAN driver

Software that establishes communication between a file server's network board and the NetWare operating system.

LAN Requester

The term used to refer to a workstation on a LAN Server network. It is also the name of LAN Server's primary management utility.

Landing zone

On fixed disk drives, the read/write heads must return to a specific position when the drive is not operating (or when the system is powered off). This position is referred to as the landing zone. Early fixed disk drives (for instance, those introduced in the IBM XT systems) had problems with the heads falling on the surface of the disk drive platters when the systems lost power, causing a head crash. The landing zone is a portion of the disk where no data is read or written, thereby ensuring no damage to the data if the heads accidentally touch the disk platter surface.

Landscape

A document orientation that has a vertical dimension greater than its horizontal dimension.

LaserWriter

The original Apple laser printer based on the Canon laser engine. Also the name of the standard PostScript laser printer driver used by the Macintosh operating system.

Latency

The delay between an update occurring on the Publisher and the update being applied to the Subscriber.

Latin-1

Also known, more cryptically, as ISO 8879. Latin-1 is an 8-bit character set (containing, therefore, 256 characters, of which the first 32 are nonprinting or "control" characters like tab and linefeed) that includes the diacritically marked characters used in European languages like French and German. (It does not, however, include the Polish barred L, the Czech r and s, the Turkish dotless i.) HTML browsers vary in how well they support Latin-1. Generally speaking, accented letters will work everywhere; special characters may not. In HTML source code, non-ASCII characters are denoted by "escape sequences" like é or §.

Launcher

1. An application that simplifies access to Macintosh programs and files. This application is standard with Macintosh Operating System 8.

2. Any application (or user interface structure) that presents a convenient way to access programs and files, such as the panel device in KDE and GNOME.

Layout manager

A class that implements the layout management interface. Layout managers perform the visual layout of components within a container.

Leaf node

SQL Server index node pointing to data records.

Leaf object

A type of NetWare object that does not contain other objects. Examples are user, printer, or server objects.

Leased line

A telephone line reserved for the exclusive use of leasing customers, without interexchange switching arrangements. Also called a Private Line.

Legacy

1. Older, non-Plug-and-Play hardware in use.

2. Older applications, such as those running on IBM Mainframes.

Legacy hardware

Term referring to hardware devices that require continued support in a new operating system environment.

Library

A group of programs or objects in a file.

License Interchange Format

A standard format for software licensing.

Licensing system

The software that provides copy protection and licensing for an application.

Lifetime

Variable lifetime refers to how long a variable remains in memory.

Lightweight Directory Access Protocol (LDAP)

A platform-independent service that may be employed to provide directories of information (such as e-mail addresses) using TCP/IP. Modeled from X.500 and DAP, LDAP is a scaled-down version of its predecessor, Directory Access Protocol (DAP), which was unsuccessful because it was too inefficient (heavy) with thin clients, personal computers, and Internet use. It is functionally similar to Microsoft's Active Directory and Novell's NDS.

LILO

Linux Loader–a boot loader for the Linux kernel.

lilo.conf

The /etc/lilo.conf file contains configuration parameters used by LILO to bring up Linux or other operating systems.

Lines per inch (lpi)

Lpi dictates how many typewritten lines will be placed in the height of an inch on the paper.

Link

Any part of a Web page that is connected to something else. Clicking on or selecting a link will make that something else appear. (This is one major difference between virtual reality and real reality.) The first part of the URL named in a link denotes the method or kind of link. The methods include file (for local files), ftp, gopher, http, mailto, news, and wais (for some kinds of searches).

Link Access Procedure Balanced (LAPB)

An alternative protocol developed after LAP. LAPB allows the DTE/DCE interface to operate in *balanced mode.*

Link Support Layer (LSL)

A component of the Open Data-link Interface (ODI) software implementation on a workstation. Link Support Layer functions between the LAN driver and IPX, TCP/IP, or other communications protocol. LSL.COM is a NetWare program file used for communication between the device driver (LAN DRIVER) and IPX or other protocol on the client workstation.

Linked list

A dynamic series of objects, each of which contains a pointer to the next object in the list.

Linked server

An association established between the local server and a remote server.

Linux

A UNIX-like operating system originally created by Linus Torvalds at the University of Finland with the assistance of developers around the world. The goal of Linux is to provide the PC with a free or very low-cost operating system comparable to high-priced UNIX system software. Linux conforms to the POSIX standard user and programming interfaces and comes in different versions that can run on Intel-based, PowerPC, Sparc, and Alpha-based computers.

Linux Documentation Project (LDP)

A project to write documentation for all facets of Linux.

linuxconf

A program to configure a Linux system; has terminal, X, and Web interfaces.

Liquid Crystal Diode (LCD)

LCD monitors are typically used in laptop and notebook systems as well as other devices, such as pocket calculators. Their light weight, small size, and low power consumption make them ideal for these applications. Most PC systems using LCD monitors now use backlit displays, which allow them to be read in low light conditions. Color LCD displays are also available.

LISTDIR

A NetWare command-line utility that lists a directory's Inherited Rights Filter, a user's effective rights in the directory, the name of each subdirectory, and the date or time the subdirectory was created.

Listserv

Listserv is an electronic mail-based discussion forum organized around topics of interest to subscribers. Internet users may subscribe to a listserv.

A listserv program maintains the list of subscribers and routes all messages to the subscriber's electronic mailboxes. Responses sent by subscribers are sent to all other subscribers.

The most common kind of mail list, Listserv originated on BITNET but is now common on the Internet.

Little-endian

A format for storage or transmission of binary data in which the least significant byte (bit) comes first. From a story in Gulliver's Travels (Swift) in which two warring factions disputed over which end of an egg should be opened. The reverse convention is called big-endian.

LMHOSTS

The LMHOSTS file lists the IP address and NetBIOS name for each network machine with which the local machine may need to communicate.

Load

Under SQL Server, this is the process of restoring a database from a backup (dump). LOAD is also a NetWare 3.x and 4.x console command that loads NetWare Loadable Modules, including disk and LAN drivers, name space for storing non-DOS files, and NLM utilities.

Loadable module

A program, usually an NLM or VLM program, users can load and unload from a server or workstation while the attendant operating system is running.

Loading and unloading

The process of linking and unlinking NLM programs to the NetWare operating system. NLM programs can be loaded and unloaded while NetWare is running.

Local Access and Transport Area (LATA)

Within a LATA, a local exchange common carrier provides connections, service, and a dial tone to all telephone subscribers. A LATA typically includes all of the local exchanges and interoffice trunks and toll offices required to service a metropolitan area that may include several small cities and towns. The U.S. has been divided into more than 200 Local Access and Transport Areas in order to define areas of responsibility.

Local account

A Windows NT Server user account not authorized for interactive logon but supporting resource access.

Local Area Network (LAN)

A group of computers running specialized communications software and joined through an external data path.

A LAN will cover a small geographic area, usually no larger than a single building. The computers have a direct high-speed connection between all workstations and servers, and share hardware resources and data files. A LAN has centralized management of resources and network security.

PC-based networks can trace their heritage back to what are now often referred to as legacy systems. These systems were mainframe and minicomputer hosts accessed through dumb terminals.

There are a number of similarities between LANs and these legacy systems, such as centralized storage and backup, access security, and central management of resources. There are, however, a number of differences.

Traditional host systems are characterized by centralized processing, dumb terminals, custom applications, and high expansion costs and management overhead. LANs are characterized by distributed processing, intelligent workstations (PCs), and off-the-shelf applications. LANs are modular, are inexpensive to expand, and have more moderate management costs.

Local caching

Storage of a copy of a user's personal profile on a local hard disk.

Local Descriptor Table (LDT)

An element of 80286/80386 memory management hardware. The LDT holds the descriptions of as many as 4,095 local segments. Each press has its own LDT and cannot access the LDTs of other processes.

Local drive

The common name for a physical drive attached to a workstation.

Local group

1. Group scope supported by Windows 2000 that defines its members as being local to the machine. Local groups are valid only on nondomain/stand-alone servers and workstations.

2. When discussing Windows NT Server domains, it is a group definition supporting local domain resource management. When discussing Workstations, it is a group definition supporting local management of a Windows NT workstation.

Local Group Policy Object

Group Policy Object used for setting and managing policies for stand-alone and workgroup member Windows 2000 systems. A system will have only one local Group Policy Object.

Local printer

A printer directly connected to one of the ports on the computer. The opposite is one connected through a network, which would be a remote printer.

Local profile

User profile stored on and specific to a particular Windows NT workstation.

Local Security Authority (LSA)

Windows 2000 component that maintains information about local system security and the local security policy.

Local server

The server a user is logged in to, located on the Local Area Network (LAN).

Local unwind

The process by which the compiler generates code to save a return value and guarantee that the final block is executed before the guarded block terminates.

Local user account

A user account created on a workstation, member server, or stand-alone system and used for local logon authentication.

Local variable

A SQL Server variable declared with the Declare statement and assigned a value with the Select statement. Local variables have names beginning with an @ character, for example, @count.

LocalTalk

A 230.4-Kbps serial interface found on all Macintosh systems. Originally intended as a vehicle for sharing a LaserWriter printer in small Mac-based workgroups, LocalTalk can also be used to build Local Area Networks (LANs). However, its relatively slow data transmission speed makes it a poor choice for networking considering the wide availability of Token-Ring (4 or 16 Mbps), Ethernet (10 Mbps), and Fast-Ethernet (100 Mbps) hardware.

LocalTalk Link Access Protocol (LLAP)

Provides the physical connection of LocalTalk and to various hardware including EtherTalk (ELAP) and TokenTalk (TLAP).

locate

In Linux, a program used to locate files using a database usually updated daily; similar in some ways to find.

Locked files

1. Files protected against user access.

2. Files that were in use during an installation or software removal. The files will be processed the next time the system is restarted.

Locks

A mechanism used by an application to prevent multiple concurrent user updates from interfering with one another and causing update anomalies.

Log file

1. Transaction log containing a record of database transactions.

2. In Linux, a file in the /var/log/ directory that tracks any of a number of events.

Log Reader Agent

Replication agent that moves transactions for replication from the published database to the distribution database.

Logging in

The process of gaining access to a computer system by providing an authorized username and then a password.

Logging out

The process of ending a user's connection to the operating system, closing all resources for that user.

Logic Board

The electronic circuit board containing the primary system components such as CPU, RAM, ROMs, etc.

Logic bomb

A kind of attack based on software that is deliberately faulty; for example, a program that deliberately consumes network bandwidth.

Logic error

Error occurring due to poorly designed applications or improperly applied functions and operators.

Logical data independence

When a change in the logical structure of a database, as in relationships among tables, columns, and rows, do not affect the function of application programs and ad hoc queries.

Logical operators

Also called Boolean operators, they include AND (joins two or more conditions and returns results when all of the conditions are true), OR (connects two or more conditions and returns results when either or both of the conditions are true), and NOT (negates a condition).

Logical Unit (LU)

The element within a network based on IBM's Systems Network Architecture (SNA) by which a user (terminal or program) attaches to the network. LUs are described by type to indicate their functional capabilities. LU2, for example, is a 3270-type device.

Login

The process of initiating and authenticating a connection to a computer system, usually requiring a password, and identification of the user by a unique username.

LOGIN directory

The SYS:LOGIN directory is created during network installation. It contains that LOGIN and NLIST utilities, which allow users to log in and view a list of available NetWare servers. The directory for OS/2 users is SYS:LOGIN/OS2.

Login restrictions

These control access to the network by requiring a password, setting account limits, limiting disk space, limiting the number of connections, and setting time restrictions. An account can be set to lock if a user violates login restrictions, allowing no logins using that username and preventing unauthorized users from logging in until unlocked by an administrator.

Logoff script

Executable file that runs when a user logs off.

Logon script

DOS or NT batch file or executable that may run when a user logs on to a computer system. Logon scripts can be used to map drives and search drives to directories, display messages, set environment variables, and execute programs or menus.

Logon server

Any site server that is added to the SMS system. It assists with inventory collection, package installation, etc., for its domain.

LOGOUT

A NetWare 3.x, 4.x, and Portable NetWare command-line utility that is used to close communication with one or more file servers.

Loop

1. A series of program statements running in cyclic repetition.
2. An iterative programming construct. Loops are used to repeatedly execute a block of code.

Lost update

An update anomaly in multiuser concurrent environments where one user's update overwrites another user's update, thus causing it to be lost.

Low Entry Networking (LEN)

A form of IBM's Systems Network Architecture (SNA) that permits PCs and minicomputers to communicate when a network does not contain an IBM mainframe.

Low priority category

A classification of processes that consists of processes that get CPU time only when no other thread in higher priorities needs it. This category is lower in priority than the general priority category. In Linux, a process can have any of several priorities.

lpd

In Linux, the daemon that controls print jobs and spools each one to a printer.

LPT port

Also known as a parallel port, it is a connection on the computer, usually LPT1, where the cable for a parallel printer is connected. Generally, LPT1 through LPT3 can exist on a personal computer (in Linux, referenced as /dev/lp0, lp1, and lp2). Special equipment can be added to extend this capability.

LS

Determines the number of link stations for a Token-Ring driver. This parameter may be required on a Novell network in the SHELL.CFG file depending on the network interface card.

ls

In Linux, the command to list contents of a directory.

lsmod

The command to list loaded Linux kernel modules.

LU6.2

A communication protocol. IBM has identified LU6.2 as the transport mechanism for applications using the future Enhanced Connectivity Facilities (ECF) within SAA.

Luminosity

A value between 0 and 240 that indicates the amount of black or white contained in a particular color. A value of 0 indicates all black. A value of 240 indicates all white.

Lycos

Lycos is a search engine on the Internet located at www.lycos.com.

Lynx

A text-based interface to the World Wide Web.

M

MacBinary

A file transfer format used to exchange Macintosh files over modem or direct serial port connections. This format maintains all Macintosh file information contained in both Data and Resource Forks.

MACHINE

NetWare login script command that specifies the workstation's long machine name as assigned in SHELL.CFG or NET.CFG. The MACHINE command is required to run NetBIOS.

Machine group

A group of computers. Can be used as a shortcut instead of specifying computers individually.

Macintosh client

A Macintosh computer that attaches to the network. A Linux server running netatalk support allows the Macintosh client to store data on and retrieve data from the network. A NetWare server running NetWare for Macintosh namespace support modules allows the Macintosh client to store data on and retrieve data from the network. The client can also run executable Macintosh network files, share files with other clients (DOS, MS Windows, OS/2, and UNIX/Linux), and monitor print queues.

Macintosh files

Files used on Macintosh computers. They contain two parts: the data fork, which contains information specified by the user, and the resource fork, which contains Macintosh-specific information such as the windows and icons used with the file. The Macintosh namespace module must be linked with the NetWare operating system container for Macintosh files to be stored on a NetWare server.

Macintosh files can be shared transparently in a number of ways. The Linux file server should run netatalk to make files transparently available to the Macintosh client. Use of Macintosh files by non-Macintosh clients only requires that the resource fork be ignored.

Magnetic stripe reader

The device that reads magnetic stripes on credit cards and bank cards.

Mail bomb

A type of attack designed to create an exponentially growing cascade of e-mail, as in a chain reaction.

MAIL directory

NetWare directory that provides electronic mail boxes. The MAIL directory is automatically created in the SYS volume when the network is installed and contains a subdirectory for each user. The subdirectory serves as a mailbox with the user ID as an address.

In NetWare 3.x or lower, the subdirectory also contains user login scripts and PRINTCON definition files.

Mail programs compatible with NetWare use the SYS:MAIL directory.

Mail exploder

Part of an electronic mail delivery system that allows a message to be delivered to a list of addressees. Mail exploders are used to implement mailing lists. Users send messages to a single address (e.g., hacks@somehost.edu) and the mail exploder takes care of delivery to the individual mailboxes in the list.

Mail gateway

A machine that connects to two or more electronic mail systems, including those on different networks, and transfers mail messages among them.

Mail Transport Agent (MTA)

A systems software component designed to forward and receive e-mail from remote sites.

Mailbox

An area on a computer used to receive and store electronic mail messages.

Mailbox ID

A unique name that specifies the directory where all of the object's in-bound mail is placed.

Mailbox location

An object's mailbox resides in this messaging server.

Mailing list

A list of electronic mail addresses. A mailing list can be maintained by an individual user to send messages to groups of people. The mailing list is also used by listserv and other mail exploder programs to forward electronic mail messages on a specific topic to the listserv subscriber list.

Mailing lists are like newsletters except that any subscriber may contribute. A message sent to the list will automatically be sent to everyone who has subscribed to the list. A series of messages with the same subject line is called a thread.

Mailto

In a URL, mailto indicates a link that will allow a user to send e-mail to the person whose address follows in the URL.

Mainframe

A legacy computer that is capable of multitasking and other robust operations. It is generally used as a host for a large number of users.

Maintenance Manager

A component within the SMS Executive service. It maintains the SMS components housed on logon servers.

Makeboot.exe

A utility used to create Setup boot disks for Windows 2000. Makeboot.exe runs on MS-DOS and 16-bit Windows-family systems.

Makebt32.exe

A utility used to create Setup boot disks for Windows 2000. Makebt32.exe runs on 32-bit Windows-family operating systems.

Makepipe

Named pipe test utility.

MAKEUSER

A NetWare menu utility used to add and remove network users. A USR script file is created defining users to be created along with the user's defined parameters. The file can be written with the MAKEUSER menu utility or as an ASCII/DOS file using a text editor or word processing program.

man

In Linux, the command to display man (manual) pages.

man pages

In Linux, manual entries; most commands have a man page to document how they work.

Management Information Base (MIB)

A collection of objects that can be accessed via a network management protocol.

Mandatory package

UA users must accept (execute) an SMS mandatory package command from within the Package Command Manager in order to continue using their computers.

Mandatory profile

A server-based profile defined for the user by the domain administrator. Users cannot store changes made to a mandatory profile.

Mandatory user profile

Roaming user profile that does not allow the user to save changes made to the profile while logged on.

Manual recovery

The process by which database(s) are recovered in the event of a database media failure. Manual recovery requires the use of prior database and/or transaction log dumps.

Manufacturing Automation Protocol (MAP)

A token-passing bus designed for factory environments by General Motors; standard IEEE 802.4 is nearly identical to MAP.

Many-to-many

Relationships such as those between authors and titles in which an author can have several books and a book can have several authors.

MAP

A NetWare command-line utility and login script command. It is used for creating, viewing, or changing drive mappings or search drive mappings. It may also be used to map a false Root directory. Drive mappings are not saved from session to session. They are installed during execution of a login script or at the command prompt.

Mapping

1. The transferring of data between a disk and a computer's RAM.
2. Attaching to a server-based directory using the local drive ID.

Marshaling

The process by which arguments are packaged for transport between threads, processes, or machines.

Martian

Humorous term applied to packets that turn up unexpectedly on the wrong network because of bogus routing entries. Also used as a name for a packet that has an altogether bogus (nonregistered or ill-formed) Internet address.

Master

An instance where the highest privileges reside in a device (usually a computer) where they have control of other devices or servers.

Master Boot Record (MBR)

The physical section of a hard drive closest to the spindle and the first block on the hard drive that is read and executed by the BIOS of a PC system. The MBR stores configuration and partition information that tells it how to load the operating system.

Master database

SQL Server database controlling all user databases and the SQL Server program.

Master Domain Model

Windows NT Server domain model where one domain provides user and global group management for a set of trusting domains. Resources and local groups are managed individually at the trusting domains.

Master replica

The Directory replica that is used to create a new Directory partition in the Directory database. It also allows users to read and update Directory information. Although many Directory replicas of the same partition can exist, only one can be the master replica.

Master table

A database table that holds the top level of information for a particular activity and is associated with one or more detail tables. An intrinsic part of SQL Server that should involve limited direct access.

Math coprocessor

A specialized chip that supplements the mathematical operations of the CPU or microprocessor. Older systems had a separate chip for this purpose, while newer systems incorporate it into the microprocessor.

MATHLIB

An abbreviation for MATH LIBrary, it is a NetWare 3.11 loadable module to be used with the CLIB loadable module on a server with an 80387 math co-processor or 80486 processor.

MATHLIBC

A NetWare 3.11 MATH LIBrary C loadable module to be used with the CLIB loadable module on a server that does not have a math co-processor.

Maximum Transmission Unit (MTU)

The largest possible unit of data that can be sent on a given physical medium. For example, the MTU of Ethernet is 1,500 bytes.

Media

A generic term for the medium that is used to record data. Media can be a floppy diskette, a hard disk, or other similar recording surface (an audio tape, for instance).

Media Acess Control (MAC) address

The hardware address of a device connected to a channel, such as the address of a terminal connected to an Ethernet.

Media Access Control (MAC) sublayer

The level of the IEEE 802 data station that controls and mediates access to media.

Media Access Unit (MAU)

An Ethernet transceiver.

Megabit (Mb)

1,048,576 bits.

Megabits per second (Mbps)

Millions of bits per second (bps).

Megabyte (MB)

1,048,576 bytes.

Megabytes per second (MBps)

Millions of bytes per second (Bps).

Megahertz (MHz)

A million cycles per second. A CPU that operates at 200 Mhz uses a clock oscillator that runs at 200 million cycles per second.

Memory

A hardware component of a computer system that can store information and applications for later retrieval. Types of memory are RAM (Random Access Memory), ROM (Read-Only Memory), conventional, expanded, and extended memory.

Memory manager

The section of an operating system that allocates both physical memory and virtual memory.

Memory model

A compiler setting for 16-bit application development that determines various memory allocation variables, such as the number of bits in a particular data type.

Memory overcommit

Allocating more memory to the running program than physically exists.

Memory segmentation

The requirement on 16-bit platforms to allocate memory as either near or far.

Memory suballocation

An operating system facility that allocates pieces of memory from within an application's segment.

Menu

1. A displayed list of items from which a user can make a selection.

2. A NetWare menu utility in 3.x that allows for the use of customized menus created as ASCII text files.

Menu bar

1. The bar of selections found at the top of a Macintosh application or the Finder.

2. The bar of selections found at the top of a window in a GUI environment such as KDE or GNOME.

Merge agent

Replication agent that applies the initial Snapshot to Subscribers and merges changes occurring after the initial synchronization.

Merge replication

Replication method that merges changes occurring at the Publisher and Subscribers.

Mesh topology

A mesh configuration consists of a network in which each device has a point-to-point connection to every other device on the network. This gives the dedicated capacity of a point-to-point link to each device and provides significant fault tolerance.

Troubleshooting and isolation of network failures are easy with this type of network. Fault tolerance is maximized by rerouting traffic around failed links.

The complexity and cost make this configuration impractical. It is difficult to install or reconfigure and is expensive because of redundant connections and wasted bandwidth.

For these reasons, mesh topologies are generally used for interconnecting only the most important sites with multiple links. This is called a hybrid mesh or partial mesh.

Message

A notification from one object to another that some event has occurred.

Message Application Programming Interface (MAPI)

One of the primary ways that people use the computer to communicate with each other. This is accomplished by sending messages and documents to each other via an electronic mail system.

Most companies are using at least one type of electronic mail system. Unfortunately, many companies are not using a single unified mail system for all of their employees, and other companies need interconnectivity with users who work for different companies.

Traditionally, corporations have installed gateways to get around this problem. However, gateways are highly specialized and can only be used to connect a particular pair of mail systems. Corporations often need a number of gateways to handle the different combinations of mail systems used by their employees and other contacts.

To resolve this problem, an API was developed that allowed for connectivity between various mail service providers and mail-aware/mail-enabled client applications. The result was the Messaging API, otherwise known as MAPI.

MAPI has a layered architecture that allows various client applications to communicate with multiple messaging systems. The main components are the client application, the MAPI subsystem, the MAP spooler, service providers, and the messaging system.

The client application is a front-end application that makes MAPI calls.

The MAPI subsystem, also known as the messaging subsystem, handles the client application's calls and provides standard user interface objects, such as dialog boxes and forms.

The MAPI spooler is responsible for forwarding the message to the appropriate transport service provider.

Service providers are responsible for translating MAPI methods to a format the messaging system can understand.

The messaging system is a back-end application that is responsible for routing messages over the network or across phone lines. Messaging systems currently available include Microsoft Mail, cc:Mail, IBM PROFS, X.400, and Novell MHS.

Message Handling System (MHS)

The system of message user agents, message transfer agents, message stores, and access units, which together provide OSI electronic mail. MHS is specified in the CCITT X.400 series of Recommendations.

Message Routing Group object

A leaf object representing a messaging server, which resides on a NetWare server. When you install NetWare MHS on a NetWare Server, a Messaging Server object is automatically created in the Directory tree. The Messaging Server object is automatically placed in the same context as the NetWare Server object. The amount of disk space available is the only limiting factor in how many mailboxes a messaging server can service.

Message store

A server component of an electronic mail system. The Postoffice is the message store under Microsoft Mail.

Message Transfer Agent (MTA)

Electronic mail component that transfers messages between message stores. The external program is the MTA for Microsoft Mail.

Messages

A term used to refer to errors or messages generated by SQL Server.

Method

A defined behavior for a particular interface. An object that owns an interface must implement its methods.

Metropolitan Area Network (MAN)

A complete communications network set up by a local telephone company. This network services customers in regional locations, providing them with microwave and satellite relay stations, fiber optics, and cellular radio services with a 50-kilometer range operating at speeds from 1 megabit per second to 200 megabits per second.

A MAN is larger than a LAN (Local Area Network) but smaller than a WAN (Wide Area Network). A MAN may be made up of several LANs. MANs provide an integrated set of services for real-time voice, data, and image transmission.

Microsoft Management Console (MMC)

A framework that hosts Microsoft and third-party management tools, called snap-ins, that are used to administer computers, services, networks, users, and other components of the Windows system. The MMC does not provide any management functionality itself, but instead hosts the tools (snap-ins) that do.

The MMC provides the user with a simplified, single interface to the snap-ins. An MMC can be customized and the administrative tasks delegated with limited or full functionality of the included snap-ins.

Microsoft Point-to-Point Encryption (MPPE) protocol

Protocol used for data encryption between RAS servers and clients. Encryption is supported for the MS-CHAP and EAP-TLS remote access protocols.

Microsoft Software Installer (MSI) file

MSI file type used with the Windows Installer Service. This type of file contains installation instructions and is capable of actively tracking and repairing application installation.

Micro-to-mainframe link

The connection of personal computers to mainframe-based networks.

Mid-level network

Mid-level or regional networks operate at the middle level of the Internet hierarchy of networks. A mid-level network handles data from the backbone networks and passes them through to local or stub networks and from the local area networks to the backbones.

Migrated attribute

A NetWare status flag (M) that is set automatically to indicate a file has been migrated.

Migration

1. Conversion of NetWare servers from NetWare 2, NetWare 3, or from another operating system, to NetWare 4. Operating system migration is different from data migration, which is the moving of files to near-line or offline storage devices.

2. Transfer of users, groups, directories, and files from a NetWare Server to a Windows NT Server.

3. Transfer of users, groups, and application data from one application to another.

Mil

A part of an Internet address used to identify a military domain. For example, cop@army.mil.

Military Network (MILNET)

Originally part of the ARPANET, MILNET was split off in 1984 to make it possible for military installations to have reliable network service, while ARPANET continued to be used for research.

Million Instructions Per Second (MIPS)

A measure of the speed of execution of a computer's central processsing unit.

Milliseconds (ms)

A thousandth of a second. Access rates are expressed in milliseconds.

Minicomputer

A legacy computer that is capable of multitasking but can support fewer users than a mainframe. An IBM AS/400 is a minicomputer.

Mirror

1. Mirroring is the type of data redundancy provided at RAID level 1 and entails copying a hard disk's partition and data and duplicating it on another hard disk at the same time it is written on the original disk.

2. A site that replicates data from a popular, busy, or remote location to another location. Unlike RAID mirroring, which is done simultaneously, site mirrors are often updated only at night or during periods of lower network usage.

Mirror set

Basic disk fault-tolerant configuration using two physical hard disks with identical data. This is an implementation of RAID 1.

Mirrored volume

Dynamic disk fault-tolerant configuration using two physical hard disks with identical data. This is an implementation of RAID 1.

Mixed mode

A domain mode that includes a PDC upgraded to Windows 2000 and BDCs that have not been upgraded. Mixed mode also refers to the upgraded PDC and upgraded BDCs but without the native mode switch turned on.

Mixed-mode authentication

SQL Server authentication method using both Windows NT and SQL Server accounts for authentication.

Modal dialog box

A dialog box that must be closed before the user can continue working in an application.

Model database

SQL Server used as a template in creating user databases.

Modeless dialog box

A dialog box from which the user can shift focus.

Modem

An abbreviation for modulator/demodulator. A modem is a peripheral device that permits a personal computer, microcomputer, or mainframe to receive and transmit data in digital format across voice-oriented communications links such as telephone lines.

Modem eliminator

Also known as a modem emulator, it is a device used to connect a local terminal and a computer port in lieu of the pair of modems that would be expected to connect these. Allows DTE-to-DTE data and control signal connections otherwise not easily achieved by standard cables or connectors. Modified cables (crossover cables) or connectors (adapters) can also perform this function.

Modem port

A Macintosh serial interface port designed for use with a modem or serial printer.

Moderator

A person who monitors the content of a listserv, newsgroup, or bulletin board. The moderator determines which messages to pass on to subscribers.

Modified comparison operators

Comparison operators used to introduce subqueries that are modified by the keywords ANY or ALL, for example, >ALL.

modprobe

The command to load Linux kernel modules and their dependencies.

Modulation

The process of changing the amplitude, frequency, or phase of a carrier wave in a periodic or intermittent way from a digital signal to an analog signal for the purpose of transmitting information.

MODULES

A NetWare 3.x and 4.x console command used to display the short and long names of modules and the version number of NLMs loaded on a file server.

Modules

Parts of a system that can be loaded as needed; usually refers to kernel modules in Linux.

modules.conf

One of the two configuration files used by the kernel module tools to load modules. The modules.conf file specifies any aliases and parameters that may be needed to load modules.

modules.dep

In Linux, the file containing kernel module dependency information.

Modulo

An arithmetic operator (the percentage symbol %) that gives the integer remainder after a division operation on two integers. For example, 9 modulo 2 is 1 because 9 divided by 2 equals 4 with a remainder of 1.

MONITOR

In NetWare 3.x, 4.x, and 5.x, MONITOR is a loadable module used to list connections, locks, and open files. It provides hard disk and LAN information, lists modules and the resources they use, locks and unlocks the console, and describes the file server memory and its use.

Monitors

Enforce mutually exclusive access to methods, particularly synchronized methods.

Monochrome

Refers to one color (mono=one, chrome=color). Early PC adapters and monitors were able to send only a single color to be displayed on the black background of the screen. Although the term "black and white" is commonly used to describe monochrome, studies have shown that other popular monochrome colors, like amber and green, actually create less eye strain than white. While only a single color appears on the black background, many monochrome monitors do support multiple shades of "gray."

Mosaic

A software program that supports text and GUI (Graphical User Interface) access to the World Wide Web. Mosaic supports hypertext links to graphics and text.

Mosaic was developed at the National Center for Supercomputing Applications at the University of Illinois. It was the first WWW browser that was available for the Macintosh, Windows, and UNIX with a common user interface. Mosaic started the popularity of the Web.

The source code to Mosaic has been licensed by several companies, and several other pieces of software are as good or better than Mosaic. The most notable are Netscape and Internet Explorer.

Motherboard

The electronic circuit board containing the primary computer components such as CPU, RAM, ROMs, etc.

MOUNT

A NetWare 3.x and 4.x console command used to make a volume available to users. The MOUNT command can be used for a new volume or one that has been made inactive with the DISMOUNT console command.

mount

In Linux, the command used to load a file system; also the process of making a file system available. Used as a noun to refer to the mounted file system, e.g., a mount; look at the list of mounts.

Mount point

In Linux, the directory under which a file system will be located when it is mounted. A common mount for removable file systems is in /mnt.

Mounting point

A folder in one volume that another volume's data may be accessed through. The folder specified as a mounting point must be empty.

Moving Pictures Experts Group (MPEG)

MPEG is a method of storing movie files in digital format.

MS Windows client

A workstation that boots with DOS and accesses the network through the NetWare DOS Requester and its VLM programs (for NetWare 4.x) or a NetWare shell (for NetWare versions earlier than NetWare 4.x). While on the network, users can map drives, capture printer ports, send messages, and change context with MS Windows software.

Msdb database

SQL Server database containing recurring task and alert information.

MS-DOS

MS-DOS is Microsoft's version of the DOS operating system.

MUD Object Oriented (MOO)

One of several kinds of multiuser role-playing environments. MOO is a text-based environment.

Multicast

A special form of broadcast where copies of the packet are delivered to only a subset of all possible destinations.

Multicolor Graphics Array (MCGA)

Also known as Memory Controller Gate Array, the MCGA graphics adapter was introduced by IBM to support CGA and some VGA modes.

Multidrop

Referring to a circuit in a communications line that is a multipoint link where the telephone company *drops* several sets of local loops into various customer sites at secondary stations. Multidrop is in contrast to a standard multipoint link where there is only one set of local-loop connections at each end of the telephone network.

MultiFinder

A Macintosh Operating System 6 utility allowing multiple applications to be loaded concurrently. Later versions of the Mac OS incorporate this capability in the core operating system software.

Multihomed host

A computer connected to more than one network or having more than one network address. The network addresses may or may not be on the same network and could even be on different kinds of networks.

Multilink

Windows NT Remote Access Server connection method whereby multiple serial lines are treated as a single virtual connection.

Multimedia

In computing, multimedia refers to the presentation of information using sound, graphics, animation, and text.

Multiple Document Interface (MDI)

An application that allows the user to have more than one document open at a time.

Multiple inheritance

An object-oriented feature that allows a class to have more than one superclass. It is not supported in Java.

Multiple Link Interface Driver

A device driver written to the ODI specification that handles sending and receiving packets to and from a physical or logical LAN medium.

Multiple-Master Domain Model

Windows NT Server domain model when multiple trusted domains provide user and global group administration for a set of trusting domains. Resources and local groups are managed individually at the trusting domains.

Multiplexer

A device that takes several input signals and combines them into a single output signal in such a manner that each of the input signals can be recovered.

A device used to transmit information more efficiently and economically across a network. A multiplexer combines a number of low-speed inputs into a smaller number of high-speed outputs. Some multiplexers temporarily store information in buffers, so all of the information can be sent at once when the line becomes free.

Multiplexing

In data transmission, a function that permits two or more data sources to share a common transmission medium in such a way that each data source has its own channel.

Multipoint line

A circuit established between one primary station and multiple secondary stations simultaneously. This type of network groups devices together so they can share the same communications line.

Multiprocessing

The ability to execute more than one thread simultaneously.

Multiprogramming

A mode of operation that provides for the interleaved execution of two or more computer programs by a single processor.

Multiprotocol routing

Windows 2000 RRAS configuration supporting any combination of IP routing, IPX routing, and AppleTalk routing.

Multipurpose Internet Mail Extensions (MIME)

The standard for attaching non-text files to standard Internet mail messages. Non-text files include graphics, spreadsheets, formatted word-processor documents, sound files, etc. An e-mail program is said to be "MIME compliant" if it can both send and receive files using the MIME standard. When non-text files are sent using the MIME standard they are converted (encoded) into text, although the resulting text is not really readable. Generally speaking, the MIME standard is a way of specifying both the type of file being sent (e.g., a QuicktimeTM video file) and the method that should be used to turn it back into its original form. Besides e-mail software, the MIME standard is also universally used by Web servers to identify the files they are sending to Web clients; in this way, new file formats can be accommodated simply by updating the browsers' list of pairs of MIME types and appropriate software for handling each type.

Multistation Access Unit (MSAU)

The central hub where drop cables attach to the Token-Ring network. MSAUs are typically located in central locations, such as a wiring closet.

Multisynch

Multiscanning or multisynch monitors adapt to the incoming horizontal and vertical frequency signal sent by the computer. By adapting rather than being fixed at a particular setting, multisynch monitors earn their name and can work with almost any other video standard. Multisynch monitors were first introduced as EGA displays.

Multitasking

A mode of operation that provides for the concurrent performance or interleaved execution of two or more tasks.

Multithreaded

A feature by which applications can execute multiple sets of instructions at a time.

Multithreaded application

An executable that activates more than one thread of execution, for example, a thread to handle user input and one to perform background operations.

Multiuser

The ability of a computer to support several interactive terminals at the same time. This allows several users to access the computer's resources, usually at the same time; each user will have an account to keep individual resources for different users separate.

Multiuser Dungeon (MUD)

A multiuser simulation environment that is usually text-based. Some MUDs are purely for fun and flirting, others are used for serious software development or education purposes and all that lies in between.

A significant feature of most MUDs is that users can create objects that stay in the environment after the user leaves. Other users can interact with this object in the originator's absence, thus allowing a *world* to be built gradually and collectively.

MUSE

One kind of MUD, usually with little or no violence.

Musical Instrument Digital Interface (MIDI)

A standard communications protocol for the connection of a computer to a musical synthesizer. MIDI enables musicians to compose complex music on a piano-style keyboard and then capture that information using a computer that can be used to automatically write the score.

N

NAME

A NetWare 3.x and 4.x console command to display the file server's name.

Name Binding Protocol (NBP)

NBP is responsible for resolving naming schemes contained within network addresses.

Name context

The position of an object in a NetWare Directory tree.

Name resolution

The process of mapping a node name into the corresponding network address. The name of a file can be resolved to the file itself through the Windows NT file system forming a namespace.

Named pipe

1. An Application Program Interface that allows an unlimited number of sessions on the network. Named pipe is a much higher-level interface than NetBIOS (Network Basic Input/Output System). A single named pipe function is equal to many NetBIOS calls.

2. In GNU/Linux, an InterProcess Communication (IPC) facility that allows data to be exchanged from one application to another either over a network or running within the same computer. The use of the term pipes for interprocess communication was coined in UNIX.

Named shared memory

A memory segment that can be accessed simultaneously by more than one process. Its name allows processes to request access to it.

Namespace

TCP/IP term for a given subnet assigned by an authoritative body; refers to a group of addresses within a given range associated with a name. There can be only one authoritative DNS server for each domain namespace.

Namespace support

NLM files that allow you to store non-DOS filenames on a NetWare 3.x, 4.x, or 5.x server. Users at different types of workstations see the files in native mode. Namespace NLM files have a .nam extension, for example, MAC.NAM and OS2.NAM.

Narrowband

In data communications, narrowband refers to a bandwidth or circuit capable of handling digital signals up to 2,400 bps.

National Center for Supercomputer Applications (NCSA)

Located at the University of Illinois in Urbana-Champaign, Illinois.

National Information Standards Organization

An organization that develops standards and promotes the voluntary use of technical standards in libraries, publishing, and information services.

National Institute of Standards and Technology (NIST)

U.S. governmental agency that assists in developing standards. Formerly the National Bureau of Standards.

National Research and Education Network (NREN)

A U.S. national computer network outlined in the initiative signed into law in December 1991. NREN is to be built on NSFnet, the National Science Foundation Network connecting national and regional networks. NREN will be able to transmit data at more than 40 times the rate of NSFnet.

National Science Foundation (NSF)

A U.S. government agency that promotes the advancement of science.

This foundation funded NSFNET, a high-speed network connecting supercomputing and research facilities in the United States. NFSNET also has connections to Canada, Mexico, Europe, and other geographic locations.

NSFNET is part of the Internet.

National Science Foundation Network (NSFNET)

An Internet backbone that began as a project with the National Science Foundation in cooperation with corporate partners IBM, MCI, and the Michigan Strategic Fund. It is now owned by America Online.

NSFNET was established to enable researchers and scientists working on complex problems to instantaneously access library resources, supercomputer computation, and databases, as well as to exchange information with colleagues worldwide.

NSFNET links regional networks to each other and to the NSF-sponsored supercomputer networks. These other networks include BARRNET (Stanford University), NCAR/USAN (National Center for Atmospheric Research), NorthWestNet (University of Washington), SDSCNET (San Diego Supercomputer Center), Sesquinet (Rice University), Westnet (Colorado State University), MIDnet (University of Nebraska-Lincoln), NDSA/UIUC (University of Illinois), CNSF (Cornell Theory Center), JvNC (John von Neumann Supercomputer Center), NYSERNet (Syracuse, New York), PSCnet (Pittsburgh Supercomputing Center), and SURAnet (University of Maryland). These networks are based on TCP/IP and are part of the Internet.

Native mode

Domain mode that only has Windows 2000 domain controllers and doesn't contain any PDC or BDCs.

Native SQL

The SQL dialect used by a particular DBMS.

Natural join

An equijoin in which one of the two columns used in the join is deleted from the result table (removes the redundancy).

NBACKUP

NetWare menu utility that backs up and restores MS-DOS and Macintosh files on file servers and local drives. NBACKUP is also used to change the current file server attachments. Up to eight file servers can be attached, and only attached servers can be backed up or act as backups.

NBF

Windows NT-enhanced implementation of NetBEUI.

NCOPY

An abbreviation for Network COPY. It is a NetWare command-line utility used to copy files to another directory.

NDIR

An abbreviation for Network DIRectory. It is a NetWare command-line utility that provides information about files and subdirectories. NDIR can manipulate information about a directory's subdirectories and files like a database. It sorts, limits, and displays special information such as name, file size, date and time created, etc.

NDIS

The modular network driver interface standard, developed by Microsoft and 3-COM. It has become an industry standard.

NDS container object types

There are three container object types in the NDS: Country, Organization, and Organizational Unit.

It is important to note that in the [ROOT], you can create only Country, Organization, or Alias objects.

A Country container object identifies the name of the country. This allows multiple countries to be identified for Wide Area Networks (WANs). A Country container object can contain only Organization and Alias objects. The Country object is a two-character field and is identified by "C=."

An Organization container object identifies the name of the company, divisions within a company, or departments. Each [ROOT] of the NDS requires a minimum of one Organization object. An Organization container object can only contain Organizational Units and Leaf objects. The Organization object name can be up to 64 characters and is identified by "O=."

The Organizational Unit container object identifies different divisions or departments within the company. The Organizational Unit is a sublevel of the Organization container object and can only contain Leaf objects or other organizational units. Organizational Unit objects are optional within the directory tree. The Organizational Unit can be up to 64 characters and is identified by "OU=."

NDS object types

The NetWare Directory Services (NDS) is a database containing all network information, such as users, printers, and servers. It is important to divorce the concept of individual printers, servers, and users being on a particular server. NDS maintains these objects globally for the whole network, not on a server basis.

In the NetWare Directory Services (NDS) database, each object represents a defined item. Each object contains properties and their values for identification purposes. For example, a user is an object with a property called name; the value is the actual name itself.

Some object properties, such as name, are mandatory; other properties, such as phone number, are optional.

The three types of objects are [ROOT], Container, and Leaf.

All objects make up the directory tree. This is a logical organization for the NDS.

At the top of each directory tree is the [ROOT] object, which is created at the time of installation. Only one [ROOT] should be created for each LAN/WAN, due to the inability of [ROOT] objects to communicate with each other. When referring to the root, it is necessary to place brackets around the object name ("[ROOT]"). Because the [ROOT] contains all objects, it can be considered a Container object.

Container objects are objects that hold (or *contain*) other objects and are used to build the NDS and align it with an organization's work flow or structure.

Near Letter Quality (NLQ)

By striking the paper several times to create a character, dot matrix printers can give the impression of non-dot matrix quality output.

Negative Acknowledgment (NAK)

Notifies a packet sender that a corrupted packet of information has been received. If a packet is correctly received over a network, an acknowledgment (ACK) is sent to the packet originator.

Nested if

"If" statements appearing within "if" statements.

Nested loops

Embedding one loop inside another.

Net

An Internet domain designated for networks that include network service centers, network information centers, and others items. Examples are nyser.net or concentric.net.

NET$DOS.SYS

A NetWare remote boot image file in the file server's SYS:LOGIN directory, containing a workstation's boot files. The file is generated with the DOSGEN command-line utility. The boot files allow the workstation to be booted from the file server rather than from a hard or floppy drive at the workstation.

NET$OBJ.SYS

In NetWare 3.x, one of three files that make up the server's bindery. This file is in the SYS:SYSTEM directory, which contains the objects for the bindery.

NET$PROP.SYS

NetWare 3.x file in the SYS:SYSTEM directory that contains the properties for the bindery.

NET$VAL.SYS

NetWare 3.x file in the SYS:SYSTEM directory that contains the property data sets for the bindery.

NETADMIN

A text-based utility in NetWare 4.x that is used to create and manage objects, properties, and rights.

NetBIOS

Standard programming interface for the development of distributed applications.

NetBIOS Extended User Interface (NetBEUI)

This is a nonroutable transport protocol written to the NetBIOS interface.

NetBIOS name

Microsoft networks, including workgroups and NT Server domains, always use NetBIOS names to identify workstations and servers. Machines recognize each other through unique machine names. Shared resources, files, and printers are accessed using NetBIOS names. For example, resources are identified by their Universal Naming Convention (UNC) name, which uses the format \\server\share_name.

In a UNC name, "server" is the NetBIOS name of the machine where the resource is physically located, and "share_name" is the name uniquely identifying the resource.

Microsoft NetBIOS names may contain up to 15 characters and are used to identify entities to NetBIOS. These entities include computers, domain names, workgroup names, and users.

In an internetwork TCP/IP environment, it is necessary to support resolution between NetBIOS names and IP addresses. Microsoft provides two methods of supporting this name resolution: LMHOSTS and Windows Internet Name Service (WINS).

LMHOSTS name resolution is based on a locally stored ASCII text file.

WINS Name resolution is based on WINS servers.

When designing your network, you will need to select the most appropriate method for your organizational requirements.

NET.CFG

A NetWare shell configuration file that can be created with a text editor and used to customize the parameters a workstation is given through the NetWare shell or DOS Requester. It is used for managing its interactions with the network, including data transmission packet handling, print jobs, and network drives.

Netiquette

Describes the code of conduct or etiquette governing personal behavior on the Internet. For example, it is considered poor netiquette to use all upper-case letters for casual conversations or messages. Upper case normally conveys the meaning that the originator is shouting angrily.

Netizen

Derived from the term citizen, it referrs to a citizen of the Internet or someone who uses networked resources. The term implies civic responsibility and participation.

Net-Library

Library of functions allowing SQL Server servers and clients to communicate by way of a network protocol.

Netscape Communications Corporation

The company that produces Netscape Navigator and Netscape Server products. Purchased by AOL in 1999.

netstat

A network utility that displays network information such as network connections, interface statistics, routing tables, masquerade connections, netlink messages, and multicast memberships.

NETSYNC cluster

Includes one NetWare 4.1 server running NETSYNC4 and up to twelve NetWare 3.1x servers attached to it.

NetWare

One of the first widespread LAN programs, still widespread as a file and print server.

NetWare Administrator (NWADMIN)

A Windows-based utility in NetWare 4.x that can be used to create and manage objects, properties, and rights.

NetWare Client for DOS and MS Windows

Software that connects DOS and MS Windows workstations to NetWare networks and allows their users to share network resources.

NetWare Client for OS/2

Software that connects OS/2 workstations to NetWare networks and allows users to share network resources.

NetWare Control Center (NCC)

NetWare for Macintosh utility that allows the management of users and security via a Macintosh client.

NetWare Core Protocol (NCP)

These are procedures a server's NetWare operating system follows to accept and respond to workstation requests. They exist for every service a workstation might request from a server, including creating or destroying a service connection, manipulating directories and files, opening semaphores, altering the Directory, and printing.

NetWare Desk Accessory (NetWare DA)

NetWare for Macintosh utility that allows a Macintosh user to view print jobs, send messages, and set rights.

NetWare Directory database

The database (commonly referred to as the Directory) that organizes NetWare Directory Services objects in a hierarchical tree setup called the Directory tree.

NetWare Directory Services (NDS)

A database containing all network information, such as users, printers, and servers. It is important to divorce the concept of individual printers, servers, and users being on a particular server. NDS maintains these objects globally for the whole network and not on a server basis.

Each server on the network *looks* to the global NDS for information on objects. Therefore, all servers and clients have access to the same information. When a network administrator makes any changes to the NDS, it is made once, and all servers *see* the new information.

This is sometimes referred to as the Directory Tree.

NetWare Directory Services management request

A request that controls the physical distribution of the Directory database. In this manner, network administrators can create new Directory partitions and manage Directory replicas.

NetWare Directory Services request

Users or network supervisors request information from the Directory database.

NetWare Directory Trustee Rights

In NetWare, the eight Directory Trustee Rights are Supervisory (S), Read (R), Write (W), Create (C), Erase (E), Modify (M), File Scan (F), and Access Control (A).

The Supervisory (S) right grants all rights to a directory and overrides any restrictions placed on subdirectories or files with an Inherited Rights Filter. A user with the Supervisory right can assign the Supervisory right to another user and can modify space restrictions in subdirectories. Caution must be used when assigning this right.

Read (R) grants the right to open files in a directory. This allows the user to view file contents or execute a program file.

Write (W) grants the right to open a file and write to (or modify the contents of) a file.

Create (C) allows the user to create files or subdirectories. If the Create right is granted, but not Write, the user can create a file, open, and write the initial contents of the file. Once closed, however, the user cannot reopen or modify the file contents.

Erase (E) grants the right to delete a directory, its subdirectories, and all files contained within.

Modify (M) allows the user to change directory and file attributes, including the directory, subdirectory, and filenames. This does not allow the user to modify the contents of a file.

File Scan (F) grants the right to see the subdirectories and files when the user views the directory contents.

Access Control (A) allows the user to modify trustee rights and the Inherited Rights Filter (IRF) for a directory. All rights (except Supervisory) may be assigned to other users. If a user has the Access Control right, they can give more rights to another user than they have themselves.

NetWare disk partitions

NetWare server hard disks can be divided into these logical units. NetWare 4.x creates a partition on each hard disk. Volumes are created from the pool of NetWare partitions.

NetWare DOS requester

A group of files providing NetWare support for DOS and MS Windows clients. They consist of VLM programs and a single executable file (VLM.EXE) that manages their operation.

NetWare effective rights

In NetWare 4, effective rights are the available rights to any object. They include all rights allowed through trustee assignments except those removed through the Inherited Rights Filter (IRF). To calculate effective rights, there are several steps.

First, you add the user and group membership rights, both inherited and explicit. If a user inherits rights and also has explicit rights, the rights are added together. If a group inherits rights and also has explicit rights, the rights are added together. You then add a user's rights inherited from group membership to the user's explicit rights.

In NetWare 3, the definition is slightly different as there are no *objects* with which to contend. Effective rights are the available rights at any directory, subdirectory, or file. They include all rights allowed through trustee assignments except those removed through the Inherited Rights Filter (IRF).

Except for the SUPERVISOR, a user has no rights in a directory unless assigned through a trustee assignment (user or group). If the parent directory has trustee assignment supervisory rights, the user has all rights in the subdirectory.

If there is a subdirectory trustee assignment, the user's effective rights are equal to the trustee assignment, plus any inherited rights.

If the IRF allows all rights to be assigned, the effective rights equals the effective rights of the parent directory.

The effective rights are equal to the effective rights of the parent directory minus those revoked through the IRF. Note that trustee assignments can be added.

A second trustee assignment in a lower subdirectory made to the same user or group will override the previous trustee assignment.

NetWare file allocation tables

NetWare's method for tracking the location of files on a disk is through File Allocation Tables (FATs). FATs are index tables that show the location of all files on a disk. If a file is spread out among several random blocks on the disk, the FAT is the index that allows the computer to reassemble the file blocks in the proper sequence to be retrieved from the disk.

If a file exceeds 64 FAT entries, NetWare creates a special FAT for that specific file, called a Turbo FAT. Using Turbo FATs, Novell can retrieve large files off the disk much faster than by using the normal FAT table.

FATs are stored in Directory Entry Tables (DETs). DETs also store information about the files, such as who created them, the creation date, date last modified, and who has rights to the file. The operating system stores two copies of the DET on the disk. If one DET gets corrupted, the backup copy can be used to repair the damaged DET by use of the VREPAIR utility.

There are two DETs per NetWare volume, per name space. If you add the Mac name space to a volume, NetWare warns you that it is going to use additional disk space. This is because it is creating additional DETs.

NetWare file trustee rights

There are eight NetWare 4 File Trustee Rights: Supervisory (S), Read (R), Write (W), Create (C), Erase (E), Modify (M), File Scan (F), and Access Control (A).

The Supervisory (S) right grants all rights to the file and allows the user to grant rights to other users or modify the Inherited Rights Filter (IRF). Read (R) allows the user to open a file, view the contents, or execute a program file. Write (W) allows the user to open and modify the contents of the file. Create (C) allows the user to salvage the file after it has been deleted. To be able to create new files, this right must be assigned at the directory level.

Erase (E) grants the user the right to delete the file. Modify (M) grants the right to change the file attributes or name but not the file contents. File Scan (F) allows the user to see the file when viewing a directory. Access Control (A) allows the user to modify the Inherited Rights Filter (IRF) for this file or assign all rights except Supervisory to other users.

NetWare for Macintosh

A version of NetWare that allows Apple Macintosh computers to run on NetWare networks. NetWare for Macintosh consists of software for the Macintosh Desktop and for the NetWare file server.

NetWare for UNIX

A version of NetWare for use with UNIX and other non-DOS operating systems. In UNIX systems, the Portable NetWare file server runs as a set of processes on the host computer rather than on a dedicated file server.

NetWare Link Services Protocol (NLSP)

This is a link-state routing protocol designed by Novell for IPX internetworks. It transfers routing information between routers and makes decisions based on the information. NLSP routers exchange link information on network connectivity, path costs, IPX network numbers, media types, etc. By exchanging this information with its peer routers, each router builds and maintains a complete logical map of the network. Unlike RIP and SAP, which broadcast routing and service information on a regular basis, NLSP multicasts routing information only when a change occurs in a route or service on the network. NLSP uses RIP to communicate with NetWare clients.

NetWare Loadable Modules (NLMs)

Link disk drivers, LAN drivers, and other file server management utilities and enhancements with the NetWare operating system. NLMs may be loaded (linked) from a DOS drive on the file server through entries in the AUTOEXEC.NCF file.

Available NLMs include disk drivers, which control communications with the hard disk(s). This NLM type is identified by a .DSK extension.

NLMs also include LAN drivers, which control communications with the network interface card(s). This type of NLM is identified by a .LAN extension.

NetWare Loadable Modules with an .NLM extension identify server files such as utilities and server applications. These can be both Novell and third-party files. For example, some files bundled with NetWare are the INSTALL.NLM installation utility, the MONITOR.NLM monitor program, and the VREPAIR.NLM disk test utility program.

All NLMs, with the exception of VREPAIR, can be loaded dynamically, used as necessary, and unloaded to free server memory for other tasks. Volumes must be unmounted to use the VREPAIR NLM.

Name Space NLM Modules allow non-DOS names to be stored in the directory system. This type of NLM is identified by a .NAM extension.

NetWare MHS services

Services that allow users to communicate electronically across a network by exchanging electronic mail, sharing calendars, and scheduling facilities. To provide these messaging services, NetWare uses a messaging server, a Distribution list object, a Message Routing Group object, an External Entity object, and a Postmaster.

NetWare Name Service (NNS)

NetWare global naming of directory service product allowing the network to handle requests for services. NetWare Name Service permits creation of a domain of a file server and resources so that logging in to one server in the domain makes all of its servers and resources available. NetWare Name Service consists of a program and utilities that are loaded on top of the NetWare operating system. This product was the predecessor to the NDS in NetWare 4.x.

NetWare NFS

Software that transparently integrates UNIX systems with NetWare 4 file systems.

NetWare object rights

The NetWare object rights are Browse (B), Create (C), Delete (D), Rename (R), and Supervisor (S).

Browse (B) grants the right to view an object in the directory tree. This does not include viewing property values.

Create (C) grants the right to create new objects below the current object level in the directory tree. The Create right is only available for container objects. (Leaf objects cannot contain other objects.)

Delete (D) allows the object to be deleted from the directory tree. If the object contains other objects, they must be deleted first.

Rename (R) grants the right to modify or change the object's name.

Supervisor (S) grants full access privileges. This includes access to all properties. The Supervisor right can be blocked.

To access an object and use the resource it represents (for example, a printer object), users will need only the Browse right. The remainder of the rights are required to manage the object. While users will need to access a printer (Browse), they do not need to change the name (Rename) or delete the printer object (Delete).

NetWare operating system

Novell, Inc., developed this system to run on a server and provide several functions to a network and the applications running on it. The functions include file and record locking, security, print spooling, and interprocess communications.

NetWare partition

NetWare volumes are created from this partition, which is created on each network hard disk at installation.

NetWare property rights

In NetWare, property rights determine who has access to the property values specified for an object.

The NetWare property rights are Compare (C), Read (R), Write (W), Add or Delete Self (A), and Supervisor (S).

Compare (C) allows comparison of a value to a value of the property. The comparison will only return a True or False value, and the actual value of the property will not be seen.

Read (R) grants the right to read the property's values. The Read right incorporates the Compare right.

Write (W) grants the ability to add, modify, or remove any of the property's values. Write incorporates the Add or Delete Self right.

Add or Delete Self (A) grants the right to add or remove oneself as a value of the property. This property right only pertains to objects that contain an object name as a value, such as a list of group membership.

Supervisor (S) grants all rights to the object's property. This can be blocked by the Inherited Rights Filter (IRF).

NetWare Server for OS/2

Device driver allowing the NetWare 4.x operating system to run as a nondedicated server on an OS/2 computer.

NetWare UAM

Allows the use of password encryption.

NetWare user tools

Software that provides a graphical means of accessing network resources like volumes, directories, printers, and users. NetWare user tools allow you to manage drive mappings, printer connections and setup, and server connections; display network users; and send messages. The user tools are available for all client types.

NetWare volumes

Similar to logical drives in DOS. Each of the volumes within a single NetWare file server must have unique names of 2 to 15 characters.

NetWare 4.x can support up to 64 volumes, with a maximum storage space of 32 TB. A single volume can span multiple physical drives, up to a maximum of 32 TB. A maximum of 1,024 physical drives is supported.

Volumes should be created with short names because they will frequently need to be typed.

It is advantageous to divide a file server into multiple volumes. This provides a more flexible way to set up and manage the system. Multiple volumes allow more detailed control over rights and drive access for security purposes.

Multiple volumes aid in simplifying system requirements. Application files, which seldom change, can be kept on a separate volume. This volume will not require a daily backup, just a routine weekly backup. All of the data can be placed in a separate volume and backed up daily.

Multiple volumes can also help protect against the spread of viruses. Viruses are seldom capable of crossing NetWare volumes. It is advisable to set up a small (50-100-MB) volume as a quarantine area for testing new software.

NetWire

An online information service, accessed through the CompuServe Information Service, providing access to Novell product news and information on services and technical issues for NetWare users.

Network

A group of computers and other devices connected together so they can communicate with each other.

Network adapter

The card that allows a computer to interface with the network. Also known as a Network Interface Card (NIC).

Network address

1. A network number that uniquely identifies a network cable segment.

2. A network address can also be the network portion of an IP address. For a Class A network, the network address is the first byte of the IP address. For a Class B network, the network address is the first two bytes of the IP address. For a Class C network, the network address is the first three bytes of the IP address, e.g., 192.168.1.0 is the network address for the hosts 192.168.1.1-192.168.1.254. In each case, the remainder is the host address.

Network Address Translation (NAT)

A routing protocol that allows network administrators to connect a local network to an external network with only a single external IP address. NAT is performed packet by packet, translating each local IP address to the external, globally routable IP address and back. The translation tables may be static or dynamic and may be combined with policies in conjunction with firewall rules.

Network administrator

The person in charge of all facets of a computer network.

Network application

A computer program housed on a server and designed to run over the network instead of being installed and run locally.

Network backbone

A central cabling system that provides connection to other cable segments. The central cable handles all internetwork traffic, decreasing packet transmission time and traffic on the network.

Network Basic Input/Output System (NetBIOS)

A standard programming interface for the development of distributed applications. Used primarily by IBM and Microsoft.

Network board

A circuit board installed in each computer allowing workstations to communicate with each other and the network server. Printers that contain their own network boards can attach directly to the network cabling. NetWare documentation uses the term network board; it can also be referred to as an NIC, LAN card, or network adapter card.

Network drive

The common name for a logical drive.

Network File System (NFS)

Software developed by Sun Microsystems that allows you to use files on another computer or network as if they were on your local computer. A method of sharing disk drives native to UNIX.

Network Information Center (NIC)

A resource providing network administrative support as well as information services and support to users. The most famous of these on the Internet is the InterNIC, which is where new domain names are registered.

Network Information Service (NIS)

A system for sharing configuration files (such as password files) over a network.

Network installation

The process of installing an operating system by pulling installation files from a network file server.

Network Interface Card (NIC)

The card that allows a computer to interface with a network. Workstations communicate with each other and the network server via this circuit board, which is installed in each computer. It can also be referred to as a network adapter, NIC, LAN card, LAN adapter, or network card.

Network layer

The OSI layer that is responsible for routing, switching, and subnetwork access across the entire OSI environment.

Network library

Library of functions allowing SQL Server servers and clients to communicate by way of a network protocol.

Network Management Station (NMS)

The system responsible for managing a (portion of a) network. The NMS talks to network management agents, which reside in the managed nodes, via a network management protocol.

Network Monitor

An SMS utility that functions as a *sniffer* and is used to capture, transmit, and display network packets.

Network news

Network news (also called newsgroups) is a misleading name for this popular function of the Internet. Network news has no relation to the world or local news reports. Although it includes news coverage, a newsgroup's function is far broader than simply reporting events.

Network news is made up of discussion groups, or forums, where Internet users can browse a multitude of articles (postings) that cover a variety of topics. USENET is a term often used in conjunction with Network news. Network news grew out of USENET, which is a UNIX function that services discussion groups. The two terms are generally used interchangeably.

Users can choose articles on a variety of subjects. In 1995, more than 7,000 topics were covered by newsgroups, and new groups are constantly being created. The group "new.announce.newuser" lists new newsgroup additions. Though the address is similar to the domain name system, it has no relation to domain names. This format is just a convention for identifying newsgroups.

Because there are so many topics, some Internet providers will not download all of the possible newsgroups. For example, many providers prohibit any newsgroup with a name that includes the words "sex" or "alt" (which stands for alternative). System administrators also decide how long to maintain postings on network servers. A day's worth of postings may require 50 megabytes or more of disk space. It is unusual for administrators to keep articles that are older than one or two weeks.

The major newsgroup divisions are biz (business and commerce), comp (computers, computer science, and software), sci (scientific subjects, such as astronomy and biology), soc (socializing and social issues), talk (debate on various topics), news (general news and topical subjects), rec (arts, hobbies, and recreational activities), alt (extremely varied subjects), and misc (topics that don't fall under the other categories). These abbreviations are the first part of a newsgroup's name and provide a very general idea of the newsgroup's subject matter.

The second part of a newsgroup's name identifies the major subject area or topic. For example, one of the "misc" subcategories is "misc.jobs." More additions to the name increase the newsgroup's focus. For example, the following subcategories of "misc.jobs" offer very specific discussion groups, such as "misc.jobs.contract," "misc.jobs.resume," "misc.jobs.offered," "misc.jobs.offered.entry," and "misc.jobs.misc."

If a user is interested in a particular discussion group, he or she can subscribe to that newsgroup and read or post articles as desired. While no one limits the number of newsgroups in which a user can participate, the amount of time required to read and respond to the thousands of daily postings can become prohibitive.

Network news is a separate application from electronic mail. Although e-mail might seem like a convenient way to read newsgroup postings, users would find their mailboxes flooded with thousands of postings daily. The storage space needed to maintain these postings would be enormous. Network news gives users the ability to view unread postings at their leisure and keeps e-mail inboxes free of clutter.

Anyone on the Internet can post an article to a news group, as can people from other sources. When someone posts an article to a newsgroup, the local system sends the article to the central server for that newsgroup. The central server distributes the article to the other network news servers throughout the Internet.

Some discussion groups are moderated. In moderated news groups, someone reviews each article before it is sent to the other servers. The reviewer for a newsgroup does not censor articles but ensures that articles posted are relevant to that group. Although this method slows down the posting process, the postings on moderated discussion groups stay focused on the issue.

Unmoderated newsgroups have no screening process. Discussions can and do follow a variety of tangents. Junk-mail postings are prevalent. However, unmoderated newsgroups are somewhat policed by the subscribers to that group. For example, if someone were to advertise a car for sale in the middle of a newsgroup on popular music, the poster of the advertisement would find his e-mail inbox flooded with angry letters from subscribers. This can be frustrating for the offender as he will need to delete hundreds of messages a day. It can also be devastating if the offender uses a provider that charges a fee for each item of e-mail received.

Network News Transfer Protocol (NNTP)

A protocol that defines the distribution, inquiry, and retrieval of news articles on the Internet from TCP/IP sites.

Network node

A server, workstation, router, printer, or fax machine connected to a network by a network board and a LAN driver.

Network number

A number that uniquely identifies a network cable segment. In TCP/IP networks, the network address is determined by the IP address and subnet mask. In IPX/SPX networks, it is also referred to as the IPX external network number.

Network numbering

A system of numbers, including IPX external network number, IPX internal network number, and node number, identifying servers, network boards, and cable segments.

Network Operations Center (NOC)

The authority for monitoring network or Internet operations. Each Internet service provider (organization providing Internet connections) maintains its own network operations center and is responsible for users' connectivity.

Network printer

A printer shared by multiple computers over a network.

Network server

A network node that provides file management, printing, or other services to other nodes or workstations. A node can function as a file server exclusively or as both a file server and a workstation.

Network Service Access Point (NSAP)

The point at which the OSI Network Service is made available to a Transport entity. The NSAPs are identified by OSI Network Addresses.

Network supervisor

The person responsible for configuring a network server, workstations, user access, printing, etc. He or she may also be referred to as network administrator.

Network Support Encyclopedia Professional Edition (NSEPro)

Novell's database of information is based on the Folio hypertext system. It is distributed on CD-ROM and can be run from a hard disk or a CD-ROM. To find information, select a subject or search for keywords.

The NSEPro contents include the NetWare Buyers Guide, Novell Product Manuals, information about Novell Education Certification Programs and NetWire, Technical Information Documents (TIDs), Bulletins, NetWare Application Notes (AppNotes), and FYIs (For Your Information). It includes files, patches, and fixes for NetWare products.

Network Time Protocol (NTP)

A protocol that ensures accurate local timekeeping with reference to radio and atomic clocks located on the Internet.

NETx.COM

A NetWare shell file. The x represents the station's version of DOS. NET3.COM is used for DOS 3.x, NET5.COM for DOS 5.x. Novell has also released a universal version of this program called NETX.COM. (In this case, the X is the character "X," not representative of a number.) This version of the program works with DOS versions 3.x through 6.x. The file is automatically executed when the filename is included in the Autoexec.bat file. Novell's VLM files replace this program.

New Technology File System (NTFS)

A fast and reliable file system provided with Windows NT. It is fully recoverable and allows the implementation of local security.

Newbie

A novice Internet user.

Newsgroups

Message centers devoted to a particular topic, such as history or science. They resemble mailing lists except that no one need subscribe to them. Anyone with access to a computer that receives Usenet news may both read and contribute to every newsgroup to which they have access. In URLs, newsgroups are denoted by the prefix "news."

nfsstat

A program that displays NFS server statistics.

nice

In Linux, a command to change scheduling priority of a process.

NMENU

A subset of Saber Systems Menus. A utility used by NetWare to execute a compiled menu file.

Node

A device at a physical location that performs a control function and influences the flow of data in a network. Node can also refer to the points of connection in the links of a network. Any single computer connected to a network.

Node address

A number that uniquely identifies a network board. It is also referred to as the node number.

Node number

A number that uniquely identifies a network board. It may also be referred to as a station address, physical node address, or node address. Every node must have at least one network board connecting it to the network. Each board must have a unique node number to distinguish it from other network boards on the network.

Noise

In data transmission, any unwanted electrical signal that interferes with a communications channel. Noise is often a random transmission of varying frequency, amplitude, and phase. Such noise may radiate from fluorescent lights and electric motors, and can also be caused by static, temperature changes, electric or magnetic fields, or from the sun and the stars.

Nonclustered index

Indexing method where data is not necessarily stored in the index sort order.

Nondense indexes

An index that has an entry for each data page that exists in the table. Only clustered indexes can be nondense since the physical rows are in the same order as the index.

Nondomain Local group

Any group created on a Windows 2000 system configured as a stand-alone system, workstation member, or domain member will be created as a Local group.

Nonpre-emptive multitasking

Windows handles the multitasking of 16-bit applications nonpreemptively. There is one thread of execution to be shared between all 16-bit applications. An application will control the thread until the application either terminates or returns control to the operating system. Unless the application was terminated, the contents of the registers will be saved and another application will take control of the thread of execution. The contents of the registers will be restored to the values held when the controlling application was last suspended.

It is up to an application to return control to the operating system. This means that the application developer needs to divide the application into minuscule tasks or scatter PeekMessage calls throughout the application.

Dividing the application into minuscule tasks can sometimes be difficult. Some tasks, particularly those that involve nested loops, are difficult to subdivide. Writing code to handle multitasking in this manner is unnatural and unnecessarily complicated.

The PeekMessage function offers control to the operating system, which can then give control to another application. There can be a long delay between the user action and the desired response depending on the placement of PeekMessage calls. For example, if a spreadsheet application performs a complicated recalculation without calling PeekMessage, a user who clicks on a background window may not receive a response for an extended period of time.

Nonpre-emptive multitasking involves switching between applications, also known as tasks. It often seems that tasks are running simultaneously, but it only appears that way to the user. Each application is offering control to the operating system often enough that the user cannot distinguish the time lapse between the task from which the user is expecting response and the task that actually has control of the thread.

Problems with the nonpre-emptive multitasking approach are evident when the following situations occur:

One problem arises when an application has a long task to perform. For example, a user chooses to reformat a large document. If the application was written so the reformat command completes before giving control back to the operating system, the user cannot access any other 16-bit application until the operation is complete. If the user is running Windows 3.x, the user cannot access any part of the operating system.

Another problem is with application bugs. Often, a bug in an application causes a loop to be executed continuously. If there is no PeekMessage in the loop and the loop's exit condition can never be met, the operating system will never regain control of the thread of execution and the computer will appear to have *hung* or stopped.

The altering of data can be another problem. For example, a user could be running both a word processing program and a presentation program. This particular presentation program allows the user to edit word processing files. The user has opened a file with the word processing program and changed some text but not saved it. The user then runs the presentation program and notices that the text has not been changed. Next, the user opens the word processing file in the presentation program to change the text, but the file is not saved. Each version of the text is slightly different. When the user switches back to the word processing program and saves the changes, the changes made in the presentation program are lost.

Nonpriority Scheme

A Token Ring can be used on a priority or nonpriority basis. When a station receives a free token it transmits the data units it needs to send. Opposite of Priority Scheme.

Nonresident attribute

An attribute that is not stored in the NTFS directory entry but elsewhere on the hard disk.

Nontrusted connection

SQL Server connection by an IPC method other than named pipes, such as IPX/SPX or TCP/IP sockets.

Non-Windows application

An application designed to run with DOS but not specifically with Microsoft Windows. The application may not be able to take full advantage of all Windows features, such as memory management.

Normal attribute

A file system attribute (N) that indicates that no NetWare attributes have been set.

Normalization

Normalization guidelines are a set of data design standards called the Normal Forms. Five normal forms are widely accepted, although more have been proposed.

In SQL Server, normalization protects your data integrity by avoiding duplicate data, while still providing acceptable data access speeds. The process, called nonloss decomposition, is the process of splitting a table into two or more smaller tables that contain like or grouped data without losing information. This often involves splitting a table into two or more smaller tables, then using a rejoining process and setting up a relationship between the tables to put them back together.

Achieving a well-designed database is usually a process of following the widely accepted five normal forms.

With the First Normal Form, there can be only one value for each attribute or column heading. This means that you don't *stuff* a column. In other words, each column will contain one unique attribute only. When creating a table for employee records, you would be in violation of the first normal form if you placed both the first and last names in the same columns. They should be stored in separate columns.

Progress from the first form to the second form is achieved only when all of the rules of the first form are met. As you move into higher-level forms, all of the rules of lower forms must be met.

With the Second Normal Form, all nonkey columns (that is, columns not defined as primary keys) must directly relate to the primary key and not just to another column within that table. This rule is irrelevant if the primary key is one column only. Violations of this type can sometimes be a little harder to catch.

In the Third Normal Form, no nonkey column can depend on another nonkey column.

The Fourth Normal Form forbids independent one-to-many relationships between primary key columns and nonkey columns.

The Fifth Normal Form breaks tables into their smallest possible pieces in order to eliminate redundancy (duplication) within a table. Often, tables normalized to this extent contain few columns other than the primary key itself. One advantage of this form is the control of database integrity as you are assured that all data is likely to occur only once, making updates of data very easy. The disadvantage is the number of times keys are used to join tables. Changes to primary key values should not be allowed. If a change is made, you must ensure that every occurrence of it is also changed. This can be extremely difficult to control when the keys are referenced in many tables and may appear as unreferenced values in some other tables.

The main problem with the Fifth Normal Form is that *no* data is duplicated anywhere else in the system. While this ensures data is stored and therefore updated only once, it causes significant problems in database speed, programming, and complex SQL strings. The Fifth Normal Form is too perfect to be efficient.

Northwind database

SQL Server 7.0 sample database.

NPRINT

A NetWare print service utility that allows DOS files or other files to be printed on a specific printer rather than from an application.

NPRINTER

In NetWare 4.x, there are two NPRINTER files. NPRINTER.EXE is a TSR that runs at a DOS workstation to support a remote printer on the network. NPRINTER.NLM is a Network Loadable Module that runs at the file server to support local printers attached to the server.

nslookup

A program used to query domain name servers.

NT Lan Manager (NTLM) protocol

Authentication protocol used with Windows 2000 and earlier Windows-family products.

NuBus

The original expansion bus designed at MIT and adopted by Apple Computer for use in the Macintosh line, from the Macintosh II through the early PowerPC models. This has been replaced by the PCI bus. Supported by MKLinux, but not by LinuxPPC, which requires the PCI bus.

Null

Represents a missing or unknown value in a column of a database table. Columns must be set up to allow or disallow null values.

Null modem

A device that connects two DTE devices directly by emulating the physical connections of a DCE device.

Null variable

A variable set specifically to a value of null.

Numeric variable

A variable used to store numeric values, such as integer or real.

NVER

NetWare command-line utility that displays current versions of NetBIOS, IPX, SPX, LAN driver, shell, and workstation and file server operating systems.

O

Object

1. In Novell networking, an object contains information about network resources. An object is made up of categories of information, called properties, and the data in those properties. Some objects represent physical entities, like a user or printer. Others represent logical entities, like groups and print queues.

2. In SQL Server, objects are tables, data types, views, stored procedures, indexes, triggers, rules, and constraints.

3. Objects can be compound documents that incorporate data of different formats.

4. An object can also be any program, file, or utility that can be accessed by the user.

5. In some environments, an object is an item that is contained in the site database.

Object Linking and Embedding (OLE)

Microsoft's specification that allows applications to transfer and share data.

Object Linking and Embedding in Visual Basic

Object Linking and Embedding (OLE) is Microsoft's open object model. It is also the foundation on which Visual Basic 4.0 is built.

Visual Basic OLE support features include prebuilt OLE controls, OLE automation, and OLE object creation. Prebuilt OLE controls provide access to existing libraries of prebuilt OLE objects. OLE automation gives the ability to control an object inside of other applications if it is an OLE Automation object. OLE object creation allows creation of a code library containing reusable OLE objects.

Any Visual Basic 4.0 edition can make use of prebuilt OLE components. OLE object creation requires either the Professional or Enterprise edition.

Object manager

The part of the operating system responsible for handling the allocation and access of objects.

Object ownership

The login username of the object's creator becomes the object owner. The owner has full privileges on that object. The system administrator can set up aliases for object creators to ensure that all objects within a database have the same owner's name.

Object permission

Defines the operations a database user can perform on the data within a database object. This typically means that DML statements are allowed on the object—Insert, Update or Delete for tables and views, and Execute for stored procedures.

Object right

Qualifiers that are assigned to an object and specify what it can do with directories, files, or other objects.

Object variable

A variable used to store a reference to an instance of a class in memory.

Object-Oriented Programming (OOP)

Component-based application development. C++ is a popular object-oriented language, providing classes that combine data and functionality in a single object.

Octet

A set of 8 bits or one byte.

ODBC SQL

The SQL dialect used by ODBC.

OFF

A NetWare console command that clears the file server console screen.

OLE Automation controller

An application that calls the exposed methods of automation servers to perform various tasks.

OLE container

An application that can accept OLE objects and/or controls.

OLE server

An application that provides and manages OLE objects.

One-to-many

A master-detail relationship in which one row in the first table may relate to many in the second, but a row in the second table can relate to only one row in the first.

One-Way Trust

A trust relationship where trust exists in one direction only.

Online access

Refers to direct interaction with a host computer through local or long-distance telecommunications links.

Online documentation

Refers to help documents in electronic format. Linux provides extensive online documentation in the /usr/doc directory. The information is written in a number of styles, including HOWTO documents, FAQs, and manuals, and is available in different languages and formats, such as HTML and plain text.

More online documentation can be found on the Internet. On the Internet, information can be found by using search engines or visiting Linux help sites such as http://www.linux.org/.

Online Public Access Catalog (OPAC)

A computerized library catalog. OPACs worldwide are accessible through the Internet.

OnNow

The specification that defines how hardware and software should be designed to allow for the computer to turn on instantly instead of requiring a long startup sequence.

Open Data Services

An API set that extends the capabilities of SQL Server.

Open Data-link Interface (ODI)

NetWare software used in open systems. ODI allows one network board, LAN driver, and cabling system to support multiple connections to communications protocols, such as AppleTalk, IPX/SPX, and TCP/IP, and uses them interchangeably.

Open Host Controller Interface (OpenHCI)

The specification that describes the capabilities required for a PC to utilize a Universal Serial Bus (USB). It also defines a standard programming interface for accessing a USB device.

Open Network Computing (ONC)

A distributed applications architecture promoted and controlled by a consortium led by Sun Microsystems.

Open Shortest Path First (OSPF)

A proposed standard IGP for the Internet.

Open Source

Development, licensing, and marketing strategy in which software source is open to a vast community of developers. Product can be sold at any price, but source must be included.

Open Systems Interconnection (OSI)

To support international standardization of network terminology and protocols, the International Organization for Standardization (ISO) proposed a reference model of open systems interconnection. Currently under development, OSI ensures that any open system will communicate with any other OSI-compliant system.

Open Token Foundation

A private nonprofit organization composed of users and vendors of Token-Ring products who are dedicated to expanding the interoperability of multivendor Token-Ring products and broadening their use. Founded in 1988 by such companies as 3Com, Momorex Telex, Madge Networks LTD., Proteon Corp., NCR, and Texas Instruments.

OpenDoc

A cross-platform, component software architecture developed by Apple Computer. Although included as part of Mac OS 8, further OpenDoc development has been halted by Apple due primarily to a lack of interest among developers.

OpenType

Allows a TrueType font file to contain an Adobe Postcript file.

Operating system

The software program that controls all system hardware and provides the user interface.

Operations Master

Active Directory operations that are not permitted to occur at different places in the network at the same time (i.e., single-master).

Operator

A SQL Server user designated to receive alert and job notifications.

Operator precedence

The order in which operators are executed.

Optical fiber

A thin filament of glass or other transparent material through which a signal-encoded light beam may be transmitted by means of total internal reflection.

Optimizer

The component in the DBMS responsible for generating the optimal execution plan for a query.

Optional package

A package command that can be executed from within the Package Command Manager if and when a user chooses to do so.

Orange Book

A book in the Department of Defense's *Rainbow Series* that defines a hierarchy of security levels for *stand-alone* computer systems. The levels range from A1 (most secure) to D (least secure).

Org

An Internet domain that identifies nonprofit organizations. An example is ddn.internic.org.

Organization object

A container object that allows users to organize other objects in the Directory and to set template information for users created in it. The Organization object is located below the Country object, if a Country object is used, and above the Organizational Unit object.

Organizational role object

A leaf object that defines a position or role in an organization that can be filled by different people, such as Team Leader or Vice President.

Organizational unit object

A container object that helps to further organize objects in the Directory and allows users to set template information for users created in it. It is located below the Organization object.

Orientation

A setting that indicates whether the vertical or horizontal dimension is longer.

OS/2 Client

An OS/2 computer that connects to the network and can store and retrieve data from the network and run executable network files using NetWare Client for OS/2 software. OS/2 client workstations support IPX/SPX, NetBIOS, and Named Pipes, allowing users access to OS/2-based applications such as SQL Server.

OS/2 Requester

Connects OS/2 workstations to NetWare networks. This allows OS/2 users to share network resources.

OSI Implementors Workshop (OIW)

Frequently called NIST OIW or the NIST Workshop, this is the North American regional forum at which OSI implementation agreements are decided. It is equivalent to EWOS in Europe and AOW in the Pacific.

OSI Layer 1

The Physical layer. It is the lowest of the seven defined layers of the generalized network architecture. It defines the transmission of bits over a communication channel, ensuring that 1s and 0s are recognized as such. The Physical layer accepts and transmits a bit stream without recognizing or defining any structure or meaning.

OSI Layer 2

The Data link layer. It provides methodologies for transforming the new Physical layer link into a channel that appears free of errors to the Network layer (the next higher layer). The Data link layer accomplishes this by splitting the input or data stream provided in the Physical layer into data frames that are transmitted sequentially as messages and by processing the acknowledgment (ACK) frames sent back over the channel by the receiver.

OSI Layer 3

The Network layer. It accepts messages of data frames from the transmitting host, converts the messages to packets, and routes the packets to their destination.

OSI Layer 4

The Transport layer. It accepts data from the Session layer (the next layer up, which is the human user's interface to the network), splits this data into smaller units, passes these units down to the Network layer, and ensures that all of the pieces arrive at the destination in the correct order. The Transport layer is a true end-to-end process. A program on the source transmitter carries on a conversation with a similar program at the end receiver. This end-to-end consideration in layers 4 to 7 is different from the protocols in layers 1 to 3, which regulates subnetworks at intermediate stages of a true end-to-end transmission.

OSI Layer 5

The Session layer. It is the user's interface into the network through which the user establishes a connection with a process on another distant machine. Once the connection is established, the Session layer manages the end-to-end dialog in an orderly manner, supplementing the application-oriented user functions to the data units provided by the Transport layer. The Session layer connection is typically a multistep operation involving addressing the host, authenticating password access, stating communications options to be used, and billing arrangements. Once the session is underway, the Session layer manages the interaction.

OSI Layer 6

The Presentation layer protocols format the data to meet the needs of different computers, terminals, or presentation media in the user's end-to-end communications. The protocols at this layer may also provide data encryption for security purposes in transmission over networks or data compression for efficiency and economy.

OSI Layer 7

The Application layer specifies the protocols for the user's intended interaction with the distant computer, including such applications as database access, document interchange, or financial transactions. Certain industry-specific end-to-end application protocols, such as banking or airline reservations, require specific configurations, from the Physical layer through and including the Application layer.

OSI network address

The address, consisting of up to 20 octets, used to locate an OSI Transport entity. The address is formatted into an Initial Domain Part, which is standardized for each of several addressing domains, and a Domain Specific Part, which is the responsibility of the addressing authority for that domain.

OSI presentation address

The address used to locate an OSI Application entity. It consists of an OSI Network Address and up to three selectors, one each for use by the Transport, Session, and Presentation entities.

OSI Reference Model

The Open Systems Interconnection (OSI) Reference Model was developed by the International Organization for Standardization (ISO). The OSI model provides a standard means of describing the data flow in a network and how it is managed.

While a number of companies have endorsed and agreed to apply this model within their own products, few follow its guidelines exactly. Some use their own networking model, most of which closely parallels the OSI standard. It is still a helpful tool, allowing a common point of reference for discussing network devices and concepts.

OSI Transport Protocol Class 0 (TP0)

Also known as Simple Class, this is the simplest OSI Transport Protocol, useful only on top of an X.25 network (or other network that does not lose or damage data).

OSI Transport Protocol Class 4 (TP4)

Also known as Error Detection and Recovery Class, this is the most powerful OSI Transport Protocol, useful on top of any type of network. TP4 is the OSI equivalent to TCP.

osql

SQL Server text-based utility. Replaces isql.

Outboxes

Directories that can store send-request files.

Outer join

A join that includes all nonmatching rows from one of the join tables in the result table.

Outer query

A DML statement (including a subquery) that contains a subquery.

Overlapped window

An application window.

Overloading

A feature that allows two methods to have the same name if their signatures have a different number or type of parameters.

Over-the-network installation

Windows NT and Windows 2000 installations where a shared network directory is used as the installation source.

Owner

An object that creates and/or manages some other object. For example, a dialog box is the owner of the controls that appear on it.

P

Pacing

A technique by which a receiving station controls the rate of transmission of a sending station to prevent overrun.

Package

1. An object that contains software installation information. Used to distribute software to client computers.

2. Data Transformation Services (DTS) object defining tasks to be executed.

3. A collection of documentation, configuration files, source code, and executable binary files that together provide functional applications or utilities.

Package Command Manager

An SMS program that runs on SMS clients. It provides users with a list of optional packages that can be executed by the user. It will also automatically install any mandatory packages.

Packet

A unit of data transmitted at the OSI Network layer; or any addressed segment of data transmitted on a network.

Packet Assembler/Disassembler (PAD)

Device that accepts dial-in access for a client system over the PSTN and connects the client to the X.25 public data network.

A PAD could be a translating computer that provides access for asynchronous character-at-a-time terminals to a synchronous packet-switching network.

Packet filter

A software component that can alter packets as they pass through; for example, by modifying the source IP address. Used in *firewalls*.

Packet Internet Groper (Ping)

A program used to test reachability of destinations by sending them an ICMP echo request and waiting for a reply. The term is used as a verb: "Ping host X to see if it is operational!"

Packet receive buffer

In the NetWare server's memory, buffers are set aside to temporarily hold data packets arriving from various workstations. Packets remain until the server is ready to process them and forward them to their destination, ensuring a smooth flow of data into the server even when there is particularly heavy input/output.

Packet Switching Node (PSN)

A computer that accepts, routes, and forwards packets in a packet-switching network.

Packet-switching network

A communications network that breaks a message into small units called packets in order to transmit data from one computer to another. Each packet contains destination (header) information and a part of the message. The packets are routed from the sending computer to the receiving computer through switching points, where each of the switches (nodes) is a computer capable of recognizing the address information and routing the packet to its destination.

The Packet-Switching Nodes can dynamically select the best route for each packet so that later packets may arrive prior to earlier packets. The switch at the receiving end reassembles the packets in the proper order. Packet-switching networks do not establish a real connection between transmitter and receiver but, instead, create a virtual circuit that emulates the connection created by a physical link.

Page

1. A basic SQL Server I/O unit, 2 KB in size.

2. A Web *page* isn't literally a page but an entire document, however long. A home page (often called "home.html" or "index.html") is the first page called up when you enter a Web site or if the URL doesn't give a filename.

Pages per minute (ppm)

A term used to describe the output speed of printers.

Paging file

Dedicated hard disk space used to emulate RAM for virtual memory.

Palette

1. The palette is a set of colors that can be displayed on a particular device such as a video monitor.

2. A movable tool bar within an application (known as a *tool palette).*

Panic

An unpredictable termination of a process being controlled by the kernel.

Parallel interface

A connection between a parallel device, such as a printer, and a computer. The computer sends multiple bits of information to the device simultaneously. This is also known as a Centronics interface.

Parallel multitasking

The process whereby programs execute simultaneously.

Parallel ports

In a parallel interface, eight data bits of data are sent at the same time, in parallel, on eight separate wires. Therefore, parallel transmissions are faster than serial transmissions.

Parallel ports, also called LPT ports, were originally used to connect line printers and terminals. Most systems have at least one parallel port, which is called LPT1 in DOS and Windows and /dev/lp0 in Linux.

There are two parallel standards: Bi-Tronics and Centronics (IEEE 1284). Centronics cables support a higher data rate. The Centronics connector is a 25-pin D-shell connector and is considered the standard.

Printers generally use parallel communications, as do some early notebook PC network adapters. Devices are available that allow the connection of SCSI devices to a parallel port.

Parallel transmission

In computer communications, parallel transmission is the transmission of data (binary digits) simultaneously (in parallel with each other) using separate lines. In contrast, serial transmission sends only one bit after the other using only one communications line.

Parameter

A variable that is given a constant value for a specified application and that may denote the application; or a variable that is given a constant value for a specific document processing program instruction.

Parameter RAM (PRAM)

The permanent memory on a Macintosh system board that stores information such as system name, LocalTalk address, and hardware configuration. Similar in function to CMOS Memory used by IBM-compatible systems. To reset the PRAM to factory-set default values, hold down the Command and Option keys while depressing the "P" and "R" keys when first booting up. The Mac startup chime will sound multiple times, indicating the PRAM has been successfully *zapped.*

Parent directory

This is the term for the directory immediately above any subdirectory. For example, SALES would be the parent of the SALES/NEW.

Parent object

Container objects that hold other objects.

Parent partition

The partition immediately toward the [ROOT] of another partition.

Parent process

1. A process that creates other processes.
2. An independent process. Contrast with child process.

Parent site

A site that has another site directly below it in the SMS hierarchy.

Parent VLM

A VLM acts as a multiplexer, routing calls to the correct child VLM and ensuring that each request reaches its destination.

Parity bit

A check bit that is added to each byte to signal the computer that the bits in a byte have transmitted correctly.

Parity check

A technique used to quickly check the integrity of data received after a transmission, or from memory. Parity checking can apply to bytes, words, long words, and other units of information.

Parser

The component of a DBMS that is responsible for verifying the syntactic and semantic correctness of a query, and generating a processed form of the query that is decomposed into simpler functions.

Partition

1. An area of storage on a fixed disk that contains a particular operating system or a logical drive where data and programs can be stored.

2. The NetWare Directory database is divided into these logical divisions. A partition represents a distinct unit of data in the Directory tree that can store and replicate Directory information. Each Directory partition has a container object. All objects and data about the objects are contained in it. Directory partitions do not include any information about the file system, directories, or files located therein.

Partition management

A method of management that allows users to divide the Directory into partitions and manage various Directory replicas of these Directory partitions.

Pass-through query

A query that is passed to a remote server for execution without being evaluated by the local server.

Pass-through validation

A process where a logon attempt that cannot be validated by the local domain is passed to trusted domains for validation.

passwd

In Linux, file in the /etc directory that contains user account information, including username, user ID number, user's primary group ID, miscellaneous information in the GECOS field, home pathname, and login shell. When the shadow feature is not enabled, this record also includes the encrypted password.

Password

A word or set of letters, numbers, and symbols allowing access to a facility, computer, or network. Must be kept as a close personal secret. Should not appear in a dictionary nor be a personal name, nor an item of personal information. Insertion or substitution of numbers and symbols can make a password harder to guess. A password may be accompanied by some other unique identifier before the user is allowed to log in.

Path

1. In hierarchical data structures, such as operating system directories, the path is the chain from a root directory (as in MS-DOS or Linux) or volume (as in NetWare) to a specific subdirectory or file. For example, from the root (/) directory down the etc directory to the file passwd is /etc/passwd.

2. In data communications, the path is the transmission route from sending node to receiving node.

Pathname

The pathname is information that uniquely designates an item on a server. Pathnames have the form "volume/folder/.../name," where the volume is the storage device (typically a hard disk) on which the file resides, and "folder/.../" designates the series of nested folders (or, in the DOS and UNIX worlds, directories) containing the file.

Because pathnames use the slash (/) to separate the labels they contain, it is a good idea not to use slashes in the names of HTML files even when, as on Macs, it is legal to do so. A URL will typically include a pathname.

PAUDIT

NetWare command-line utility in the SYS:SYSTEM directory that displays in chronological order the system's accounting records contained in the NET$ACCT.DAT file.

PAUSE

A NetWare login script and DOS batch file command that stops execution of the script and displays a "Strike a key when ready" message. Execution will resume after any key is pressed. WAIT can also be used instead of PAUSE.

PC Card (PCMCIA)

A bus definition that defines a hardware interface that supports very small peripherals, such as credit-card-sized modems, network interface cards, hard drives, and memory cards. Sometimes referred to by the acronym "People Can't Memorize Computer Industry Acronyms."

PCCOMPATIBLE

A NetWare login script command that must be included if the workstation is IBM-compatible, but the long machine name in the workstation's NET.CFG file reads otherwise.

PCONSOLE

An abbreviation for Print CONSOLE. A NetWare menu utility used to define queue and print server configurations and to provide print queue and print server information and control.

PC-DOS

IBM's version of the DOS operating system. Often referred to simply as DOS.

Peer

A Windows Socket application that functions as both a server and a client.

Peer-to-peer

Communication in which two communications systems communicate as equal partners sharing the processing and control of the exchange, as opposed to host-terminal communication in which the host does most of the processing and controls the exchange.

Performance Monitor

Windows NT utility for tracking and reporting performance counters.

Perimeter-based security

Network security based on controlled access at all transfer points from internal to external networks.

Peripheral Component Interconnect (PCI)

A high-speed expansion bus technology used by PC and Apple computers.

Perl

Practical Extraction and Report Language. A popular scripting language used almost universally to control system processes and script Web sites. Designed to make scripting faster and easier, perl features relatively clear syntax and is readily extensible.

Also, Pathologically Eclectic Rubbish Lister.

Permanent Virtual Circuit (PVC)

Provides for a fixed logical connection between two network subscribers by reserving buffer space in the switching nodes. A connection between two subscribers can be established by either a virtual call or a permanent virtual circuit. The permanent virtual circuit is established by prior arrangement between the network subscribers and the network provider. On a permanent virtual circuit, the network is aware of the fixed association between two stations. Permanent logical channel numbers are assigned exclusively to the permanent circuit.

Permissions

1. Authority to run certain actions on certain database objects or to run certain commands. Permissions may be set within an operating system or within a database. SQL Server permissions are generated using Grant and Revoke commands.

2. In Linux, three sets of flags attached to each file and directory: one each for owner, group, and other users on the system. Permissions include read, write, and execute.

Per-seat licensing

Microsoft software licensing option where license tracking is based on individual client systems with unlimited server connections supported.

Per-server licensing

Microsoft software licensing option where license tracking is based on concurrent server connections.

Persistence

Permanent storage of property values.

Persistence APIs

These APIs specify a way to store and retrieve components in the context of a containing document.

Persistent connection

A network connection that is restored each time the workstation or user logs on to the network.

Personal address list

User-specific private address list.

Personal profile

The server-based, user-specific profile applied when a user logs in from any domain workstation. Users are allowed to make changes to local profiles.

Phase modulation

The time difference between two identical wave forms that are delayed (phased) to represent the binary digits 0 and 1.

PhoneNet

A low-cost implementation of LocalTalk developed by Farallon. PhoneNet uses inexpensive telephone wiring as opposed to the relatively expensive shielded twisted-pair (STP) cabling required by Apple's LocalTalk network technology.

Physical data independence

The independence of the physical storage of data from a database's logical design.

Physical layer

It is OSI Layer 1, and it is the OSI layer that provides the means to activate and use physical connections for bit transmission. In plain terms, the Physical layer provides the procedures for transferring a single bit across a physical medium.

Physical media

Any means in the physical world for transferring signals between OSI systems. Considered to be outside the OSI model and, therefore, sometimes referred to as *Layer 0.* The physical connector to the media can be considered as defining the bottom interface of the Physical layer, i.e., the bottom of the OSI Reference Model.

Physical Unit (PU)

An input/output unit identified by its actual label or number.

PICS

A file format used by some animation applications.

PICT

A file format developed by Apple Computer that is used by vector and/or bitmapped graphics applications.

PIN pad

The numeric pad that allows a customer to enter his PIN number when using a bank card. A PIN number is similar to a password, ensuring that the person with the card is authorized to perform the transaction.

Ping

A user command to test the presence of other computers on the network. You can use IP addresses or names. Either DNS names or NetBIOS names may be used, provided appropriate entries have been made in DNS or WINS servers or in a hosts file. Colloquially, any call that is sent out in order to solicit a response.

Pipe

1. To start execution of an instruction sequence before the previous instruction sequence is completed to increase processing speed.

2. Using the pipe symbol (|), Linux commands that read and write to the standard input and standard output can be chained together to create pipelines.

Pitch

In printing, pitch refers to the number of characters per horizontal inch and is related to the character point size. Some fonts use a fixed pitch, where the spacing is the same for each character. Many fonts use a variable or proportional pitch, where each character has a different width. Overall, controlling the pitch makes for a better document appearance.

Pixel

Sometimes called a pel, it is an individual picture element. This is the smallest single element that can be displayed on the screen. Screen resolution is given in horizontal and vertical pixel counts. The more pixels, the greater the resolution.

Plain Old Telephone Service (POTS)

A term used by the telecom industry to denote the service has not been upgraded to support higher-level data transmissions.

PlainTalk

Macintosh system software that provides voice recognition and text-to-speech capabilities.

Plasma display

Plasma video displays operate by exciting a heated gas and tend to get very warm with extended usage. Formerly, these distinctive orange displays were often used in laptop and portable systems. Plasma screens allowed for a thin screen, but the high power consumption made them not suited to battery-powered systems.

Platters

In hard disks, platters are rigid aluminum disks covered with metal particles that are magnetized. When read/write heads sweep across the platter, the magnetized particles form patterns that represent stored data. Platters are similar to floppy diskettes except that there are multiple platters in each hard disk. Data can be written to both sides of the platter's surface. The term platters refers specifically to hard (fixed) disk drives. Most drives have at least four platters; some have as many as ten.

Plug and Play

The specification for a hardware and software architecture that allows automatic device identification and configuration.

Pluggable Authentication Modules (PAM)

A programming interface that enables third-party security methods to be used in UNIX. For example, smart cards, Kerberos, and RSA technologies can be integrated with various UNIX functions such as rlogin, telnet, and ftp.

Plug-in

A software utility that conforms to a specific application's add-on software architecture. For example, Adobe Photoshop can be extended through the use of third-party plug-ins such as Kai's Power Tools from MetaCreations, Inc.

Point of Presence (POP)

The access point to a Packet Data Network (PDN). It is a location where a network can be connected to the PDN, often with dial-up phone lines.

If an Internet company says they will soon have a POP in Belgrade, it means that they will soon have a local phone number in Belgrade and/or a place where leased lines can connect to their network.

Point size

In printing, characters are measured in points. There are 72 points per inch. The point size refers to the maximum size for any character, measured top-to-bottom.

Pointer

1. Represents the memory address of a data variable.

2. A screen symbol used to point to some element on the screen, erroneously referred to as the cursor.

3. In database programming, an address embedded in a record that specifies the location of data in another record or file.

Point-to-point

Data communications links are divided into two main categories, depending on how the line is structured: either point-to-point or multipoint. Point-to-point describes a channel that is established between two, and only two, stations. The link may be a dedicated or a dial-up line connecting a processor and a terminal, two processors, or two terminals.

Point-to-Point Protocol (PPP)

The successor to the SLIP protocol, PPP allows a computer to use a regular telephone line and a modem to make IP connections. PPP can also carry other routable protocols such as IPX.

Point-to-Point Tunneling Protocol (PPTP)

Provides secure client connections over the Internet.

Policy

A set of rules regarding resources that are applied to individuals or groups.

Polling

The process by which a computer periodically asks each terminal or device on a LAN if it has a message to send and then allows each to send data in turn. On a multipoint connection or a point-to-point connection, polling is the process whereby data stations are invited one at a time to transmit.

Polymorphism

The ability to provide type-specific behavior for a given operation.

Port

1. A memory address that identifies the physical circuit used to transfer information between a microprocessor and a peripheral or a physical interface allowing connection between devices, e.g., "Connect your modem to the DB25 serial port..."

2. On the Internet, *port* often refers to a number that is part of a URL, appearing after a colon (:) immediately after the domain name. Every service on an Internet server listens on a particular port number on that server. Most services have standard port numbers. Web servers normally listen on port 80. Services can also listen on nonstandard ports, in which case the port number must be specified in a URL when accessing the server. You might see a URL of the form: gopher://peg.cwis.uci.edu:7000/, which shows a gopher server running on a nonstandard port (the standard gopher port is 70).

3. Port also refers to translating a piece of software from one type of computer system to another, for example, translating the source code written for a program to run on the i386 architecture to the Alpha architecture.

Port mapper

A system program that matches TCP/IP services such as Telnet and FTP with IP port numbers.

Port scanner

A system tool that probes a range of ports to determine whether they are active and, if possible, what protocols or services match up with what ports.

Portable NetWare

A version of NetWare for use with UNIX and other non-DOS operating systems. In UNIX systems, the Portable NetWare file server runs as a set of processes on the host computer rather than on a dedicated file server.

Portrait

The orientation setting in which the vertical dimension is longer than the horizontal dimension.

Post

To send a message to a network newsgroup or electronic bulletin board.

Post Office Protocol (POP)

Refers to the way e-mail software, such as Eudora, gets mail from a mail server. When you obtain a SLIP, PPP, or shell account, you normally get a POP account. You set your e-mail software to use this account for receiving mail.

Postoffice

Microsoft Mail message store element.

Postoffice Address List

Local users at a Microsoft Mail postoffice.

Postoffice Network List

External postoffice list.

PostScript

A registered trademark of Adobe Corporation and the accepted language standard for high-resolution printing on laser printers. PostScript is a language used to tell the printer how to print a character on the page. PostScript uses vector information to define graphics. Some printers, such as Apple LaserWriter printers, are true PostScript printers. Some printers use PostScript emulation, either at the system or in the printer. A free emulation of PostScript included with Linux is Ghostscript.

Power On Self Test (POST)

When you first start a PC, it will go through a Power On Self Test (POST). The various parts of the computer are checked in a particular order. If errors are detected, they are reported to the user.

The first part tested is the basic system. This includes the microprocessor, bus, and system memory. The extended system is checked next (the system timer and, if installed, the ROM BASIC interpreter).

The third group tested is related to the video display. The video signals and display-adapter memory are tested. If there is more than one display adapter installed, only the primary adapter is tested.

The memory is tested next. All addressable memory (conventional and extended) is tested through a write/read test.

The keyboard interface is tested, and the keyboard is checked for malfunctioning (stuck) keys.

Finally, the system will then determine if any disk drives (floppy and/or hard disks) are installed. If so, they are then tested.

POST errors are reported as audio beeps and numeric error codes. While many manufacturer's codes are similar, you will want to refer to documentation for your particular system to identify any error messages.

Power supply

A PC's power supply is a device that takes the AC (alternating current) electric current from the wall and converts it into the DC (direct current) current required by the computer.

The power supply outputs four discreet voltages: +5 VDC, -5 VDC, +12 VDC, and -12 VDC. Spikes are smoothed out with capacitors connected across the power supply leads.

For a list of power supply manufacturers and their home pages, see www.yahoo.com/Business_and_Economy/Companies/Computers/Hardware/Components/Power_Supplies.

PowerPC

The microprocessor family jointly developed by Apple, IBM, and Motorola. These processors are found in Power Macintosh and compatible computers.

Precompiled queries

In Transact-SQL, named collections of SQL statements for which execution plans have already been figured out.

Pre-emptive multitasking

A multitasking method where the operating system allocates processor time to tasks according to their relative priority.

Preferences

A folder contained in the Macintosh System folder. This folder holds application software preferences established by the system's user.

Presentation layer

OSI Layer 6. It is the OSI layer that determines how application information is represented (i.e., encoded) while in transit between two end systems.

Presentation services

The application services that format data, present it to the user, and receive user input.

Pretty Good Privacy (PGP)

A public domain (i.e., unpatented) form of public key encryption.

Primary data file

Initial database data file and initial default for database objects. Each database will have one primary data file.

Primary Domain Controller (PDC)

The first domain controller created in a Windows NT domain.

Primary identity

A client application can specify that one of the service providers should be considered the primary identity for the session. This is particularly important when there are multiple service providers of the same type installed.

Primary key

In database terminology, the purpose of the primary key is to ensure that each row in a table is unique. The primary key will contain one or more columns defining a unique value. Normally, you will want to protect the column(s) defining the key so that a value cannot be changed after it is entered.

Primary partition

A basic disk partition that will have one logical drive ID. A primary partition marked Active is a bootable partition. A basic disk can have multiple primary partitions, but only one may be marked as Active.

Primary Rate ISDN

ISDN connection providing up to twenty-three 64-Kbps channels.

Primary site

Contains a site server and an SQL server that houses the site database and a copy of the databases of all of the sites below it in the hierarchy. It has administrative tools that provide for management of itself and all sites below it in the hierarchy.

Primary time server

This server synchronizes the time with at least one other Primary or Reference time server. It also provides the time to Secondary time servers and workstations.

PRINT

A NetWare command followed by the path and filename used to print an ASCII file.

Print device

Term used to refer to a physical printer, fax, or other device that can be associated with a logical printer.

Print Monitor

The print spooling software included with Macintosh operating system.

Print queue

A directory that stores print jobs. The print server takes the print job out of the queue and sends it when the printer is ready. It can hold as many print jobs as disk space allows.

Print server

A network computer, either dedicated or nondedicated, used to handle the printing needs of workstations.

Print server object

A Leaf object that represents a network print server in the Directory tree.

Print spooler

A program that allows background printing so that a computer may be used for other processing tasks while a print job is in progress.

printcap

In Linux, the /etc/printcap file defines all system printers. Use printtool under X environment to modify.

PRINTCON

An abbreviation for PRINT job CONfiguration. A NetWare menu utility used to edit, select, and copy print job configurations.

PRINTDEF

An abbreviation for PRINTer DEFinition. A NetWare menu utility used to create printer, plotter, and form definitions to be used with PRINTCON.

Printer

A peripheral hardware device that produces printed material (hard copy). In Windows 2000, refers to a logical printer created on a Windows 2000 system and to the physical print device itself.

Printer Access Protocol (PAP)

Responsible for handling all print requests/transactions on the network.

Printer Control Language (PCL)

Hewlett-Packard developed PCL for its own LaserJet printers. PCL instructs the printer on how to construct the output on a page. A large number of other manufacturers also support the HP PCL language.

Printer Definition File (PDF)

NetWare PDF files contain definitions for printers. NetWare provides some files that are placed in SYS:PUBLIC during the installation of the operating system. Definitions can also be created or imported from other file servers.

Printer driver

A program that translates the printed file into the language the printer understands. A printer cannot be used unless the correct driver is installed.

Printer fonts

Fonts that are built into the printer. They may also be downloadable soft fonts.

Printer languages

In addition to simple control characters, more advanced printers (such as laser printers) support a command and control language, which allows for even greater application support. PCL (Hewlett-Packard) and PostScript (Adobe) are two primary, de facto industry standards for printer languages.

Printer object

A Leaf object that represents a physical printing device on the network.

Printer port

A communications port located on the rear panel of a computer, designed for the connection of a printer.

Priority

Sometimes abbreviated as PRI, PRIO, or PRTY; a rank assigned to a task that determines its precedence in receiving system resources.

Priority class

A priority setting for an entire process.

Priority level

A priority setting for a thread within a process.

Priority scheme

A Token Ring can be used on a priority or nonpriority basis. When a station receives a free token, it compares the priority value with the priority of any data unit it has to transmit. If the data unit's priority is equal to or higher than the token priority, the data unit is transmitted. If the data unit's priority is lower than that of the token, the data unit is not transmitted.

Private

An access modifier that specifies class members to be accessible only by other members of the class in which they are defined.

Private Branch Exchange (PBX)

A telephone exchange on the user's premises. Provides a switching facility for telephones on extension lines within the building and access to the public telephone network. May be manual (PMBX) or automatic (PABX). A digital PBX that also handles data devices without modems is called a CBX.

Private Key Cryptography

A type of encryption system using only one key for both encryption and decryption.

Private Management Domain (PRMD)

An X.400 Message Handling System, or private organization mail system. Example: NASAmail.

Privilege mode

A special execution mode (also known as ring 0) supported by the 80286/80386 hardware. Code executing in this mode can execute restricted instructions that are used to manipulate key system structures and tables. Only the kernel and device drivers run in this mode.

Problem determination

The process of identifying the source of a problem, such as machine failure, power loss, or user error.

Proc

In Linux, a pseudo file system. It provides information on currently running processes, system statistics such as memory availability and processor usage, and hardware information, including interrupts and addresses used by adapters.

Procedural languages

In these languages, large programs are divided into small tasks. For each clearly defined task, one procedure or function is written. Examples of procedural languages are C, Pascal, Basic, and Cobol.

Procedure

1. A block of program code with or without formal parameters (the execution of which is invoked by means of a procedure call). In C, a procedure is referred to as a *function*. Usually, except in C, a procedure is distinguished from a function in that a function returns a value and a procedure does not.

2. A set of executable Visual Basic program steps.

Procedure cache

Memory allocated to running compiled procedures under a SQL Server.

Procedure group

A group of related procedures. All of the procedures have the same name prefix but are identified by a semicolon followed by a unique integer within the group name, for example, proc;1, proc;2, etc. All of the procedures in a group can be dropped with a single Drop Procedure statement.

Process

1. Once a 32-bit application is launched, it is loaded into memory. It receives a block of memory addresses. A process cannot execute any commands and does not use any processor time.

2. To perform operations on data in a process; or, a course of events defined by its purpose or by its effect, achieved under given conditions. A course of events occurring according to an intended purpose or effect.

3. The basic unit of program execution. Each program consists of one or more processes.

Process Identification Number (PID)

A unique code that the operating system assigns to a process when the process is created. The PID may be any number except 0, which is reserved for the init process.

Process throttling

Limiting the amount of processor time that will be made available to a Web site's applications.

Processor

In a computer, the processor, or Central Processing Unit (CPU); this is a functional unit that interprets and executes instructions. A processor contains at least an instruction control unit and an arithmetic and logic unit.

Processor-direct slot

An expansion slot that allows direct connection to the system's CPU(s).

Profile

1. The group of settings that define a user's working environment. These settings are contained in a Registry file and within the Documents and Settings folder on a Windows 2000 computer.

2. In Linux, the file in the /etc directory that is the template for all user logins.

Profile login script

This login script sets environments for a group of users. It is best used if there are groups of users in different containers with matching login script needs. Profile login scripts are not required. They execute after the container login script and before the user's script.

Profile object

A Leaf object mainly used as a login script for users who need to share common login script commands. The users do not need to be located under the same container in the Directory tree to use the same profile login script.

Program Information File (PIF)

A file used by Microsoft Windows, Windows NT, and Windows 2000 to provide parameters necessary for running non-Windows applications.

Project

Visual Basic application and all of its components while under development.

Promiscuous mode

Enables a network adapter card to *hear* all of the frames that pass over the network.

Promotion of OSI (POSI)

The OSI arm in Japan. Consists of executives from the six major Japanese computer manufacturers and Nippon Telephone and Telegraph. They set policies and commit resources to promote OSI.

Properties

Values related to an object.

Property

A variable containing information about a particular object. Properties can be exposed or private.

Property rights

Rights that apply to the properties of an NDS object.

Property sheet

A grouping of an object's properties that can be viewed or changed.

Prospero

A distributed file system that allows the user to create multiple views of a single collection of files distributed across the Internet. Prospero provides a file naming system, and file access is provided by existing access methods (e.g., anonymous FTP). The Prospero protocol is also used for communication between clients and servers in the Archie system.

Protected

An access modifier that specifies class members to be accessible only to methods in that class and in subclasses of that class.

Protected mode

The operating mode of the 80286 microprocessor that allows the operating system to use features that protect one application from another; also called Protect Mode.

PROTOCOL

A NetWare 3.x console command that displays the protocols registered on a file server along with the names of their frame types and protocol identification numbers as included by the LAN driver when it is installed.

Protocol

A set of strict rules (usually developed by a standards committee) that govern the exchange of information between computer devices. Also, a set of semantic and syntactic rules that determine the behavior of hardware and software in achieving communication. Any set of agreed-upon methods, names, locations, and process steps to be used.

Protocol Control Information (PCI)

The protocol information added by an OSI entity to the service data unit passed down from the layer above, all together forming a Protocol Data Unit (PDU).

Protocol Data Unit (PDU)

This is OSI terminology for *packet.* A PDU is a data object exchanged by protocol machines (entities) within a given layer. PDUs consist of both Protocol Control Information (PCI) and user data.

Proxy

1. The mechanism whereby one system *fronts for* another system in responding to protocol requests. Proxy systems are used in network management to avoid implementing full protocol stacks in simple devices, such as modems.

2. A copy of an out-of-process component's interfaces. Its role is to marshal method and property calls across process boundaries.

Some *proxy servers* will *cache* results of requests so that a repeated request can be served from the proxy, reducing network traffic and server load.

Proxy ARP

The technique in which one machine, usually a router, answers ARP requests intended for another machine. By *faking* its identity, the router accepts responsibility for routing packets to the real destination.

Proxy ARP allows a site to use a single IP address with two physical networks. Subnetting is normally a better solution.

ps

In Linux, a user command to list processes.

PSC

NetWare command-line utility used by print server operators for print server and printer control. Most of the PSC commands can also be performed through PCONSOLE.

PSERVER

A NetWare file that provides print services to a network.

PUBLIC

A NetWare directory that contains files in general use, such as utilities and overlay, and other files used for running menu utilities. Public files are files available to all users and are placed in PUBLIC.

Public

An access modifier that specifies class variables and methods to be accessible to objects both inside and outside the class. Public class members have global visibility.

Public Key Cryptography

A type of encryption system based on two keys, a public one distributed in the clear, and a private one held in secret by the user who wishes to encrypt his transmissions. A message encrypted with the public key can, in practice, only be decrypted with the recipient's privately held decryption key.

Public Key Infrastructure (PKI)

An encryption scheme that uses a shared key for encryption and decryption of files.

Public switched network

Any switching communications system—such as Telex, TWX, or public telephone networks—that provides circuit-switched connections to many customers.

Publication

SQL Server database published for replication.

Published printer

This is a printer that has been published in the Active Directory. A printer must be shared before it can be published.

Publisher

SQL Server system with one or more databases published for replication.

Publishing server

In SQL Server replication, this is a server having a source database.

Pubs database

Sample database provided with SQL Server.

Pull subscription

Replication subscription where replication is controlled by the Subscriber.

Pulse Code Modulation (PCM)

A technique used by the coder/decoder to convert an analog signal into a digital bit stream. The amplitude of the analog signal is sampled and a digital code is selected to represent the sampled value. The digital code is transmitted to the receiving end, which uses it to generate an analog output signal. Encoding techniques may be used to reduce the amount of data that is transmitted between the sender and the receiver.

Pulse dialing

Older form of phone dialing, utilizing breaks in DC current to indicate the number being dialed.

PURGE

In NetWare 3.x and Portable NetWare, PURGE is a command-line utility that makes deleted files unsalvageable in the current directory.

Purge attribute

NetWare will purge the directory or file when it is deleted so it cannot be recovered when this file system attribute (P) is applied.

Push subscription

Replication subscription where replication is controlled by the Publisher.

Q

Qualification

Under SQL Server, conditions on the rows to be retrieved, described in the Where or Having clause.

Qualifier

A word or words that further define a help topic.

Quality of Service (QoS)

The ability to measure and guarantee transmission rates and error rates.

Query

1. The process where a master station asks a slave station to identify itself and to give its status.

2. In interactive systems, query is an operation at a terminal that elicits a response from the system.

3. In another usage of the term, a query specifies the criteria to be used to find database objects. When the query is executed, the objects that match the criteria of the query will be displayed in the Query Results window.

Query criteria

A set of instructions that is used to find objects in the site database.

Query language

A stand-alone language provided by the DBMS for definition and manipulation of database objects. The term query language comes from the fact that it is often used for ad-hoc querying of databases.

Queue

A holding area in which items are removed in a first in, first out (FIFO) manner. In contrast, a stack removes items in a last in, first out (LIFO) manner.

QuickDraw

System software that handles all graphical screen display chores and is built into the Macintosh ROMs.

QuickDraw GX

An enhanced version of the Macintosh QuickDraw that provides more efficient text and graphics handling as well as enhanced printing capabilities and color management.

QuickTime

Apple Computer's standard file format for digital movies. Macintosh computers load the QuickTime extension at startup in order to view or create movie files. QuickTime movie files have a .mov extension.

Quota entries

Disk quota limits set for individual users to restrict the amount of disk storage space a user may absorb on a network server.

R

RAID 5 volume

Dynamic disk fault-tolerant configuration using multiple disks with data and parity striped across multiple disks. This is an imlementation of RAID 5.

Rainbow Series books

A set of publications issued by the Department of Defense defining all aspects of computer and network security, so-called due to their colorful jackets.

RAM disk drive

Also known as a virtual drive. A portion of memory used as if it were a hard disk drive. RAM drives are faster than hard disks because the memory access time is much faster than the access time of a hard disk. Information on a RAM drive is lost when the computer is turned off.

RAM semaphore

A kind of semaphore that is based in memory accessible to a thread; fast, but with limited functionality.

Ramdrive.sys

Windows for Workgroups includes a RAM disk driver, Ramdrive.sys, that allows you to set up a disk drive emulation in either Extended Memory Specification (XMS) or Expanded Memory Specification (EMS). Though it is often not necessary or even advisable to set up a RAM disk, there are some situations when a RAM disk can improve your performance.

If a networked diskless workstation has enough memory for Windows for Workgroups and a RAM disk, the RAM disk can be used as an efficient location for application swapfiles.

Some applications create temporary files while they are working. You can usually improve application performance by having the temporary files sent to a RAM disk.

If your system has physical EMS that is not being used by any non-Windows applications, you can make use of this memory as a RAM disk. *Do not* set up a RAM disk in emulated expanded memory.

When deciding on your RAM disk configuration, keep a careful watch on memory requirements. Make sure that at least 4 MB of RAM are left available for Windows for Workgroups after creating your RAM disk and any disk caching program assignments.

Random access

File access method where data can be read from the file in any order.

Random Access Memory (RAM)

The computer's storage area to write, store, and retrieve information and program instructions so they can be used by the central processing unit. The contents of RAM are not permanent.

RAS programs

Reliability, Availability, and Serviceability programs. These programs monitor the operating system and facilitate problem determination.

Raster Image Processor (RIP)

A universal file format used to preserve formatting information such as font name, size, margins, etc., when moving a document between different applications.

rc.d

In Linux, a directory containing system startup directories, commonly located in the /etc directory.

rc.local

In Linux, a script run by init on system startup that is used for controlling network services, commonly located in the /etc directory.

RCONSOLE

An abbreviation for Remote CONSOLE. It is a NetWare 3.x, 4.x, and Portable NetWare menu utility that allows a workstation to be used as a virtual file server console.

rcp

A standard BSD-based command used for remote copying of files. Since it is known to have security issues, you should use scp instead.

rc.sysinit

In Linux, the system intialization script. First script to be run by the init process, commonly located in the /etc directory.

RDBMS

Relational Database Management System. A DBMS that is based on the relational model.

Read right

A file system right that allows users to open and read files. It is also a property right that allows the reading of values of the property.

Read-after-write verification

A way to ensure that data written to the hard disk is the same as the original data still in memory. If it matches, the data in memory is released. If it does not match, the block location is recognized as bad, and Hot Fix sends the data to a good block location within the Hot Fix Redirection Area.

Readme

Standard filename for information about installing or using a software package.

Read-Only attribute

The NetWare file system attribute (RO) prevents writing to the file.

Read-Only Memory (ROM)

Read-Only Memory is used to store permanent instructions for the computer's general housekeeping operations. A user can read and use, but not change, the data stored in the computer's ROM. ROM is stored on a nonvolatile memory chip, enabling the information to be retained even after the computer's power has been turned off.

The Apple Macintosh ROMs contain a large portion of the operating functionality in permanent storage on the system board. Macintosh clone vendors must license these ROMs in order to build Mac-compatible computer systems.

Read-only replica

This Directory replica views but does not modify Directory information.

Readpipe

Named pipes test utility.

Read/write heads

In a fixed disk drive, there is one read/write head for every side of each platter. The read/write heads are said to be *gang mounted* because they move together in unison across multiple platters.

Read/write replica

The Directory replica that reads or updates Directory information (such as adding or deleting objects).

Real mode

The operating mode of the 80286 microprocessor that runs programs designed for the 8086/8088 microprocessor.

Real time

A mode of interaction between the user and a distant facility in which the response to the user's inquiry or comment is apparently immediate.

Reboot

The process of restarting a computer system.

Record

A set of related fields that describes a specific entity. Also called a *tuple* or *row.*

Recovery Console

Windows 2000 administrative tool that can be launched instead of launching Windows 2000 at startup.

Red Hat Package Manager (RPM)

In Linux, the program that installs and queries software packages.

Redundancy check

A check made with redundant hardware or information that can provide an indication that certain errors have occurred.

Redundant Array of Independent Disks (RAID)

Usually referred to as a RAID system. The "I" originally stood for Inexpensive but was changed to Independent because RAID systems are typically expensive.

A RAID system is composed of multiple hard disks that can either act independently or emulate one large disk. A RAID disk system allows increased capacity, speed, and reliability.

RAID was defined in nine levels by the RAID Advisory Board. Each level provides a different amount of reliability and fault tolerance. The level numbers do not indicate that one level is superior to another.

For an online RAID Guide, see www.invincible.com/rguide.htm.

Re-entrant

The attribute of a program or routine that allows the same copy of a program or routine to be used concurrently by two or more tasks.

Reference time server

This server specifies the time for the synchronization of other time servers and workstations.

Referential integrity

The process by which critical data remains accurate and usable as a database changes.

Refresh rate

The rate at which a video display monitor redraws screen contents. Higher refresh rates (72 Hz and above) provide better display characteristics than lower rates (60 Hz).

Region

An area of the screen that responds to user input. It may be nonrectangular.

Registry

Windows NT and Windows 95 configuration database.

Relation

The formal term for a table.

Relationship

The *verb* part of a statement describing the association between two different entities. For example, the relationship between an author and a book is that an author writes books. There is a direct relationship between the two entities. This relationship would be described as many-to-many.

Reliable Transfer Service Element (RTSE)

A lightweight OSI application service used above X.25 networks to handshake application PDUs across the Session Service and TP0. It is not needed with TP4 and not recommended for use in the U.S. except when talking to X.400 ADMDs.

Remark (REM)

1. A nonexecutable statement in a computer program, entered as documentation or as a reminder to the programmer.

2. In a NetWare login script, REM, Remark, an asterisk, or a semicolon at the beginning of a line indicates that what follows is not to be executed.

Remote access

The ability of a computer to access an offsite or distant computer using telephone lines or a network.

Remote Access Service (RAS)

In most networks, clients are connected directly to the network. In some cases, however, remote connections are needed for your users.

In Windows NT, the standard mechanism distributed with the operating system to allow logon to Windows NT domains and individual systems from remote systems. RAS may operate over modem, ISDN connection, or through a *Virtual Private Network* supplied by a third party such as WorldCom or AT&T. The computer so authenticated behaves as any other trusted domain member in the sense of Windows NT domain semantics.

Remote Administration mode

Terminal Services server mode optimized for support of remote server management.

Remote Authentication Dial-In User Service (RADIUS)

Client/server-based authentication and authorization service for remote access. Connection criteria are passed from the remote access server to the RADIUS server, which will inform the remote access server whether access is allowed or declined.

Remote client

Remote Microsoft Mail user.

Remote control agent

An SMS utility that enables you to control a remote client or use remote troubleshooting utilities.

Remote Desktop Protocol (RDP)

Protocol used for communication between Terminal Services servers and clients.

Remote File System (RFS)

A distributed file system, similar to NFS, developed by AT&T and distributed with its UNIX System V operating system.

Remote login (rlogin)

In UNIX, the original method of activating a login procedure to a remote computer prior to accessing files and other services on that system. Generally supplanted today by telnet and ssh.

Remote management

Use of a remote console by a network supervisor or by a remote console operator to perform file server tasks.

Remote Operation Service Element (ROSE)

A lightweight RPC protocol used in OSI Message Handling, Directory, and Network Management application protocols.

Remote Procedure Call (RPC)

A protocol that standardizes initiation and control processes on remote computers. Developed initially on UNIX and later on Windows NT.

Remote stored procedure

Stored procedure stored on and executed on a remote server.

Remote workstation

A terminal or personal computer that is connected to the LAN by a remote asynchronous connection.

REMOTE.NLM

In NetWare 3.x, 4.x, or Portable NetWare, a necessary loadable module that allows a file server to be controlled from a workstation functioning as a remote console.

REMOVE

A NetWare command-line utility used to remove a user or a group as a file or directory trustee.

REMOVE DOS

A NetWare 3.x and 4.x console command that removes DOS from a file server's memory. This prevents loading of modules from DOS drives or the hard disk's DOS partition, makes the memory available to the disk cache, allows warm rebooting of the file server from EXIT, and allows remote rebooting under RCONSOLE.

Rename Inhibit attribute

This NetWare file system attribute (Ri) prevents any user from renaming the directory or file.

Rename right

This object right allows the changing of the name of an object, which results in changing the naming property.

RENDIR

An abbreviation for REName DIRectory. It is a NetWare command-line utility that allows a user with directory Modify rights to change the directory's name or the names of its subdirectories without changing any of the characteristics.

Repeaters

The earliest functional role of repeaters was to extend the physical length of a LAN. This is still the primary benefit of a repeater.

There are, however, several potential problem areas that are not addressed by repeaters. These include signal quality, time delays, network traffic, and node limitations.

Most repeaters do nothing to filter noise out of the line, so it is amplified and sent on with the signal.

Time delays can occur as signals are generated over greater distances. These delays may eventually generate timeout errors. This is why repeaters are not used for remote links.

Repeaters do nothing to reduce the network traffic load because they don't have any capacity for filtering traffic. Repeaters are "invisible" to access protocols. All nodes added through a repeater count toward the total that can be supported in a subnet.

Repeaters are typically used on bus networks. To get the best signal quality, place the repeater so that the two connected segments are approximately the same length.

Replica

A copy of the data defined by a NetWare Directory partition. The Directory database must be stored on many servers to be distributed across a network. Rather than storing a copy of the entire Directory database at each server, replicas of each Directory partition are stored on many servers. An unlimited number of Directory replicas for each Directory partition can be created and stored on any server.

Replication

The process of copying Active Directory object state to all domain controllers.

Reply

An electronic mail program feature that enables a message receiver to automatically respond to a received message without manually addressing the message.

Request For Comments (RFC)

The name of the result and process for creating a standard on the Internet. New standards are proposed and published online as a Request For Comments.

The Internet Engineering Task Force is a consensus-building body that facilitates discussion and new standards. When a new standard is established, the reference number/name for the standard retains the acronym RFC. For example, the official standard for e-mail is RFC 822.

Requester

A NetWare program on the REQUESTER diskette that allows a workstation running under OS/2 to communicate through a NetWare network by attaching to a file server.

Requester postoffice

Postoffice participating in directory synchronization.

Reseaux Associes pour la Recherche Europeene (RARE)

European Association of Research Networks.

Reseaux IP Europeene (RIPE)

European continental TCP/IP network operated by EUnet.

RESET ROUTER

NetWare 3.x and 4.x console command that immediately rebuilds a functioning file server or router's routing table. RESET ROUTER initiates a special router request for information rather than waiting for the next automatic table updating.

Resident Attribute

Attribute that is stored in the NTFS directory entry.

Resolution

1. In monitors, this refers to the sharpness of the displayed image or text on a monitor and is a direct function of the number of pixels in the display area. Resolution is the number of pixels across one line of the monitor by the number of lines down the screen (for example, 800x480). The greater the pixel count, the higher the resolution and the clearer the screen image.

2. The process of matching (or resolving) an IP address with an associated host name. In Linux, nameserver resolution order is specified in /etc/resolv.conf. In DNS, a domain name is matched to an IP address. In WINS resolution, it matches a NetBIOS name with an IP address.

Resource fork

The portion of a Macintosh file that contains information about the application that was used to create the file.

Resources

Objects an application needs, such as icons, cursors, and regions.

Restore

To bring back computer data or files that have been lost through tampering or other corruption or through hardware malfunction. Files should be backed up frequently to protect against such loss.

Restriction

One of the basic query operations in a relational system, also called selection. A restriction determines which rows will be selected from a table.

Result set

Rows returned by a SQL Server SELECT statement.

Return value

The data returned by a function. You can store a return value in a variable by the statement variable=function().

Reverse Address Resolution Protocol (RARP)

The protocol in the TCP/IP suite used to map physical hardware addresses (MAC addresses) to logical IP addresses. RARP allows a workstation to obtain an IP address by broadcasting a datagram with its MAC address. A listening RARP server, such as a DHCP server, will respond with a valid IP address for the device if the MAC is authorized.

Reverse lookup zone

DNS zone used for IP address-to-host name resolution.

REVOKE

A NetWare command-line utility used to revoke specific rights of a user or group in a directory or file.

Revoke

Removing granted or denied permissions.

RGB

When referring to the three primary colors used in all color monitors and adapters, RGB gets it name from these colors: Red, Green, and Blue.

Rich Text Format (RTF)

A universal file format used to preserve formatting information such as font name, size, margins, etc., when moving a document between different applications.

RIGHTS

A NetWare command-line utility that displays a list of a user's effective rights in a file or directory. In NetWare 4.x, it has options for GRANT, REVOKE, and REMOVE.

Ring 3

The privilege level that is used to run applications. Code executing at this level cannot modify critical system structures.

Ring insertion and exit

In Token Ring networks, insertion is accomplished by the network station applying voltage to its cable, which activates a relay in the MSAU and electrically includes the station in the ring. Exit is accomplished by removing voltage from the cable, thereby closing the relay in the MSAU.

Ring topology

Provides a closed-loop transmission medium. Repeaters at each node connection duplicate the signal. This is done to minimize signal degradation.

Traditional rings have the same failure risk as a bus topology. Any break brings down the entire network. To prevent this type of failure, most ring implementations (such as Token Ring) are wired in a star topology with an out loop and a return loop from each workstation to the wiring hub.

The Fiber Distributed Data Interface (FDDI) design specification calls for a dual fiber-optic ring. Should a break occur in either ring, it automatically converts to a bus topology.

Risk analysis

The process of balancing the strength of security measures against the relative risk of system compromise.

Rlogin

A service offered by Berkeley UNIX that allows users of one machine to log in to other UNIX systems across a network (for which they are authorized) and interact as if their terminals were connected directly. Similar to Telnet.

Roaming User Profile (RUP)

User profile that is stored in a network location and made available to the user when logging on to any system in the domain.

Role

1. A designation used to assign permissions to MTS components and SQL Server database objects. Users and groups can be members of roles.

2. An identified group of SQL Server users. Roles are used for security and access control management.

Role member

Login name or user assigned to a server or database role.

Rollback

Cancels a SQL transaction and returns the result set to the state it was in prior to the beginning of the transaction.

root

In UNIX/Linux, the superuser account that has access to all system resources.

Root directory

In general, the top-level directory of a file system or grouop of file systems.

1. In UNIX/Linux, the first level of the file system that forms the basis of the file hierarchy. Also called /. Note the distinction between the first-level directory, /, and the root user's home directory, /root.

2. In DOS, the first-level directory of a disk or partition, created when the user first formats a disk and then is able to create files and subdirectories in it.

rootkit

A set of scripts and programs distributed through secret channels in the hacker underground, designed to provide a *black bag* of tools for breaking into systems. It is called this because the goal is to obtain *root* access to a system.

Round-robin scheduling

A method of allocating CPU time in a multiuser environment, with each user being allocated a certain amount of quantum or processor time. Once a user has exhausted his quantum, control passes to the next user.

Route

To move data between multiple connected networks.

Router

1. A connection between two networks that specifies message paths and may perform other functions, such as data compression.

2. In early versions of NetWare, the term bridge was sometimes used interchangeably with the term router.

Router configuration

The settings and parameters that configure a NetWare 4 server as a router. They are set through internetwork utilities.

ROUTER.CFG

A NetWare configuration file that can be written with an ASCII text editor to customize the router boot process.

ROUTER.EXE

A NetWare executable file used to boot a NetWare stand-alone router. This product was replaced with Novell's MultiProtocol Router, which runs on a dedicated NetWare server.

Routing and Remote Access Service (RRAS)

Windows 2000 service that enables a Windows 2000 server to simultaneously support multiprotocol routing, demand-dial routing, and remote access. RRAS supports clients running Windows 2000, Windows NT, Windows 9x, UNIX variants, and Macintosh.

Routing domain

A set of routers (devices connecting hosts on a network) exchanging routing information within an administrative domain (computers and networks under a single administrative authority).

Routing Information Protocol (RIP)

1. This protocol allows routers to exchange routing details on a NetWare internetwork. Using RIP, NetWare routers can create and maintain a database, or routing table, of current information. Workstations can query the nearest router to determine the fastest route to a distant network by broadcasting a RIP request packet. Routers send periodic RIP broadcast packets with current information to keep all routers on the internetwork synchronized. They also send RIP update broadcasts when a change is detected in the internetwork configuration.

2. An Internet standard (Interior Gateway Protocol) IGP supplied with Berkeley UNIX. It is based on distance-vector algorithms that measure the shortest path between two points on a network.

Routing Table Maintenance Protocol (RTMP)

The routing protocol used by routers to share network information in an AppleTalk network. RTMP is responsible for maintaining routing table information. This information is received from broadcasts from other networks and routers on the network.

Row

The set of data values associated with one instance of the entity that the table describes; one set of columns.

RPMs

In Linux, RPM packages (plural) containing binary or source software and installation procedures.

RPRINTER

A NetWare command-line and DOS executable utility that is loaded as a Terminate and Stay Resident (TSR) program and is used to add or remove a network remote printer.

RS-232-C

A low-speed serial interface used to connect data communications equipment (such as modems and terminals) defined as a standard by the Electronic Industries Association. All standards recommended by the EIA have an RS prefix.

RSA algorithm

A patented public key encryption algorithm whose strength relies on the difficulty of factoring large integers. The acronym is generated from the names of its inventors–Rivest, Shamir, and Adleman.

RSPX

A NetWare 3.x, 4.x, and Portable NetWare loadable module that contains the SPX driver, which allows a workstation to function as a remote console.

Rule

SQL Server referential integrity feature ensuring that a value either falls within a specific range, matches a specified pattern, or matches a value from a specified list.

Run time

Visual Basic execution interface.

Runlevels

The various modes in which a Linux system can run.

Runnable

A simple interface with only one method, called run().

Runtime dynamic linking

The act of establishing a dynamic link after a process has begun execution. This is done by providing OS/2 with the module and entry point names; OS/2 returns the address of the router.

Runtime error

An error occurring when an application executes.

S

sa

The logon name for the SQL Server system administrator account.

Sad Mac

When a Macintosh system cannot complete the startup process due to some error condition, a face with an unhappy expression (Sad Mac) is displayed on the video monitor.

SALVAGE

NetWare menu utility used to recover files that have been deleted or erased but not purged with the DOS DELETE or ERASE command.

Samba

In Linux, file server system software that lets you share files and printers with MS Windows clients and servers.

SATAN

A program that provides a comprehensive assessment of vulnerabilities of hosts on an entire subnet. SATAN is an acronym for *Security Administrator Tool for Analysing Networks*. While undoubtedly created with this purpose in mind, in the wrong hands SATAN and similar programs (i.e., SAINT) can provide a powerful reconnaisance tool for hackers by automating the work of probing vulnerabilites. Modern intrusion detection software is, however, easily capable of detecting the type of scans performed by these programs.

Saturation

A value between 0 and 240 that indicates the amount of the hue contained in a particular color. A value of 0 indicates no color. A value of 240 indicates the greatest saturation of color.

Savepoint

An intermediate point within a user-defined transaction that a transaction can be rolled back to. Useful for length transactions.

SBACKUP

A NetWare 3.x and 4.x loadable module that controls the operation of Server Backup. A product used to back up a file server to a tape drive.

Scalar aggregate

An aggregate function that produces a single value from a Select statement.

Scale

Stretch or shrink the contents to fit inside a specific area.

Scan mode

When a monitor screen is refreshed by the electron gun and beam, there are two modes of scanning that may be used. With sequential scanning, all lines are scanned in order from the top left corner, across, and then down the screen. This is sometimes referred to as noninterlaced scanning. With interlaced scanning, the lines are divided into an odd and an even group. First one (the odd) and then the other (the even) group is scanned each time the screen is refreshed. As a result, interlaced scanning takes more time and the image on the display begins to deteriorate. Because it takes longer for the electron beam to return to the top corner, after the odd and even scan, to start scanning the odd group again, flicker is produced as the electron gun refreshes and excites the phosphor elements on the screen. Noninterlaced scanning is considered preferable over interlaced.

Scan rate

Screens must be refreshed several times per second to continue displaying data. This is called their refresh rate or the frame rate. This rate is expressed in Hertz (Hz). Standard rates vary from 50 to 72 Hz (or more), which means that the screen is scanned 50 to 72 times per second. The more times a refresh occurs per second, the sharper the image, the less the image decays between scans, and the less flicker can be seen.

Scanning frequency

The number of lines scanned per second on a monitor. The formula for frequency is the number of pixels scanned per second divided by the number of pixels per line. The higher the frequency, the higher the resolution.

Scheduler

Also known as a dispatcher. The part of the operating system that determines which thread should run and the relative priority of each executing thread.

Scope

1. Variable scope refers to where in the application a variable can be seen. Scope can be limited to a procedure, a module, or global (visible throughout the application).

2. Project scope refers to the definition of features, requirements, schedule, and budget for a project.

scp

A secure encrypted implementation of the rcp command. The scp program is a part of the SSH suite.

Scrapbook

A sophisticated, multipage Macintosh clipboard utility that allows the storage of text, graphics, audio, and video for later retrieval.

Screen font

A bitmapped font used for on-screen representation of a printing font. Screen fonts allow users to preview printed output on the system's video monitor.

Screen group

A group of one or more processes that share (generally in a serial fashion) a single logical screen and keyboard.

Screen saver

A system utility used to prevent monitor damage by powering the video monitor down or displaying a moving graphic.

Script

1. A file that contains a sequence of system commands used to automate common tasks.

2. In Linux, the **script** command generates a plaintext file containing command-line input and the screen's output.

Script kiddie

A user, often a teenager, with some computing skill but not at the level of detailed understanding implied by the term *hacker.* Nevertheless, such a user may be quite adept at using prebuilt tools (scripts), designed by skilled hackers, to compromise the security of a system.

SCSI bus

This is an interface that connects Host Bus Adapters (HBAs) to controllers and hard disks.

SEARCH

NetWare 3.x and 4.x console command used to display, add, or delete file server search paths for loadable modules and .NCF batch files. The order in which paths can be searched can also be specified.

Search drive

The operating system searches this drive when a requested file is not found in the current directory. Search drives are supported only from DOS workstations. They allow a user working in one directory to use an application or data file in another directory.

Search engine

A search engine is a computer or group of computers that provides search capabilities for resources on the Internet.

Secondary site

A site that has a site server but no SQL server. All inventory information is passed to its parent site. A secondary site can contain no subsites. Therefore, it is the *lowest* site in the SMS hierarchy.

Secondary time server

This server gets the time from a Single Reference, Primary, or Reference time server and gives workstations the time.

Sector

In disk drives, each track is divided into sectors. Sectors resemble pieces of a pie.

Sector sparing

Disk fault tolerance feature that allows remapping of bad sectors to an alternate sector when disk I/O errors occur.

SECURE CONSOLE

A NetWare 3.x and 4.x console command that protects the system against unauthorized entry. The command forbids modules from being loaded from any partition, drive, or directory except SYS:SYSTEM. SECURE CONSOLE also removes DOS from a file server, preventing access to systems that have power-on passwords.

Secure Shell (SSH)

A replacement for rsh, and an enhancement for telnet, that encrypts all transmitted data so that other users on the network cannot use packet sniffers to see information as it crosses the network.

Secure Sockets Layer (SSL)

A transmission scheme proposed by Netscape Communications Corporation. It is a low-level encryption scheme used to encrypt data sent over in high-level protocols such as HTTP and FTP. An SSL transmission over HTTP is specified by using the protocol HTTPS. The latest revision of the standard is called Transport Layer Security (TLS).

SECURITY

A NetWare command-line utility that allows a user with Supervisor rights to examine the bindery and check for possible security violations.

Security Configuration and Analysis

MMC snap-in that can be used to review and analyze local security policy, edit local security policy, and import and apply a security template on a stand-alone or workgroup member Windows 2000 system.

Security descriptor

A structure that contains information about which users can access an object and for what purpose. Only objects created under Windows NT can have security descriptors.

Security equal to

A user object property that specifies other objects, allowing the user to have all rights of an object such as user, group, or printer objects in that list.

Security group

At the time of their creation, the three kinds of groups--Domain Local, Global, and Universal--can be classified within Active Directory as a security group or a distribution group. The security classification allows rights and permissions to be assigned to the group. Distribution groups, on the other hand, are nonsecure groups that are primarily used for e-mail distribution lists or other means of nonsecure communication.

Security Identifier (SID)

Unique identifier value used in Windows NT Workstation and NT Server security management.

Security template

File representing a security configuration defined as a group of security settings. Security templates can be applied to domain or local Group Policy Objects.

Segment

1. A self-contained portion of a computer program that may be executed without the entire computer program necessarily being maintained in internal storage at any one time.

2. In computer graphics, a segment is a collection of display elements that can be manipulated as a unit. A segment may consist of several and separate dots, line segments, or other display elements.

3. In TCP/IP, a segment is a message block.

4. Named collection of SQL Server disk storage pieces.

Selector

The identifier used by an OSI entity to distinguish among multiple SAPs at which it provides services to the layer above.

Self join

A join of a table with itself. The table and column names are all aliased twice to enable a comparison of values between columns in the same table.

Semaphore

An object that limits access to a particular number of threads.

SEND

NetWare command-line utility used to send short messages from a workstation to one or more network users or groups. SEND is also a NetWare 3.x and 4.x console command used to send a message from a file server to some or all users.

Sender

A component within the SMS Executive service that is used to send data from one site to another.

Sequenced Packet Exchange (SPX)

A Novell protocol used as the resident protocol in NetWare, along with IPX.

Sequential access

File access method where data is read in the same order it appears in the file.

Serial communication

The transmission of data between devices over a single line, one bit at a time.

Serial interface

A connection point through which information is transferred one digital bit at a time. The term serial interface is sometimes applied to interfaces in which the data is transferred serially via one path, but some control signals can be transferred simultaneously via parallel paths.

Serial Line Internet Protocol (SLIP)

An Internet protocol used to run IP over serial lines such as telephone circuits or RS-232 cables interconnecting two systems. SLIP is now being replaced by PPP.

Serial multitasking

The process by which multiple programs execute, but only one at a time.

Serial port

In a serial interface, bits of information are sent in a series, one at a time. Data bits are typically surrounded by starting and ending flags, which provide synchronization.

Serial ports are also called communications (COM) ports and referenced by number; COM1 is serial port 1. Most systems come with two COM ports.

The standard serial port connector is a 9-pin D-shell connector, but some systems still have older 25-pin D-shell connectors. Adapters are available to convert between the two standard connectors. With either connector, only 9 connector pins are soldered to 9 wires inside the cable.

Most serial cables are no longer than 50 feet. Use of longer cables can result in transmission errors.

Modems, serial printers, and serial mice use serial communications.

A new bus type, the Universal Serial Bus (USB), will become more prevalent in the future. The concept behind the USB is to consolidate all desktop peripherals into a single high-speed (12-Mbps) access route.

The USB allows up to 64 devices to be daisy-chained together. The single USB connector type will support many devices, including some that in the past used the serial, parallel, keyboard, mouse, or game ports.

The USB will usher in a new set of hardware peripherals and accessories, including products such as digital cameras and virtual-reality gloves.

More information about USB can be found at the Universal Bus Implementers Forum Home Page: www.usb.org.

Serial transmission

Transmission in which data (binary digits) can be transmitted only one bit at a time using only one communications line. In contrast, parallel transmission sends each byte simultaneously using separate lines. Connections exceeding one meter in distance typically use serial transmission.

Server

A computer or a software package that provides services to client software running on other computers on a network. Possible services include file sharing, printer sharing, or communications services.

Server configuration

The settings and parameters specified when using INSTALL.NLM to install a new NetWare 4.x server or perform maintenance work on an existing NetWare 4.x server.

Server Manager

In Windows NT Server, the Server Manager lets you manage domain members and provides a quick way of viewing information about your domain. With Server Manager, you can view system properties or view and manage shared directories and services running on Windows NT Workstations and Servers. It will also allow you to add member systems to, or remove member systems from, the domain, promote a backup domain controller into the role of domain controller, and broadcast messages to the domain. You can also view and manage trusting domains.

DOS, Windows 3.x, and Windows for Workgroups stations will be listed while active on the domain but are not registered as domain members.

Server mirroring

A NetWare SFT III configuration that provides a secondary, identical server to immediately take over network operations in case of failure of the primary server.

Server object

A leaf object that represents a server running NetWare on your network. A NetWare Server object can represent a server running any version of NetWare. Some objects, such as Volume objects, use a reference to a NetWare server object to pinpoint their location.

Server Requester Programming Interface (SRPI)

A subset of APPC.

Server socket

A Windows socket that listens for a stream connection, then accepts it.

Server-based profile

A user profile that is stored on a domain server.

Service Access Point (SAP)

The point at which the services of an OSI layer are made available to the next-highest layer. The SAP is named according to the layer providing the services: e.g., Transport services are provided at a Transport SAP (TSAP) at the top of the Transport Layer.

Service Access Point Stations (SAPS)

Number of service access point stations for Token Ring. This parameter may be required on a Novell network in the shell.cfg file depending on the network interface card.

Service Advertising Protocol (SAP)

The protocol used by NetWare service providers such as file server, print server, etc., to notify network elements of services provided on the network.

Service provider

A DLL that interfaces with a device or third-party application. A service provider is generally developed by the developer of the device or application it supports.

SERVMAN

A NetWare menu utility that is run at the file server to support file server configuration commands such as the SET command.

Servo voice-coil technology

Like a voice coil in a loudspeaker, this technology generates a magnetic field to move the heads across the disk platters. In general, newer, high-performance disk drives use this technology.

Session

1. That group of processes or tasks associated with an application.

2. A NetWare 3.1x menu utility used to change a user's environment while logged in to the server. It can be used to change file servers, log out, view a list of network groups or users, or send a message to a group or user. It can display, add, delete, or modify drive mappings.

Session layer

OSI Layer 5 is the OSI layer that provides means for dialogue control between end systems.

Session manager

A system utility that manages screen group switching. The session manager is used only in the absence of the presentation manager. The presentation manager replaces the session manager.

SET

A NetWare 3.x and 4.x console command used to view and change operating system parameters to fill the needs of a particular network.

set

A command used to set shell variables or to query what variables have been set.

SETPASS

An abbreviation for SET PASSword. It is a NetWare command-line utility used to create or change a user's password to the file server. The password can have up to 127 characters.

Sets

Groups of rows aggregates apply to.

SETTIME

A NetWare 3.x and 4.x console command used to set the time and date on a file server.

SETTTS

SET Transaction Tracking System. A NetWare 3.x and 4.x command-line utility used to turn the NetWare TTS capabilities on or off.

Setup Manager

Utility that can be used to automatically create answer files and distribution folders for unattended Windows 2000 installations.

Setupact.log

File created during Windows 2000 Setup listing all file operations taking place during GUI mode Setup.

Setuperr.log

File created during Windows 2000 Setup listing errors reported by devices or services during Setup.

Setuplog.txt

File created during Windows 2000 Setup listing each driver and service loaded and each DLL registered by Setup.

Shadow passwords

In UNIX/Linux, a method of storing passwords so that users cannot see the encrypted form, making passwords more difficult to crack. Restricting access to the encrypted copy of the password makes it more difficult for a cracker to guess the password. Without shadow passwords, anyone who manages to obtain a copy of the (world-readable) /etc/passwd password file could potentially run a *cracking program* to *brute-force* decrypt the passwords.

Shadowing

A set of rules used to determine variable usage when variables at different scope levels have identical names.

Share name

The name given to a shared resource. The universal naming convention references machine name and share name.

Share point

A shared resource identified by a UNC name.

Shareable attribute

A NetWare file system attribute (Sh) that allows a file to be accessed by more than one user at a time.

Shared lock

Lock set at the start of a read operation allowing further read access to the page, but no write access.

Shared memory

The use of the same portion of memory by two distinct processes, or the memory so shared. Shared memory is used for interprocess communication and for purposes that lead to compactness of memory, such as common subroutines.

Shared printer

This is a printer that has been shared to the network and can be accessed by its UNC path.

Shareware

Software publicly available for downloading. If the shareware is copied and used, the author of the software is expected to receive compensation.

Shell

In general, a program or portion of a program that interprets commands on behalf of a user or process. Under UNIX, a command-line interpreter such as the Bourne or C shell; under Windows, the Windows Explorer program, from which all other programs are interactively started.

1. In DOS, the command shell is loaded as a Terminate and Stay Resident (TSR) program.
2. In Linux, a command-line interpreter; examples include bash and tcsh.

SHELL.CFG

Older versions of NetWare used this shell configuration file that can be created with a text editor and used to customize the parameters a workstation is given through the NetWare shell. The file manages the workstation's interactions with the network, including data transmission packet handling, print jobs, and search drives. SHELL.CFG has been replaced by the NET.CFG file.

Shortcut

A technique that allows a Windows 95 or Windows NT user to create a link to a file or program in an alternative location.

Short-haul modem

A signal converter that conditions a digital signal to ensure reliable transmission over DC-continuous private-line metallic circuits without interfering with adjacent pairs in the same telephone cable.

Shutting down

The process of preparing the machine to power off in an orderly manner. Includes termination of all processes in the proper sequence and closing all files so that data is preserved.

Signaling

Using semaphores to notify threads that certain events or activities have taken place.

Signals

Notification mechanisms implemented in software that operate in a fashion analogous to hardware interrupts.

Signature

The three- or four-line message at the bottom of a piece of electronic mail or a USENET article identifying the sender.

Signed driver

A device driver that has been digitally signed by Microsoft certifying that the driver has passed the WHQL Windows 2000 certification tests. The digital signature is recognized natively by Windows 2000 systems.

Simple Gateway Management Protocol (SGMP)

The predecessor to SNMP.

Simple Mail Transfer Protocol (SMTP)

The standard protocol for transferring electronic mail messages between computers. SMTP originated in the UNIX world but has since become a cross-platform mail exchange standard.

Simple Network Management Protocol (SNMP)

One of the most comprehensive tools available for TCP/IP network management. It operates through conversations between SNMP agents and management systems. Through these conversations, the SNMP management systems can collect statistics from and modify configuration parameters on agents.

The agents are any components running the SNMP agent service and are capable of being managed remotely. Agents can include minicomputers, mainframes, workstations, servers, bridges, routers, gateways, terminal servers, and wiring hubs.

Management stations are typically more powerful workstations. Common implementations are Windows NT or UNIX stations running a product such as HP OpenView, IBM Systemview/6000, or Cabletron Spectrum. The software provides a graphic representation of the network, allowing you to move through the network hierarchy to the individual device level.

There are three basic commands used in SNMP conversations: GET, SET, and TRAP.

The GET command is used by the management station to retrieve a specific parameter value from an SNMP agent. If a combination of parameters is grouped together on an agent, GET-NEXT retrieves the next item in a group. For example, a management system's graphic representation of a hub includes the state of all status lights. This information is gathered through GET and GET-NEXT.

The management system uses SET to change a selected parameter on an SNMP agent. For example, SET would be used by the management system to disable a failing port on a hub.

SNMP agents send TRAP packets to the management system in response to extraordinary events, such as a line failure on a hub. When the hub status light goes red on the management systems representation, it is in response to a TRAP.

An SNMP management station generates GET and SET commands. Agents are able to respond to SET and GET and to generate TRAP commands.

Simple volume

Dynamic disk configuration with all disk space coming from one hard disk. Disk space assigned to the volume does not have to be contiguous.

SimpleText

A widely distributed, low-functionality ASCII text editor included with the Macintosh operating system and many software applications to ensure that users can view associated README files. Formerly known as TeachText.

Simplex transmission

Data transmission in one direction only.

Single Domain Model

Simplest Windows NT Server domain model where only one domain exists on the network.

Single Reference time server

This server provides time to Secondary time servers and workstations. It is the sole source of time of the network.

Single, In-Line Memory Module (SIMM)

A standard package for dynamic RAM.

Site

1. Any location of Internet files and services.

2. A site is a group of domains and/or computers. A site can be either a primary or secondary site. The Central site is the highest site in the hierarchy and can administer all sites in the system.

Site database

The Microsoft SQL server database that houses inventory information for the site and its subsites.

Site server

Every site has a site server. It contains the SMS components that are used to manage the site.

Slave

Opposite of master. The device that is controlled by the master.

Slipstreaming

A process whereby a Windows 2000 service pack is applied to an installation file set. This allows the service pack to be applied automatically to the destination system during installation.

SLIST

A NetWare command-line utility that provides information about internetwork file servers. This command is obsolete in NetWare 4.x and is replaced by NLIST.

Small Computer Systems Interface (SCSI)

A high-speed interface bus used for disk drives, scanners, printers, CD-ROM drives, digital cameras, and other devices. Available in several versions including SCSI-I, SCSI-II (Fast SCSI), Wide (16-bit data path), or UltraWide.

Smart

Containing microprocessor intelligence. A modem or adapter is smart if it has its own computer chip. A dumb device is limited in functions and features and takes processing power from a high-level system.

SMODE

Abbreviation for Search MODE, it is a NetWare command-line utility that defines a program's method of looking for a data file. Eight search modes are possible.

SMS Administrator

The program that is used to administer the SMS system.

SMS client

A member of the SMS system.

Snail mail

A term used to describe conventional postal service mail delivery. This contrasts with the speed of near instantaneous electronic mail delivery.

Snap-in

A management tool designed to run in the Microsoft Management Console (MMC) environment.

Sniffer

A device for monitoring network traffic, usually for the purpose of diagnosing problems. In the context of hacking, it is used for gaining information surreptitiously about hosts and users on that network.

Sniffing

The process of monitoring network traffic in order to compile information about hosts and users generating traffic on that network. For example, if passwords are transmitted unencrypted on a network, an intelligent sniffing program can pluck them out of the background traffic.

Socket

1. The network programming idiom for the TCP/IP suite of protocols. Processes are said to create sockets–a second process on the same machine or on a remote machine communicates with the first process by *plugging into* or *connecting to* the socket. The socket programming idiom first appeared in BSD UNIX in the late 1970s.

2. The destination of an IPX packet is represented by this part of an IPX internetwork address in a network node. Some sockets are reserved by Novell for specific applications; all NCP request packets are delivered to socket 451h. By registering those numbers with Novell, third-party developers can reserve socket numbers for specific purposes.

Software

A computer program, or a set of instructions written in a specific language, that commands the computer to perform various operations on data contained in the program or supplied by the user.

Sort order

A collating sequence (or collation) for a character set, determining which characters come before and after other characters.

Source code

Programming instructions (text) in human-readable form.

Source routing

A means IBM uses to route data across source-routing bridges. NetWare source-routing programs enable IBM Token-Ring network bridges to forward NetWare packets (or frames).

Spam

Large quantities of traffic, usually unwelcome and/or repetitive, on any of a number of transmission media, frequently in the form of an excessive number of e-mail messages. An inappropriate attempt to use a mailing list, USENET, or other networked communications facility as a broadcast medium (which it is not) by sending the same message to a large number of people who didn't request it.

Spam probably comes from a famous Monty Python skit that featured the word "spam" repeated over and over. The term may also have come from someone's low opinion of the food product with the same name, which is generally perceived as a generic, content-free waste of resources. Spam is a registered trademark of Hormel Corporation for its processed meat product.

Spanned volume

Dynamic disk configuration using disk space from multiple hard disks.

SPEED

NetWare 3.x and 4.x console command that displays the file server's speed, which is determined by the clock speed in hertz (Hz), processor type, and number of memory wait states.

Spoofing

The processs of altering network packets to make them appear to a remote system to have originated from a trusted host. Also, more generally, any attack based on falsely assuming the identity of a trusted user or host.

SPOOL

NetWare 3.x console command used to list, create, or change spooler assignments.

Spool directory

In Linux, the location in /var/spool/ where print jobs are stored on a disk while waiting to be printed.

Spooler

System software used to provide background printing.

SPXS

A NetWare 3.x and 4.x loadable module that provides SPX protocol services under the STREAMS loadable module.

SQL batch file

A series of executable SQL statements and control-of-flow language.

SQL Enterprise Manager

A full-featured management utility. It gives you the ability to manage all of the SQL Servers in your enterprise from any server or 32-bit client location. You can create and manage server groups and register servers for management. You can manage database devices, databases, objects, users, and services on any of your servers. You can also view the activity at any server and kill processes remotely.

SQL Mail

Mail service used by SQL Server to process queries via e-mail.

SQL Profiler

Management tool that catures real-time SQL Server activity.

SQL Server Manager

SQL Server utility able to start and stop SQL Server and related services.

SQLServerAgentMail

Mail system used for operator notifications.

ST506

An old interface standard for connecting disk drives to PCs.

Stack frame

A temporary area of memory that stores the variables and parameters for a function. When the function ends, the memory is freed and the variables are no longer accessible.

Stallman, Richard

Founder of the Free Software Foundation and the GNU project; often referred to as RMS.

Stand-alone Dfs root

Dfs root hosted on a server and stored in the server's Registry. Root and link replicas are not supported by a stand-alone Dfs root.

Stand-alone snap-in

A single management utility designed to run in the Microsoft Management Console (MMC) environment.

Standard Generalized Markup Language (SGML)

An international standard, it is an encoding scheme for creating textual information. HTML is a subset of SGML.

Standard Login Security

Term referring to SQL Server validation of login attempts.

Standard mode

A mode of operation used by Microsoft Windows 3.x that can be used with an 80286 or higher processor. Standard mode provides access to extended memory and also enables the user to switch between non-Windows applications. It does not provide virtual memory or allow non-Windows applications to be run in a window or in the background.

Standard module

A Visual Basic module used for defining procedures and variables.

Standard primary

Zone name server configuration option where the zone database is stored locally as a text file. This is the master (read/write) copy of the DNS database.

Standard secondary

Zone name server with a read-only replica of a standard zone database file.

Standards Promotion and Application Group (SPAG)

A group of European OSI manufacturers that chooses option subsets and publishes these in a "Guide to the Use of Standards" (GUS).

Standby server

Duplicate SQL Server available to be brought online after failure of the primary server.

Star topology

Star/hub networks connect the peripheral devices via point-to-point links to a central location. An Active Hub regenerates signals while Passive Hubs simply act as a terminating point for the network. Star topologies provide architectural flexibility but can require more cable than traditional bus and ring topologies.

Most modern data networks are configured with hubs. This allows for simplified adds, moves, and changes. System failure from any individual segment break is minimized. Examples of hub configurations for traditional bus and ring topologies include the use of the wiring closet in Ethernet 10BaseT networks or multiport repeaters in both Ethernet 10BaseT and 10Base5 networks. The use of MAU hubs in Token-Ring networks is another example.

A star may be wired with twisted pair or coax cabling. Most current implementations use twisted pair.

Start menu

The pop-up menu containing Windows 95 functions that is accessed by pressing the **Start** button on the Taskbar.

Start/stop bits

Additional bits inserted to mark the beginning and the end of transmitted characters. Start bits and stop bits are used in asynchronous communications.

Startup disk

The system boot drive. May be a floppy disk, hard disk, CD-ROM, or other drive.

Startup form

First form loaded when a Visual Basic application executes.

STARTUP.NCF

A NetWare 3.x, 4.x, and 5.x bootfile that loads disk drivers and name space support.

Statement

A SQL Data definition, data manipulation, or data administration command.

Statement block

A sequence of Transact-SQL statements enclosed within a BEGIN and END statement that is treated as a single unit.

Static heap

A block of memory that is set aside to allow allocation of smaller variables. Since it is static, it cannot shrink or grow.

Static Random Access Memory (SRAM)

RAM built from active electronic components (transistors). Does not require periodic refreshing as does Dynamic RAM.

Station

A term used as a shortened form of workstation, but it can also refer to a server, router, printer, fax machine, or any computer device connected to a network by a network board and communication medium.

Station address

A number that uniquely identifies a network board. It is also referred to as a node number.

Statistical multiplexor

An apparatus that serves as a time-division multiplexor and contains a microprocessor control unit for allocating the available bandwidth dynamically to improve the utilization of the channel.

Still Image Interface (STI)

An API designed to allow applications to obtain digital images from scanners and other devices that capture still images.

Storage compaction

A hardware feature allowing the dynamic relocation of programs residing in the central storage unit to provide an efficient multiprogramming environment.

Storage Device Interface (SDI)

A set of routines that will allow SBACKUP to access different storage (backup) devices and media.

Storage dump

The copying of all or a portion of a storage.

Storage Management Services (SMS)

A combination of services that allows data to be stored and retrieved.

Stored procedures

Custom SQL Server procedures that have been compiled, for which an execution plan has been created, and have been stored in the current database.

Stream transmission

A connection-oriented transfer of data between two sockets.

Stream-oriented

A type of transport service that allows its client to send data in a continuous stream in the same order as sent and without duplicates.

STREAMS

A NetWare 3.x and 4.x loadable module that acts as an interface between NetWare and the network's transport protocols, such as IPX/SPX. STREAMS requires that the CLIB, IPXS, SPXS, and TLI modules are loaded.

String

A sequence of characters, whether they make sense or not. For example, "dogcow" is a string, but so is "z@x#tt!." Every word is a string, but relatively few strings are words. A search form will sometimes ask you to enter a search string, meaning a keyword or keywords to search on. Sometimes string means a sequence that does not include space, tab, return, and other blank or nonprinting characters.

String variable

A variable used to store text.

Stripe set

Basic disk configuration using multiple disks with data striped across the disks for performance improvement. This is an implementation of RAID 0.

Stripe set with parity

Basic disk fault-tolerant configuration using multiple disks with data and parity striped across multiple disks. This is an imlementation of RAID 5.

Striped volume

Dynamic disk configuration using multiple disks with data striped across the disks for performance improvement. This is an implementation of RAID 0.

Structural programming language

A programming language that revolves around a control mechanism, such as a main loop. Execution proceeds through the code along a predefined path. PASCAL and C are structural programming languages.

Structure of Management Information (SMI)

The rules used to define the objects that can be accessed via a network management protocol.

Structured Query Language (SQL)

An ISO data-definition and data-manipulation language for relational databases. Variations of SQL are offered by most major vendors for their relational database products. SQL is consistent with IBM's Systems Application Architecture and has been standardized by the American National Standards Institute (ANSI).

Stub

An object that impersonates an ActiveX client. The operating system creates it in the address space of an out-of-process component.

Stub network

A local network that carries data to and from local hosts exclusively. Even if connected to other networks, a stub network depends on other levels in the Internet hierarchy of networks, the mid-level and backbone networks, to carry traffic for other networks.

su

In UNIX/Linux, the command to switch users (if a username is specified) or temporarily invoke superuser privileges while maintaining the same user environment.

Sub procedure

A procedure that does not return a value to the calling procedure.

Subclass

A class derived from a parent class or superclass. A subclass inherits public and protected data and methods from its parent class.

Subdirectory

This is a directory that lies below another in the file system structure. For example, in SALES/NEW, NEW is a subdirectory of SALES.

Subnet

The primary reason to divide a network into subnets is network performance and available bandwidth. Without separate networks, each transmission would be broadcast across the entire internetwork, waiting for the destination system to respond. As the network grows, this causes increases in traffic until it exceeds the available bandwidth.

Routers divide, as well as provide, communications between the networks. Packets bound for a destination within the local network are kept local. Only packets bound for other networks are broadcast across the network, moving from router to router. Overall traffic levels are reduced.

Subnet mask

A bit mask used to select bits from an Internet (TCP/IP) address for subnet addressing. The mask is 32 bits long and selects the network portion of the Internet address and two or more bits of the local portion. It is sometimes called address mask. Local systems have subnet masks so they can restrict the broadcast to be received on the local network only.

Subnetting

When a complex network is recognized as a single address from outside of the network.

Subnetwork

A collection of OSI end systems and intermediate systems under the control of a single administrative domain and utilizing a single network access protocol. For example, private X.25 networks amid a collection of bridged LANs.

Subordinate reference replica

The Directory replica is automatically placed on a server if the server holds a replica of a parent partition but not of its child. These replicas cannot be changed.

Subquery

A Select statement that nests inside the WHERE clause of another Select statement.

Subscription server

In SQL Server replication, this is a server receiving updates.

Subsite

A site that is below another site in the SMS hierarchy.

sudo

In UNIX/Linux, a command that allows a user to perform a specified command (or list of commands) with the privilege level of the superuser while maintaining the same user environment.

SUID/GUID

In UNIX, a mechanism by which restricted privilege accounts may execute commands at a higher privilege level, under the aegis of a privileged account–often the superuser account itself. This opens a dangerous security hole in that a fault in the program executing at the high privilege level may lead to the restricted privilege account gaining administrative access to the system.

Suitcase

On a Macintosh, a collection of fonts from a particular font family.

Super VGA

Also known as VGA Plus, Extended VGA, and abbreviated SVGA. It provides analog output by varying the intensity of the three primary colors. SVGA provides higher resolutions than VGA.

Superclass

A parent class that subclasses are derived from.

SuperDrive

A high-density Macintosh floppy disk drive that can read the following diskette formats: Macintosh single-sided (400-KB), double-sided (800-KB), and high-density (1.4-MB) diskettes; PC double-density (720-KB) and high-density (1.44-MB) diskettes.

Superuser

The highest privilege level account on a system. Under UNIX, the root account; under Windows NT, the Administrator account.

In Linux, the account that has access to all system resources.

Supervisor right

A NetWare file system right that allows all rights to the respective directory and files. As an object right, it allows access privileges to all objects.

Suspend

An action that causes an active program to become temporarily inactive. In effect, the suspended program is waiting for the user to reactivate it.

Swap file

A file that contains temporary data moved out of main storage to the swap file on disk. A swap file is sometimes known as a paging file.

Swapping

A process that interchanges the contents of an area of main storage with the contents of an area of auxiliary storage. Swapping is sometimes known as paging.

Switch

1. A statement that selects an action from a number of alternatives. Switch compares the value of an integer test-expression with each of several case labels.

2. In Linux, on the shell command line, switches are often separated by a hyphen, e.g., **ls -a** and **ls -al** display different results of the **ls** command.

Switched line

A communications link for which the physical path may vary with each usage, such as the public telephone network.

Switched Multimegabit Data Service (SMDS)

A high-speed packet-switching application that enables users (primarily businesses) to communicate at speeds ranging from 1.5 megabits per second (Mbps) to as high as 155 Mbps. This type of service is most beneficial to organizations distributed in regional, national, and/or international configurations, often with separate local area networks at each end.

Symmetric Multiprocessing (SMP)

In an SMP operating system such as Windows NT, the operating system can run on any processor or can share tasks between several processors. User and applications threads can also be shared between processors, making best use of processor time and reducing bottlenecks. The Linux kernel supports SMP.

SYN flooding

A type of Denial of Service attack in which the transmission bandwidth of a remote system is consumed by inducing runaway broadcasts or SYN–SYN/ACK exchanges. SYN flooding usually relies on some amplification factor by which a few low-bandwidth machines can induce a large amount of network traffic.

SYN packet

A packet sent to a remote site to initiate a TCP/IP connection. If the traffic is from an authorized host, an ACK packet is returned, instructing the host to proceed with the connection. If not, the packet may simply be discarded or a RESET packet sent, which informs the sender that the connection has been terminated.

sync

In Linux, the command to force memory buffers to write to hard drives so that all changed information is saved.

Synchronization

1. Replica synchronization is a way to ensure that replicas of a NetWare Directory partition have the same information as other replicas of the same partition. Time synchronization is a way to ensure all servers in a NetWare Directory tree register the same time.

2. Under SQL Server replication, this is the process of copying database schema and data from a publishing server to a subscription server.

3. When discussing the Internet, it is the process of setting the same clock or data rate in the receiving terminal as in the sending terminal. This is a requirement to enable the receiving device to read the incoming bits and to translate them into characters. Synchronization, accomplished by a signal from the sending terminal, enables the receiving band to recognize any single bit and to identify which group of bits belongs in which characters. Once the first bit of a character is recognized, the receiver can count off the required number of bits and identify each character if it learns the number of bits in the character and the speed at which the bits are coming. Two common approaches to synchronized transmission between devices are synchronous transmission and asynchronous transmission.

Synchronized modifier

Specifies that a method is thread safe. Only one path of execution is allowed into a synchronized method at a time.

Synchronous

Pertaining to two or more processes that depend upon the occurrence of a specific event such as a common timing signal.

Synchronous Data Link Control (SDLC)

A communications standard controlled by the American National Standards Institute.

Synchronous modem

Modem that carries timing information with data.

Synchronous terminal

A data terminal that operates at a fixed rate with transmitter and receiver in synchronization.

Synchronous transmission

Process of sending blocks of data characters without any pause between the characters. The source and receiving terminals establish synchronization (the rate of data transmission) at the beginning of each block of data. The synchronization is generally accomplished by having the source terminal send at least two synchronizing characters (SYN characters) preceding each block of data. The receiver is designed to recognize the SYN characters. Synchronous transmission is generally done with buffers the blocks are held in until sent and is more efficient than asynchronous transmission.

SYSCON

An abbreviation for SYStem CONfiguration. It is a NetWare menu utility used to control network accounting and information.

syslog

In Linux, the command to start/stop system logging services.

Sysprep

A Windows 2000 utility that prepares the hard drive of a fully configured reference computer for duplication and deployment. Sysprep requires that the reference and target computers have identical HALs, ACPI support, and mass storage controllers.

A third-party disk-imaging tool is necessary to both create the actual image of the installation and deploy it to other computers.

Sysprep removes system-specific information such as computer name, users, and Security ID (SID).

Sysprep.inf

Answer file used by the Mini-Setup Wizard as an unattended installation of a Windows 2000 image created using Sysprep.

SYSTEM

A directory automatically created in NetWare's SYS volume when a network is installed. SYSTEM contains NetWare utilities that are used only by network supervisors and must not be deleted.

System attribute

A NetWare files system attribute (Sy) that marks directories or files for operating system use only.

System catalog

The set of system tables in the Master database containing descriptions of the database objects and how they are structured.

System configuration

A process that specifies the devices and programs that form a particular data-processing system.

System data types

Predefined data types.

System Default Profile

A Windows NT profile defining background color, screen saver, and wallpaper settings when no user is logged on.

System dump

A dump of all active programs and their associated data after an error stops the system.

System Fault Tolerance (SFT)

Novell's method of protecting data by providing ways to recover from hardware failures. The three levels of SFT are hot fix, disk mirroring or duplexing, and server mirroring.

System file

The file located in the Macintosh System Folder that contains the operating system.

System folder

On a Macintosh, a folder at the root of a startup disk containing the System File, Extensions, Control Panels, Preferences, Fonts, printer drivers, and other important system resources.

System Information snap-in

MMC snap-in that displays system information including, but not limited to, the system configuration summary, resource usage, and resource conflicts.

System login script

In NetWare 3.x, this login script sets general environment for all users who log in to a server. It is replaced by the container login script in NetWare 4.x.

System Monitor snap-in

MMC snap-in that is used to view and record activity from performance counters.

System Operator (Sysop)

Anyone responsible for the physical operations of a computer system or network resource. A System Administrator decides how often backups and maintenance should be performed, and the System Operator performs those tasks.

System procedures

Predefined procedures provided with SQL Server.

System state data

Critical Windows 2000 local system components such as the Registry and system boot files.

System software

The operating system software.

System tables

Special predefined tables in each database used to track information about the server as a whole and user objects within the databases.

SYSTEM.INI

An initialization file used by Microsoft Windows. It contains hardware- and setup-specific information used for the operation of Windows. It includes printer driver references and other device driver information.

System *x*

The abbreviation used to indicate a particular version of the Macintosh operating system software.

Systems Application Architecture (SAA)

Created by IBM in 1987 to help developers standardize applications so that software can function in different operating environments with minimal program modifications and retraining of users. SAA provides a common programming interface, common user access, and common communications support for IBM operating systems.

Systems Network Architecture (SNA)

A proprietary network that links IBM and non-IBM devices together. Introduced in 1974 before the OSI Reference Model was defined, SNA was originally a mainframe-centered hierarchical network architecture. SNA is an architecture or design specification that defines the data communications facilities, functions, and procedures that are distributed throughout the network. It also defines the formats and protocols used to support communication between programs, device operators, storage media, and workstations that may be located anywhere in the network. Before SNA, there were no formalized architecture standards or guidelines for computer-based online data-processing systems.

System-stored procedures

Predefined procedures provided with SQL Server.

SYSTIME

A NetWare command-line utility that displays a file server's date and time settings and synchronizes the workstation's date and time settings with those on the server.

T

T1

A leased-line connection capable of carrying data at 1,544,000 bits per second. At maximum theoretical capacity, a T1 line could move a megabyte in less than 10 seconds. That is still not fast enough for full-screen, full-motion video, for which you need at least 10,000,000 bits per second. T1 is the fastest speed commonly used to connect networks to the Internet.

T2

A leased-line connection capable of carrying data at 6,312,000 bits per second.

T3

A leased-line connection capable of carrying data at 45,000,000 bits per second. This is more than enough to do full-screen, full-motion video.

T4

An AT&T term for a digital circuit capable of supporting transmissions at a rate of up to 274.176 megabits per second.

Table

A rectangular display of data values shown as horizontal rows and vertical columns.

Table list

The list of tables, views, or both following the From keyword in a Select statement.

Tag

A string of characters of the form <...> or </...>. (The latter is for closing tags only.) Tags tell a Web browser how to format text or various bits of text. For example, the pair of tags <B>... </B> tells the browser to put the text between the two tags in boldface. The single tag <HR> tells the browser to insert a horizontal line. The tag pair <TABLE>... </TABLE> tells the browser to format the material in between as a table.

Tagged Image File Format (TIFF)

A file format used to store bitmapped graphics.

Tape backup device

This internal or external tape drive backs up data from hard disks.

Target

Any server, workstation, or service on the network that has a Target Service Agent loaded. The data can be backed up or restored on a target. When backing up and restoring to the host server, the target and host become the same.

Target Server Agent (TSA)

An executable type of program that will run in UNIX, Macintosh, or DOS systems. The program processes data moving between a target and the SBACKUP.NLM. (A target is a server that you back up data from or restore data to.)

Target service agent

The program processes data moving between a specific target and an SMS-compliant backup engine, such as SBACKUP.

Target window

The window that is directly beneath an object being dragged.

Task

In a multiprogramming or multiprocessing environment, one or more sequences of instructions created by a control program as an element of work to be accomplished by a computer.

Taskbar

1. The Windows 95 user interface element that shows the running applications and open windows.

2. The Linux KDE/GNOME user interface element that shows the running applications and open windows.

TBC

Transmit Buffer Count for Token Ring. This parameter may be required on a Novell network in the NET.CFG file, depending on the network interface card.

TBZ

Transmit Buffer Size for Token Ring. This parameter may be required on a Novell network in the NET.CFG file, depending on the network interface card.

TCP wrappers

In Linux, the daemon that controls almost all TCP network services. It checks the requesting source address of the connection. Can be used to booby trap suspected intruders.

tcpdump

A standard BSD-based command used for monitoring network traffic that passes through the client system's network segment (known as *packet sniffing*).

Teleprinter Exchange (Telex)

A teleprinter dial network offered by Western Union and the International Record Carriers. This network uses baudot code.

Teletex

A means of medium- to high-speed text transmission, from keyboard to printer, over public-switched data networks. Teletex permits a more extensive character set than telex and permits line and paragraph formatting as in normal correspondence. Teletex was expected to replace telex by 1990 but has so far had limited market acceptance.

Teletext

A noninteractive information system that preceded Videotex. Teletext terminals consist of a specially modified television set and keypad to provide 24 lines of 40-column color text and graphics. Connection is made to Teletext systems by specially assigned television broadcast channels, hence the need to use a television set.

Teletypewriter Exchange Service (TNX)

A network of teleprinters connected over a North American public-switched network that uses ASCII code.

Teletypewriter Exchange Service (TWX)

A teletypewriter dial network owned by Western Union. ASCII-coded machines are used.

Telnet

1. The Telnet protocol is a part of the TCP/IP protocol suite. Many Internet nodes support Telnet, which is similar to UNIX's rlogin program. Telnet lets users log in to any other computer on the Internet, provided that the target computer allows Telnet logins, and the user has a valid login name and password. The computers do not have to be of the same type to Telnet between them.

Some systems expect external access, and a special software package is set up to handle outside calls. This eliminates the need to *log in* once a user reaches the remote host.

The most popular reason to log in to a remote computer is to run software that is available only on the remote computer. Another reason is when a user's computer is incompatible with a particular program, operating system, available memory, or doesn't have the necessary processing power.

People with several Internet accounts can use Telnet to switch from one account to the other without logging out of any of the accounts.

Users can use Telnet as an information-gathering tool by searching databases for information. These databases include LOCIS (the Library of Congress Information System), CARL (Colorado Association of Research Libraries), ERIC (Educational Resources Information Center), and CIJE (Current Index to Journals in Education).

2. An Internet standard user-level protocol that allows a user's remote terminal to log in to computer systems on the Internet. To connect to a computer using Telnet, the user types Telnet and the address of the site or host computer.

Tempdb database

SQL Server database used as a temporary working area.

Temporary backup file

Backup file specified as path and filename during a backup or restore operation.

Temporary table

A table that exists only for the life of the current session. Temporary tables are created in tempdb.

Terminal

A device that allows you to send commands to a computer somewhere else. At a minimum, this usually means a keyboard and a display screen and some simple circuitry. Usually you will use terminal software in a personal computer. The software pretends to be ("emulates") a physical terminal and allows you to type commands to a computer somewhere else.

Terminal Access Controller (TAC)

A device that connects terminals to the Internet, usually using dial-up modem connections.

Terminal emulation

The use of hardware and software on a personal computer to duplicate the operation of a terminal device at both the operator and communications interface sides of the connection so that a mainframe computer capable of supporting the emulated terminal will also support the PC.

Terminal emulator

A program that allows a computer to act like a terminal when logged in to a remote host. The VT100 terminal is emulated by many popular communications packages.

Terminal server

A special-purpose computer that has places to plug in many modems on one side and a connection to a LAN or host machine on the other side. Thus, the terminal server does the work of answering the calls and passes the connections on to the appropriate node. Most terminal servers can provide PPP or SLIP services if connected to the Internet.

Terminal Services

Windows 2000 service providing a Windows 2000 desktop environment for clients with Win32 operating systems that are unable to fully support a local installation of Windows 2000.

Terminate and Stay Resident (TSR)

A program that is loaded into memory and remains available even when another application is active.

Termination

Placement of a load on the ends of a cable. For example, both SCSI and Ethernet bus cabling required termination.

Text fields

An input box where a user accepts a single line of text.

Thin Ethernet

Also known as 10Base2 or 802.3 networking. For many years, this was the most common type of Ethernet installation.

Thin Ethernet has a linear bus topology and uses a 0.2-inch (20 AWG) RG58A/U or TG58C/U 50-ohm cable.

Individual Thin Ethernet segments have a maximum length of 185 m (607 ft). The maximum network length is five segments (925 m or 3,035 ft). Repeaters connect segments, with up to four repeaters per network.

Workstations are attached directly to the Thin Ethernet cable with BNC T-connectors. The minimum distance between T-connectors is 0.5 m (1.6 ft). There is a maximum of 30 stations per segment.

Third normal form

Requires that each nonkey column gives information about the key column. A nonkey column may not describe another nonkey column.

This

A keyword that provides an object with a reference to itself.

Thread

The object of a process that is responsible for executing a block of code. A process can have one or multiple threads. Each process must have at least one thread. Threads are responsible for executing code.

Three-way handshake

The process whereby two protocol entities synchronize during connection establishment, typically accomplished at the initiation of a TCP/IP connection.

Thunk

The process of allowing 16-bit code to call 32-bit code and vice versa.

Tightly coupled applications

Two or more applications that have more intimate knowledge of each other than unrelated applications. Tightly coupled applications know what to expect from each other and can use interprocess communication objects that cannot be used by loosely coupled applications.

TIME

A NetWare 3.x and 4.x console command that displays the time and date used by the file server. The time is changed by using the SET TIME console command.

Time Division Multiplexing (TDM)

A device that accepts multiple channels on a single transmission line by connecting terminals, one at a time, at regular intervals, interleaving bits (bit TDM) or characters (character TDM) from each terminal.

Time out

When two computers are talking and, for whatever reason, one of the computers fails to respond.

Time sharing

The interleaved use of time on a computer system, enabling two or more users to execute computer programs concurrently. Also, a mode of operation of a data processing system that provides for the interleaving in time of two or more processes in one processor.

Time slice

An interval of time on the processing unit allocated for use in performing a task. After the interval has expired, processing unit time is allocated to another task. Therefore, a task cannot monopolize processing unit time beyond a fixed limit. In systems with time sharing, time slice is a segment of time allocated to a terminal job.

Time synchronization

A way to ensure all servers in a NetWare directory tree report the same time. Clocks in computers can lose or gain time, resulting in different times on various servers. Time synchronization corrects these differences so all servers report the same time and provide a valid timestamp to arrange NDS events.

Time to Live (TTL)

The amount of time between when a packet of data leaves its point of origin and when it reaches its destination. The TTL is encoded in the IP header and is used as a hop count (to measure the route to the packet's destination).

Time-critical priority

A classification of processes that may be interactive or noninteractive, in the foreground or background screen group, that has a higher priority than any non-time-critical thread in the system.

Title bar

A line displayed at the top of a window or dialog box.

TLIST

NetWare command-line utility that displays the list of users and groups (trustees) who have been granted rights in a directory or file on an attached file server.

Token

In a LAN (Local Area Network), the symbol of authority that is passed successively from one data station to another to indicate the station temporarily in control of the transmission medium. Each data station has an opportunity to acquire and use the token to control the medium.

Token bus

A form of network, usually a Local Area Network (LAN), in which access to the transmission medium is controlled by a token. The token is passed from station-to-station in a sequence. A station wishing to transmit will do so by removing the token from the bus and replacing it with the data to be transmitted. When transmission is complete, the transmitting station will reinitiate the token-passing process.

Token Ring

IBM originally created Token Ring (IEEE 802.5). Over the last few years, it has steadily gained popularity.

It is a network that runs as a logical ring but is usually wired as a physical star. It has a 4-Mbps or 16-Mbps transfer rate and runs on Unshielded Twisted Pair (UTP), Shielded Twisted Pair (STP), or fiber optic cabling.

A token (data frame) passes from system to system. A system can attach data to a token if the token is free (empty). In turn, each system on the ring receives, regenerates, and passes the token.

With Token Ring, it is possible to predict the passage of the token. The predictability inherent in Token Ring makes it a popular choice for timing-critical and control applications.

Token rotation time

The elapsed time for a token to rotate around the ring network.

TOKEN.LAN

LAN driver that links NetWare to a PC Adapter II, 16/4 Adapter, 16/4 Adapter/A, or PC Adapter/A Token-Ring network board. TOKEN.LAN can be used on both ISA and MicroChannel file servers.

TOKENRPLNetWare 3.x and 4.x loadable module used to remotely boot diskless and other workstations with Token-Ring network boards.

TokenTalk

The name used to describe the AppleTalk communications protocol suite operating over a Token-Ring network.

Topology

Refers to the physical layout of network components (such as cables, stations, gateways, and hubs). Major topologies are bus, star, ring, and mesh.

Trace definition file

Definition of a SQL Profiler trace identifying the information to be captured.

Trace file

Information captured by SQL Profiler and stored in an operating system file.

traceroute

A standard command that displays the route a packet of data would take to reach a target host.

TRACK OFF

A NetWare 3.x and 4.x console command that turns off the Router Tracking System display.

TRACK ON

A NetWare 3.x and 4.x console command that turns on the Router Tracking System display. Information is displayed about the file server, the network, connection requests, and incoming and outgoing information.

Track skewing

Reduces disk rotation time when reading or writing data across consecutive tracks of the same cylinder of a disk drive. With skewing, the disk rotates just one sector between reading the last sector of the first track and the first sector of the next track.

Trackball

An alternative input device, similar in function to a mouse.

Trackpad

The standard input device found on Apple's PowerBook line of portable computers. The standard input device found on many portable computers. Often recognized as a standard PS/2-style pointing device.

Tracks

On a disk, data is organized into concentric circles, or tracks, on the disk medium. One complete circle represents one track. Tracks on disks are analogous to the tracks you might see on a record used in a record player (curving lines on the record surface). Tracks are typically numbered from the outermost track to the innermost, or from the outer edge of the medium to the inner hub area. To figure out the number of tracks on a fixed disk drive, multiply the number of cylinders by the number of heads.

Traffic

The total information flow in a communications system.

Transaction

A series of SQL statements and procedures that are completed as a unit.

Transaction isolation

The process of protecting SQL Server transactions from each other's activities.

Transaction log file

SQL database log file that tracks all transaction activity for a database.

Transaction management

Ensuring that transactions are either completed or canceled so that the database is never left in an inconsistent state.

Transaction rollback

A process performed during automatic recovery that undoes changes to a database caused by incomplete transactions. This process is performed during automatic recovery, or it can be performed through the ROLLBACK TRAN statement.

Transaction rollforward

A process performed during automatic recovery that reapplies all transactions that were committed but not written to the database.

Transaction tracking system

A NetWare 3.x and 4.x protection system for bindery files and other database files. TTS monitors transactions and backs out (or rolls back transactions) that are incomplete because of hardware or software failure, error, or user preference.

Transactional attribute

A NetWare file system attribute (T) that shows a file is protected by TTS.

Transact-SQL

Microsoft SQL Server's native and enhanced SQL dialect.

Transceiver

A terminal device that can transmit and receive information signals. Transceiver is a contraction of transmitter-receiver.

Transducer

The part of a phone device that is responsible for sending and receiving data.

Transit network

Can access at least two other networks and passes data between them as well as within its own network.

Transitive trust

Trust relationships that are propagated to all domains in a Windows 2000 network. Transitive trust rules state, "If A trusts B, and B trusts C, then A trusts C."

Transmission

The electrical transfer of a message signal from one location to another.

Transmission Control Protocol (TCP)

The reliable connection-oriented protocol used by DARPA (Defense Advanced Research Projects Agency) for their internetworking research. TCP uses a three-way handshake with a clock-based sequence number selection to synchronize connecting entities and to minimize the chance of erroneous connections due to delayed messages. TCP is usually used with IP (Internet Protocol), the combination being known as TCP/IP.

Transmission Control Protocol/Internet Protocol (TCP/IP)

Originally designed for WANs (Wide Area Networks), TCP/IP was developed in the 1970s to link the research center of the U.S. Government's Defense Advanced Research Projects Agency. TCP/IP is a protocol that enables communication between the same or different types of computers on a network. TCP/IP can be carried over a wide range of communication channels. The Transmission Control Protocol is connection-oriented and monitors the correct transfer of data between computers. The Internet Protocol is stream-oriented and breaks data into packets.

Transmission rate

The transmission rate is stated in baud or bps. If the connection cannot be made at the selected transmission rate, most modems and communication software will automatically attempt to connect at a slower speed.

Transmission speed

The transmission speed of a communication device or channel is expressed as the number of information elements sent per unit of time. Data transmission speed is usually expressed in bits per second (bps).

Transmit

To send data from one place for reception elsewhere. Also, moving an entity from one place to another, as in broadcasting radio waves, dispatching data via a transmission medium, or transferring data from one data station to another via a line.

Transmit Buffer Count (TBC)

This parameter for Token Ring may be required on a Novell network in the SHELL.CFG file, depending on the network interface card.

Transmit Buffer Size (TBZ)

This parameter for Token Ring may be required on a Novell network in the SHELL.CFG file, depending on the network interface card.

Transport layer

OSI Layer 4, which is responsible for reliable end-to-end data transfer between end systems.

Transport Layer Interface (TLI)

NetWare 3.11 loadable module that provides TLI communication services as part of the STREAMS system, which provides communication between NetWare and the network's transport protocols, such as IPX/SPX. In addition to the STREAMS and TLI modules, the CLIB, IPX, and SPX modules must be loaded.

Trash

An icon on the Macintosh desktop used to delete files, folders, and aliases from a storage device. Users drag items to the Trash to delete them. Items are not physically deleted until the user selects the "Empty Trash" option in the Finder.

Tree

A collection of one or more domains that share a common namespace.

Trigger

1. A SQL Server trigger executes when the event for which it is defined (INSERT, UPDATE, and/or DELETE) occurs.

2. A trigger is used to set off an alert when specified conditions are detected.

Trojan horse

A program that purports to perform some useful function while surreptitiously compromising a system.

TrueType Fonts (TTF)

Fonts conforming to a specification developed by Microsoft and Apple. TrueType fonts can be scaled to any height and will print exactly as they appear on the screen to the highest resolution available to the output device. The fonts may be generated as bitmaps or soft fonts, depending on the output device's capabilities.

Trunk

A signal route to which several items of a computer system may be connected in parallel so that signals can be passed between them. Signals on a trunk may be only of a particular kind, or they may be intermixed. There are a number of widely used proprietary trunk systems. A trunk is also called a bus, and in the U.K., the term used is *highway.*

Trunk coupling unit

The generic name for an MAU.

Trust relationships

Only significant in a multiple-domain environment, a trust relationship is a one-way logical relationship established between two Windows NT Server domains. Once established, the domains are referred to as the trusted domain and the trusting domain.

The trusted domain can be assigned rights and permissions in the trusting domain. In other words, the trusting domain says, "I trust you to access my resources." This is a One-Way Trust Relationship.

The trusted domain does not automatically receive rights or permissions in the trusting domain. These must be explicitly assigned. The trust relationship makes it possible for these assignments to be made.

You can also have a Two-Way Trust Relationship, which is a mutual trust between domains. This is established as two one-way trusts, one in each direction.

Trusted connection

SQL Server named pipe connection.

Trusted domain

A domain receiving security rights and permissions from another (trusting) domain.

Trusted users

Users from a trusted domain.

Trustee

In NetWare, a user or group eligible to be granted rights in a directory or file. For any specific directory or file, the trustee can be granted all, some, or none of the rights available. Trustee rights in a directory or file are called trustee assignments.

Trusting domain

The domain granting security rights and permissions to another (trusted) domain.

tty

In Linux, the command to print the filename of the terminal connected to the standard input of the command, if any.

Tunneling

A method of encapsulating data for transmission between two authenticated endpoints.

In networking, the wrapping of one packet within another. For example, IP packets can be encapsulated in other IP packets. When they arrive at their destination, their structure is intact and they can be appear to have originated locally. Tunneling is used to set up *Virtual Private Networks.*

Tuple

A set of related attributes that describes a specific entity. Also called a *row* or *record.*

Turbo FAT index

This is a special FAT index that is used when a file exceeds 64 blocks (and the corresponding number of FAT entries). It allows a large file to be accessed quickly. To group together all entries for the file, NetWare creates a Turbo Fat. The first entry in the Turbo Fat's index is the first FAT number of the file, the second is the second number, etc.

Twip

Visual Basic's default unit of measure. It is equal to 1/1440 of an inch.

Twisted-pair cabling

Twisted Pair (TP) is made of insulated, copper wires that have been twisted around each other to form wire pairs. Usually the wire is 22 to 26 gauge, and more than one pair can be carried in a single jacket or sheath. When working with twisted pair, note the difference between *wire* and *pair.* A *two pair* cable has four wires.

Because any wire carrying electricity transmits and receives electromagnetic energy, nearby pairs of wires carrying signals can interfere with each other. This is called crosstalk. To reduce crosstalk and other Electromagnetic Interference (EMI), the wires are twisted. This causes any noise to be received more evenly by both wires in a pair. A voltage difference between the two wires carries the signal so noise that is equal on both wires cancels itself.

Twisted-pair wiring may or may not have an electromagnetic shield around the pairs. Therefore, it is classed into one of two types: Unshielded Twisted Pair (UTP) and Shielded Twisted Pair (STP). Unshielded Twisted Pair is a set of twisted wire pairs within a plastic sheath. The most common use for this type of cable is telephone wire. Different types of UTP cabling are suitable for different speed communications.

UTP is usually the least expensive of all of the network transmission media types.

Shielded Twisted Pair includes a protective sheathing around the conductors. This cuts down on outside interference.

Two-Phase Commit Protocol

A protocol used to guarantee the integrity of a distributed transaction across multiple servers. It has two phases. In the first phase, all servers prepare to commit or roll back. In the second phase, they perform the commit or rollback. Hence, the name two-phase commit.

Two-way trust

A trust relationship where there is mutual trust between two domains.

Tymnet

The U.S. public packet-switching carrier that developed from Tymshare Inc.'s internal terminal network used by its public time-sharing service.

Type 1 font

The font format developed by Adobe Systems for PostScript fonts.

Typeface

The style or appearance of the set of characters. Typeface examples include Times New Roman, Helvetica, Script, etc. Many font names are trademarked and may be called by different names when coming from different sources.

U

Unattended installation

An operating system installation run without end-user interaction. Answers to Setup prompts are supplied by text files called answer files.

Unattend.txt

Default name for an answer file used during over-the-network unattended Windows NT and Windows 2000 installations.

UNBIND

NetWare 3.x and 4.x console command to remove the link between an installed network board's communications protocol and its software LAN driver.

Unicode

An international standard that is used to define characters in any written language. Unicode uses a 16-bit character set.

Unicode collation

Sort order for Unicode data.

Uniform Resource Locator (URL)

A URL is the pathname of a document on the Internet. URLs can be absolute or relative. An absolute URL consists of a prefix denoting a *method* (http for Web sites, gopher for gophers, and so forth). The prefix is followed by a colon, two slashes (://), and an address. The address consists of a domain name followed by a slash and a pathname (or "username@domain name" for mailto). The last part is an optional anchor, which is preceded by a #. The # symbol points to a place within the Web page.

Uninet

A common carrier offering an X.25 PDN.

Uninterruptible Power Supply (UPS)

If power loss, surges, or drops (brownouts) are a significant concern, an Uninterruptible Power Supply (UPS) may be your best option. With a UPS, line voltage is fed into a battery, keeping it constantly charged. The computer is, in turn, powered from the battery. Because the computer is already running from the battery, there is no switching time if power is lost. UPS systems supply protection against power events more effectively than most other devices. Uninterruptible Power Supplies are considered essential for network servers. If normal power is lost or interrupted, the UPS allows time to safely shut down the file server. Many UPSs can alert network users to warn when the system is going down.

When selecting a UPS, examine the software and hardware available for the UPS. Options and features vary greatly.

Union

A relational algebra operator that combines two sets to yield the superset with the duplicates removed.

Unique index

An index that does not allow duplicate entries.

Uniqueness Database File (UDF)

A text file containing unique responses used to override answer file responses during Windows NT and Windows 2000 unattended installations.

Universal group

Active Directory domain group scope that is only supported in native mode. Members can include users from any domain in the forest, Global groups from any domain in the forest, and Universal groups from any domain in the forest.

Universal Naming Convention (UNC)

A file-naming convention that uses the *machine_name**share_name* format.

Universal Serial Bus (USB)

A standard promoted by Intel for communication between an IBM PC and an external peripharal over an inexpensive cable using biserial transmission.

USB works at 12 Mbps with specific cost consideration for low-cost peripherals. It supports up to 127 devices and both isochronous and asynchronous data transfers. Cables can be up to 5 meters long, and it includes built-in power distribution for low power devices. It supports daisy-chaining through a tiered multidrop topology.

Before March 1996, Intel started to integrate the necessary logic into PC chip sets and encourage other manufacturers to do likewise, so currently there is widespread availability and support.

Because of its relatively low speed, USB is intended to replace existing serial ports, parallel ports, keyboard and monitor connectors, and be used with keyboard, mice, monitors, printers, and possibly some low-speed scanners and removable hard drives. For faster devices, existing IDE, SCSI, or emerging FC-AL or FireWire interfaces can be used.

UNIX

A computer operating system originally developed at AT&T's Bell Research Laboratories and later at the University of California Berkeley. It is implemented in a growing number of minicomputer and microcomputer systems.

UNIX is *multiuser* because it is designed to be used by many people at the same time and has TCP/IP built into the operating system. It is the most common operating system for servers on the Internet.

UNIX-to-UNIX Copy (UUCP)

A software program that facilitates file transfer from one UNIX system to another via dial-up phone lines. The UUCP protocol also describes the international network used to transfer USENET News and electronic mail.

UNLOAD

A NetWare 3.x and 4.x console command that removes a module that was entered into the system with the LOAD command. One purpose of UNLOAD is to remove old LAN drivers to allow for installation of new ones.

Unload

Under Visual Basic, unloading is the process of removing an instance of an object from memory.

Unmodified comparison operator

A SQL comparison operator not followed by ANY or ALL.

Update

Statement to modify the content of SQL Server rows.

Upload

A process where a user copies a file *up* to a host computer. Opposite of download.

Upper Memory Area (UMA)

An area reserved for system components, it is sometimes called *Reserved Memory.* It is the area of memory located between 640 KB and 1 MB.

Shadow RAM uses this area to shadow the computer's ROM BIOS instructions and the video controller's ROM. Hardware devices store their program code here.

Upper Memory Blocks (UMBs) are free areas within the UMA. UMBs can be used to load device drivers and Terminate and Stay Resident (TSR) programs.

Accessing the UMBs requires an extended memory manager and expanded memory manager to be loaded. In Microsoft Windows, these programs are Himem.sys (extended) and Emm386.exe (expanded).

Upper Memory Blocks (UMBs)

Areas of the upper memory that contain general-purpose memory. These areas can be used to hold device drivers or other memory-resident programs. This will free conventional memory for use by applications.

UPS STATUS

NetWare 3.x and 4.x console command that allows the status of an Uninterruptible Power Supply (UPS) to be checked when using Novell's UPS.NLM.

UPS TIME

NetWare 3.x and 4.x console command that allows a network supervisor to change the amount of time an interruptible power supply can function. The UPS TIME command can also be used to change the amount of time needed to recharge its battery.

Upstream neighbor address

In Token-Ring networks, it is the address of the network station that is physically and immediately upstream from another specific node. The upstream neighbor is the location from which the signal is being received.

Usenet

A worldwide system of discussion groups, with comments passed among hundreds of thousands of machines. Not all Usenet machines are on the Internet–only about half. Usenet is completely decentralized, with more than 10,000 discussion areas, called newsgroups.

User

1. An individual permitted to access a computer, network, or other system.
2. SQL Server database access account.

User account

Security object used for logon authentication and resource access verification.

User Agent (UA)

An OSI application process that represents a human user or organization in the X.400 Message Handling System. Creates, submits, and takes delivery of messages on the user's behalf.

User Control module

A Visual Basic module used to create ActiveX controls.

User databases

Databases created by users using the Create Database statement.

User Datagram Protocol (UDP)

A transport protocol in the Internet suite of protocols. UDP, like TCP, uses IP for delivery. However, unlike TCP, UDP provides for exchange of datagrams without acknowledgements or guaranteed delivery.

User Document module

A Visual Basic module used to create ActiveX Documents.

User ID (UID)

In Linux, the unique number associated with each user in the /etc/passwd file.

User interface

A program operated by a computer user to interact with the computer. Also known as user agent.

User login script

This login script sets environment specifics for a user. It is optional but most often used for items that cannot be included in a system or profile login script. If used, it will run after container and profile login scripts.

User Manager

A Windows NT user and group administration utility.

User Manager for Domains

A utility installed on all NT Server systems. On additional servers it is operationally identical to the Windows NT Workstation version of the utility, User Manager. The utility is also installed as part of the NT Server remote management tools.

When User Manager for Domains is started, the current domain users and groups are displayed. Domain Administrators and Account Operators can view and modify users and groups by selecting the appropriate account and running Properties from the User menu, or by double-clicking on the account. Administrators can manage any account.

Additional menu selections let you create and manage accounts, select the sort order for account names, manage domain policies, and establish trust relationships.

User mode

1. The default Microsoft Management Console (MMC) mode that allows users to use, but not modify, MMC custom consoles.

2. Higher-level Windows NT, Windows 95, or Windows 98 operating system functions. The user mode includes the protected subsystems and application sessions.

User object

A leaf object in NDS that represents a person with access to the network and stores information about this person.

User object ADMIN

A user object that has rights to create and manage other objects. It is created automatically during NetWare 4.x installation. When the Directory tree is created, ADMIN has a trustee assignment to the [ROOT] object. This includes the Supervisor object right, which allows ADMIN to create and manage all objects in the tree.

User private group

In Linux, a Red Hat security scheme that involves creating a group for each user.

User profile

Collection of folders containing information about a user's desktop environment, application settings, and other personal data that is applied when a user logs on.

User program

A program that resides and runs in the outside of the operating system kernel.

User template

A file that contains default information that can be applied to new User objects to give them default property values. This is useful if you are creating many users who need the same property values.

useradd

In Linux, a utility to add or update users from the command-line interface.

USERDEF

An abbreviation for USER DEFinition. It is a NetWare menu utility used to add users to the network, restrict users' disk space, edit and view a template for adding users, or substitute a created template. Users cannot be deleted with USERDEF.

User-defined data types

Data types defined by the user and based on system data types using the sp_addtype system procedure. User-defined data types can include a null specification and have rules and defaults bound to it.

User-defined error message

A SQL error message defined as any message number above 50,000. Provides information to the users on the status of stored procedures, triggers, or any other area of database usage. An included Raiserror statement returns an error message and sets a system flag to record that an error has occurred.

User-defined transaction

The same as an explicit transaction.

User-level protocols

Examples are Telnet, Simple Mail Transfer Protocol (SMTP), and FTP, which allow users to perform operations or applications.

USERLIST

A NetWare command-line utility that allows users to view information about the file server's current logged-in users. The information includes connection number, login time, network address, and node address.

Username

The name by which a login ID is known within the context of a database or session.

Utilities

In NetWare, utilities are programs that add functions to the operating system by being added to the file server, workstation, or router. Utilities can be in the form of console commands, including screen commands, installation, maintenance, and configuration commands.

Utility

The capability of a system, program, or device to perform the functions it was designed for.

V

V.10

A CCITT interface recommendation; electrically similar to RS-423.

V.11

A CCITT interface recommendation; electrically similar to RS-422.

V.21

A CCITT modem recommendation; similar to Bell 103.

V.22

A CCITT modem recommendation; similar to Bell 212.

V.23

A CCITT modem recommendation; similar to Bell 202.

V.24

A CCITT interface recommendation that defines interchange circuits; similar to and operationally compatible with RS-232.

V.26

A CCITT modem recommendation; similar to Bell 201.

V.27

A CITT modem recommendation; similar to Bell 208.

V.28

A CCITT interface recommendation that defines electrical characteristics for the interchange circuits defined by V.24; similar to and operationally compatible with RS-232.

V.29

A CCITT modem recommendation; similar to Bell 209.

Validation rules

A rule specifies what data may be entered in a particular column; it is a way of defining the domain of the column. Rules are sometimes referred to as *validation rules* since they allow the system to check whether a value being entered in a column falls within the column's domain.

Value

A single data element, such as contents of one column-one row intersection.

Variable

In programming, a variable is used for temporary data storage. Each variable will have an identifying name, a data type, and an assigned (or assumed) value.

The term declaration is used to refer to the statement that causes a variable to be created.

The two types of variable declarations in Visual Basic are explicit and implicit.

An explicit declaration is when a variable is defined or created before it is needed. This is normally a better method of defining variables because it forces better planning and control.

With implicit declaration, the variable is defined *on the fly.* You define the variable by referring to it as part of a program statement. Any time Visual Basic encounters a name in your code that is not defined elsewhere, a new variable is created using that name.

VCACHE

A set of 32-bit cache utilities. VCACHE is shared by VFAT and *vredir in Windows for Workgroups 3.11. In some situations, VCACHE can replace Smartdrv.exe.

Vector aggregate

An aggregate that returns an array of values, one per set.

Vector font

Generally used to refer to any font that is defined mathematically and that supports scaling to any size. Vector fonts provide a smooth appearance in large font sizes.

VERSION

A NetWare command-line utility that displays the software version, copyright information, and checksum of a NetWare executable file. In NetWare 3.x and 4.x, VERSION is also a console command that displays similar information about the file server.

Vertical filter

Sets limits on replication by identifying the article columns to be published.

Vertical Redundancy Check (VRC)

An error-detection scheme in which the parity bit of each character is set to "1" or "0" so that the total number of "1" bits in the character is odd or even.

Vertical scalability

The ability to migrate an existing server environment to a more powerful server environment with minimal impact in the client applications.

Vertical spacing

Though not actually a font characteristic, the vertical spacing is also set to match the font appearance. This may be set in lines per inch or as points of space to be inserted before and after each line.

Very Easy Rodent-Oriented Network Index to Computerized Archives (Veronica)

Developed at the University of Nevada, Veronica is a constantly updated database of the names of almost every menu item on thousands of gopher servers. The Veronica database can be searched from most major gopher menus. It is an Internet search tool that uses keywords to search gopher menus for matches to the search criteria. Veronica presents the user with a list of gopher menu items that match the keyword search and, by choosing one of these items, connects the user directly to that gopher source.

Very Large-Scale Integration (VLSI)

A chip technology with 20,000 to 900,000 logic gates per chip. The flow of electrons in chips is controlled by the transistors that form switches or logic gates. Chips are categorized by the number of logic gates available.

VFAT

A protected mode virtual device driver that handles interrupt 21b.

vi

A visual display presentation editor; standard equipment on Linux and UNIX systems.

Video card

The hardware board that contains the electronic circuitry to drive a video display monitor.

Video Graphics Array (VGA)

Uses a DAC chip and sends analog signals at varying intensities to alter the three primary colors. By varying the intensity, a seemingly infinite number of color variations can be produced and displayed on the monitor.

Video port

Also known as *display port.* The port used to connect a video display monitor to a Macintosh system.

Video Random Access Memory (VRAM)

High-speed memory used on certain video cards.

Videotex

An interactive information system also known as videotext and viewdata. The system can be used for public access or broadcast to a select user/subscriber, making large volumes of information available to an authorized audience. Videotex systems usually operate over switched telephone lines and allow 40 columns by 24 lines of color text and graphics to be displayed on the screen. Information is arranged in pages.

View

A method of creating custom presentation of data stored in database tables.

View resolution

The process of resolving references to view columns into references to underlying base tables. The process also ensures that the definitions of the underlying tables have not changed.

Virtual circuit

A network service that acts like a dedicated line between a user's computer and a host. Data is processed through a virtual circuit in the order in which it is sent, regardless of the underlying network structure.

Virtual console

Allows a single machine to display more than one terminal by using a hot key to switch from one display to another.

Virtual desktop

In GNOME, a method of having multiple (four) screen images accessible by scrolling off the current display area, like looking at one pane of a window with four glass panels. In KDE, a method of having multiple screen images (four, six, or eight) selectable from the control area.

A window can appear in one of the virtual desktop areas, all of the desktops, or (in GNOME) can overlap between two or more desktops.

Virtual directory

Web site directory linked to a different physical directory location that serves as a means to extend the home directory.

Virtual DOS Machine (VDM)

Emulated DOS machine used to support DOS and WOW under Windows NT.

Virtual library

A concept describing a library whose collection includes remote access to library catalogs, the Internet, networks, and other electronic information services and resources worldwide.

Virtual Loadable Module (VLM)

A series of executable programs that run at a DOS workstation and enable communication with the NetWare server.

Virtual machine

The Windows technique used to execute an application. Virtual machines include a virtual address space, processor registers, and privileges.

Virtual memory

Some operating systems have the ability to increase the apparent physical system memory through virtual memory. Virtual memory is a file on the hard disk that emulates physical Random Access Memory (RAM). This file is called a swap file.

With virtual memory, a portion of the program and data is kept in RAM at all times, with the remainder stored on the disk. This is normally referred to as *swapping* the information to the disk. When an attempt is made to access code or data on the disk, it is swapped back into RAM, and if necessary, other code or data will be swapped out to make room available. The swapping process is controlled by the VMM (Virtual Memory Manager).

Except for a loss of performance when swapping occurs, virtual memory is transparent to the user and application.

Virtual memory gives you more memory, providing the ability to launch more concurrent applications and work with larger data files. The system's capabilities are increased, but at a small performance decrease. Adding more physical memory will still provide better system performance.

Virtual Memory Manager (VMM)

The portion of the operating system that is responsible for swapping pages between RAM and the paging file. It also keeps track of how an address in a virtual address space maps to physical memory.

Virtual Network Perimeter

The analogous logical construction for a Virtual Private Network to a border network in a physical private network.

Virtual Private Network (VPN)

A network appearing logically as a single network, but in reality, a set of physically isolated networks that use tunneling to make (encrypted) connections over untrusted networks (such as the Internet) often leased out by third parties.

This is an option for remote access configuration where users and remote networks connect to network servers across the Internet.

Virtual Reality Modeling Language (VRML)

An extension to the WWW to support platform-independent virtual reality.

Virtual table

Another term for a *view.*

Virus

A program that can destroy data and change itself to escape detection. A virus can move into other computer systems by incorporating itself into programs or files that are shared among computer systems.

Visual Basic

A general purpose programming language for the Microsoft Windows family of products.

Visual Basic forms

In Visual Basic, a form is an object data type. This is a generic term for objects defined by Visual Basic and is also used to describe objects defined by the Microsoft Jet database engine. Some important points to understand about forms include Form events and properties, and Forms collection.

Form events are the event types defined for each form. These include system events and user events. Procedures and/or program code can be attached to any or all of these events.

Each form will have a set of Form properties that defines its appearance and other controlling factors. The properties can be modified to meet a particular need.

A Forms collection is a set of related objects. A project will have a Forms collection representing each loaded form. The Forms collection has a single property named Count. This is the number of elements (loaded forms).

Visual Basic Multiple Document Interface

Many standard applications utilize the Multiple Document Interface (MDI). Examples include Microsoft Excel, Microsoft Word, Corel Draw, and PageMaker. This discussion is concerned with the MDI as it applies to Visual Basic.

An application can only have one MDI form. All child forms will be displayed inside of that form. If an MDI form is inserted in your application, the MDI Form command is no longer available from the Insert menu.

In addition to child forms, an MDI form can contain Menu and PictureBox standard Visual Basic controls. It can also contain some types of custom controls.

Other controls can be placed on an MDI form indirectly. Because a PictureBox control can act as a container for other controls, you can draw a PictureBox on the MDI form. Other controls can be placed inside the PictureBox control.

All of the controls on the MDI form are part of the form's Controls collection. The Count property returns the number of controls in the collection.

Voice frequency

Frequency in part of the audio frequency range essential for the transmission of commercial quality speech.

Voice-Grade-Line

A channel that is capable of carrying voice frequency signals.

VOLINFO

An abbreviation for VOLume INFOrmation. It is a NetWare 3.x menu utility that displays information about each volume in a file server.

Volume

A NetWare name for the amount of named storage space on a hard disk. This space is allocated when the network is installed.

Volume object

A leaf object that represents a physical volume on the network.

Volume segment

A physical division of a NetWare volume. Large volumes can be created by storing different segments of a volume on one or more hard disks. A single hard disk can store up to eight volume segments belonging to one or more volumes. Each volume extends up to 32 segments.

Volume set

Multiple dynamic disk partitions joined as one logical drive.

VOLUMES

A NetWare 3.x or 4.x console command that lists the names of volumes and name spaces available on volumes mounted on the file server.

Voluntary tunnel

A tunnel created by a client computer to a target server.

VREPAIR

A NetWare 3.x, 4.x, and 5.x loadable module that is used to recover volume data after a power failure or because of a disk defect.

VT100

A computer terminal manufactured by Digital Equipment Corporation. Many communications software packages emulate the VT100.

Vtable

An array of function pointers, generated by the compiler.

W

w

In Linux, a utility that shows who is on a system and what they are doing.

Web browser

A client program that serves as the interface between the user and the resources of the World Wide Web.

WebCrawler

A search engine on the Internet, located at www.webcrawler.com.

WebDAV

Protocol that, when used with IIS, supports Web folders. This allows clients to manage remote folders and files through the Internet using an HTTP connection. File and folder maintenance can be performed using Internet Explorer 5, a Microsoft Office 2000 application, or any network connection using Windows 2000. WebDAV is an extention of the HTTP 1.1 standard.

WebDAV Publishing Directory

Special virtual directory that supports client read, write, delete, copy, move, and search operations. The WebDAV Publishing Directory is created by using the IIS snap-in.

Well-connected sites

Sites that communicate through high-speed connections.

What You See Is What You Get (WYSIWYG)

A word processing term that means that what is seen on the computer screen will correspond to what prints out on paper. This includes typeface, layout, and size.

White pages

Directories that are accessible through the Internet. They contain information on users, such as electronic mail addresses, phone numbers, and street addresses.

who

In Linux, a utility that shows who is on the system.

WHOAMI

A NetWare command-line utility that displays information about a user's attachments to file servers.

whois

An Internet software program that enables users to query a database of registered names for people, domains, networks, and hosts. The database is maintained at the Defense Data Network Network Information Center (DDN NIC) and can be reached through telnet at nic.ddn.mil.

Wide Area Information Server (WAIS)

Search tools for finding specific information on the Internet. A WAIS is a collection of databases. By specifying one or more keywords for which to search and which WAIS servers to examine, users can see a list of all of the indexed files that contain the keywords. As this implies, the majority of indexed files are text files, but WAIS servers also track and search for graphic images and other types of files. Anyone can add another server to the WAIS collection by indexing the information on it and maintaining that index.

While people can access most WAIS servers for free, some WAIS servers (like the Dow Jones Information Service) charge a usage fee.

Users can search for files in more than 500 WAIS libraries or sources. The Thinking Machines corporation in Massachusetts (quake.think.com), one of the original developers of WAIS, has a directory of all WAIS libraries. It is a good place to begin a WAIS search.

Users can telnet directly to a WAIS server or access WAIS through a gopher. Because people create and maintain the WAIS libraries on a volunteer basis, the indexes are not always complete. In general, a search for technical or scientific information, such as computer hardware, networking solutions, or astronomical data, will be very successful, while one for articles about psychology may not be as helpful. This depends, of course, on who is maintaining the database. The quality of a database is by no means a constant across all WAIS libraries.

Unlike other search systems, such as Veronica, WAIS cannot perform boolean searches. If a user were to enter "modem and speeds" as keywords, WAIS would dutifully search for instances of the word "modem," instances of the word "speeds," and every instance of the word "and." The search results would take a significant amount of time to compile and would be practically meaningless. WAIS' inability to handle boolean searches is not as serious as it may sound.

One way in which WAIS compensates for this is by ranking the results of every search. In the search for "modem speeds," WAIS will examine all the files in the specified database(s) and count the number of occurrences of "modem" and "speeds" for each file. Then, when presenting its results, WAIS will rank them. WAIS ranks the file with the most occurrences of the keyword(s) as 1,000, and the other files with a number between 1 and 999. While the first file may not be the most helpful, the system is better than a completely unorganized list of possibilities.

Wide Area Network (WAN)

Expands the basic LAN model by linking Local Area Networks (LANs) and allowing them to communicate with each other. By traditional definition, a LAN becomes a WAN when it crosses a public right-of-way, requiring a public carrier for data transmission. More current usage of the term usually includes any situation where a network expands beyond one location/building. A WAN is characterized by low- to high-speed communication links and usually covers a wide geographic area. The remote links may be operational LANs or only groups of workstations. With the exception of a WAN's wider area of operation, the benefits and features of LANs and WANs are the same.

Wide Area Telecommunications Service (WATS)

A service provided by telephone companies in the United States that permits a customer to make calls to or from telephones in specific zones for a flat monthly charge. The monthly charges are based on the size of the zone instead of the number of calls.

Wideband

A communications channel used to transmit more than 230,000 bps for direct data transfer from one computer to another.

Wildcard characters

Characters that have special meaning when used in pattern-matching strings. They can represent one character or any number of characters or exclude certain characters.

Win32 Driver Model (WDM)

Specification defining device driver file architecture for Windows 2000 family- and Windows 98-compatible device driver files.

WIN32S

A set of APIs that allow 32-bit applications to run on Windows 3.1. Some of the functions are implemented as stubs.

Window manager

In Linux, a program to control icons, default buttons, borders, resizing, drag-and-drop feature, virtual desktops, and other aspects of X sessions.

Windowing

In routing terms, windowing refers to a flow control technique to send multiple message packets before requiring an acknowledgment from the receiver.

Windows (Microsoft)

A graphical shell operating environment that runs on top of DOS. It contains many accessories and features that access DOS functions, such as file, program, and printer management. Windows is referred to as a GUI (Graphical User Interface).

Windows 3.x swap files

In Microsoft Windows 3.x, there are two types of swap files, permanent and temporary. Permanent swap files are faster than temporary ones because only contiguous disk space can be used. Permanent swap files are only as big as the largest contiguous block on the disk. Permanent swap files cannot be created on a network drive. Two hidden files are created when the permanent swap file is created. The 386spart.par file is the actual swap file and is located in the root directory of the chosen drive. Spart.par is created in the Windows directory and identifies the size and location of the swap file.

Temporary swap files are created whenever Windows is launched and deleted when Windows is exited. The disk space used for the swap file is recovered for use in DOS. Temporary swap files support disks too fragmented for a permanent swap file. Temporary swap files can be set up to work on network drives. Each user's swap file must be in a different directory location, and users need read/write access in that directory. The PagingFile= entry in [386enh] section of the System.ini file defines the temporary swap file's name and location. The default filename is Win386.swp. The size of the temporary swap file changes dynamically, as needed, but is limited by the MaxPagingFileSize= and MinUserDiskSpace= parameters in the [386enh] section of System.ini file. At least 2 MB of space must be available on the drive specified in the PagingDrive= parameter. The MaxPagingFileSize= parameter in the [386enh] of SYSTEM.INI should be set to at least 1,024.

Regardless of the amount of physical memory, Windows requires a swap file of at least 2 MB. The more memory there is in a system, the larger the swap file should be. The 386 Enhanced icon in the Windows Control Panel is used to configure and create a swap file. To view or modify swap file information, select the Virtual Memory button. The swap file information will be displayed. To modify the settings, select Change. Select the drive location for the swap file, the swap file type and size, and whether 32-bit disk access should be used.

Windows 9x, Windows NT, Windows 2000

Microsoft's series of 32-bit operating systems. Windows 9x is actually a hybrid of 16- and 32-bit code which operates much like Windows for Workgroups 3.11 and, in fact, was originally called Windows 4.0. Similarly, Windows 2000 was originally slated to be released as Windows NT 5.0.

Windows Hardware Quality Labs (WHQL)

Testing entity for certifying WDM device drivers for digital signing.

Windows Internet Name Service (WINS)

A Windows NT utility that translates a NetBIOS name into an IP address. It is designed for use in a routed network.

Windows NT (NT)

An acronym for New Technology.

Windows NT authentication method

SQL Server authentication method based on Windows NT user accounts.

Windows on Windows (WOW)

Win16 application support is sometimes referred to as WOW. This allows Win16 applications to run under a default WOW session, or one Virtual DOS Machine.

Win.ini file

An initialization file used by Microsoft Windows. The file contains settings used to customize the Windows environment. Windows applications will sometimes store initialization information in the Win.ini file.

Winnt32.exe

Windows NT and Windows 2000 Setup program. Winnt32.exe runs on 32-bit Windows-family operating systems.

Winnt.exe

Windows NT and Windows 2000 Setup program. Winnt.exe runs on MS-DOS and 16-bit Windows-family operating systems.

Winnt.sif

Answer file used when running an unattended installation of Windows 2000 by booting from the Installation CD-ROM.

Workgroup

A defined set of Windows for Workgroups, Windows 95, or NT stations that are able to communicate and share file and print resources.

Workgroup manager

The person appointed by a NetWare network supervisor to manage data and users belonging to a group.

Workstation

A personal computer that is connected to a network. It can perform tasks through application programs or utilities. The term client or station may also be used.

World Wide Web (WWW)

A fast-growing addition to the Internet.

In 1991, Tim Berners-Lee developed the World Wide Web for the Laboratoire Europeen pour la Physique des Particules (CERN). It was designed as a means of communicating research and ideas between members of the high-energy physics community.

Browsers are the client tools that allow users to view the contents of the Web. The Web at that time had no easily accessible viewing capabilities. The browsers were text-only, line-mode tools that offered no graphical capabilities and few navigation links.

Early in 1993, a team at the National Center for Supercomputing Applications (NCSA) at the University of Illinois at Champaign-Urbana developed an Internet browsing program called Mosaic. The NCSA had no way to disseminate or market the program.

Later that year, a former NCSA graduate student (Tim Krauskopf) offered the University of Illinois a business plan and was given the rights to license Mosaic. The company is called Spyglass. Another company, with the help of former NCSA programmers, created its own Internet browser company and wanted to call it Mosaic Communications, but the NCSA would not allow this. The company was renamed Netscape, and their graphical Web browser was named Netscape Navigator. Netscape markets its browsers and servers directly to consumers, while Spyglass markets Mosaic to component suppliers such as AT&T, IBM, and Microsoft.

Because the Mosaic project initiated the graphical browser implementation, the term Mosaic is sometimes still used to describe any graphical Web browser.

The Web unifies many of the existing network tools with hypertext (also called hyperlinks). Hypertext gives users the ability to explore paths of information in nonlinear ways. Instead of reading through files in a preplanned sequential arrangement, users can move from item to item in any order they choose.

Some hyperlinks lead to ftp sites, newsgroups, gopher sites, and other Web sites that house additional graphical Web documents. To navigate these Web sites and find links, search engines are available. While current engines can only identify sites that meet the user's criteria, second-generation search engines will use artificial intelligence to report to users on information that exactly meets their needs.

The graphical interfaces make the Internet much more appealing, powerful, and simple. Besides being more intuitive than text-based tools, graphical browsers offer full hypermedia support. As recently as 1994, few trade journals mentioned the Web.

Today, Web addresses (URLs) are included in television, radio, magazine, and movie advertisements and on billboards. By 1995, Web traffic was doubling every four months and was growing more than twice as fast as general Internet traffic. Entire businesses now reside on the Web, and millions of people use it for communications and educational resources.

World Wide Web Consortium (W3C)

W3C works with the global community to produce specifications and reference software. W3C is funded by industrial members, but its products are free and available to all.

Worm

A computer program that replicates itself infinitely, filling up memory space. It can pass from one network to another.

Wrapper class

A class that allows a primitive data type to be manipulated like an object.

WRITE

A NetWare login script command that allows a user to enter text for screen display.

Write precomp

When moving toward the center of the hard disk, sectors are physically smaller. Some drives reduce the write current to these sectors to lessen the possibility of crosstalk. The Write Precomp cylinder is the cylinder at which this change takes place.

Write right

A file system right that allows users to open and write to files. As a property right, it allows the adding, changing, or removing of any values of the property.

WSGEN

NetWare 3.11 command-line utility used to create the IPX.COM file, which installs the NetWare IPX and network card driver protocol. It is provided on the WSGEN diskette.

WSUPDATE

A NetWare 3.x command-line utility that allows workstation shells and other files to be updated from the file server. WSUPDATE functions by comparing the data of the source file with the workstation file and providing the update if the source file is more recent.

X

X

X Window System.

X client

In Linux, the part of X that generates the application data that is displayed elsewhere (on the display server).

X recommendations

The CCITT documents that describe data communication network standards. Well-known ones include X.25 Packet Switching standard, X.400 Message Handling System, and X.500 Directory Services.

X series

Standards of the CCITT for communications interfaces, such as modems.

X server

In Linux, controls the keyboard, mouse, and screen for users interacting with applications that work under X Window displays.

X Window System™

A popular window system developed by MIT and implemented on a number of workstations.

X.21

A CCITT recommendation that defines the most popular physical interface for X.25; it is equivalent to RS-232 and V.24.

X.21 bis

A CCITT recommendation that defines the most popular physical interface for X.25; it is equivalent to RS-232 and V.24.

X.25

A data communications interface specification that describes how data passes into and out of packet-switching networks. The protocol suite approved by the CCITT and International Organization for Standardization (ISO) defines the origination, termination, and use of virtual circuits that connect host computers and terminals across the network.

Note that ISO is not an acronym in this instance. The word *iso* is derived from the Greek word *isos*, which means equal.

X.25 Pad

A device that permits communication between non-X.25 devices and the devices in an X.25 network.

X.28

A CCITT recommendation that defines the interchange of commands and responses between a PAD and its attached asynchronous terminals. Supplementary packet-switched protocol.

X.29

A CCITT recommendation that defines the use of packets to exchange data for control of remote PADs.

X.3

A CCITT recommendation that defines the parameters that determine the behavior of the interface between a PAD and its attached asynchronous terminals.

X.400

The CCITT (now ITU) and International Organization for Standardization (ISO) protocol for electronic mail and public data networks. X.400 wraps messages in an electronic envelope, which will then be accepted by any system that can read the envelope. Thus, a user of one electronic mail system can communicate with an individual using another because both employ the X.400 standard (and have agreed to the interconnection).

X.500

The CCITT (now ITU) and International Organization for Standardization (ISO) standard for listing names in an electronic directory (e.g., electronic white pages). This standard enables the directory to be accessed internationally and by a variety of electronic networks.

X.75

Supplementary packet-switched protocol.

x86

Term used to refer to Intel family processors, such as the 80386 and 80486.

Xconfigurator

In Linux, a utility to set up definintions needed for X to work with specific hardware.

xdm

In Linux, the X Display Manager. A program that allows users to display X Window sessions through an X terminal.

Xerox Network Systems (XNS)

A proprietary network developed by Xerox Corporation.

XF86Config

In Linux, the file that defines interfaces with keyboard, mouse, and monitor graphics card, setting resolution and pixel density in the X display, commonly located in the /etc/X11 directory.

xf86config

In Linux, a menu-driven program used to generate the XF86Config file.

XF86Setup

In Linux, a graphical configuration utility for XFree86 used to set up or adjust XFree86 servers that display to the screen.

XMODEM

A communications protocol developed in the late 1970s to perform error checking on data sent between two data transmission devices. Xmodem protocol adds a checksum to each block of data at transmission. The sum is recalculated when the block is received and the new number is compared with the received checksum. If there is a difference, this reflects an error, and the last block of data is retransmitted. Xmodem is sometimes referred to as Christensen Protocol after its designer.

XMSNETX.COM

NetWare shell file in which most of the program resides in Extended Memory Specification (XMS). This program requires the use of an extended memory manager such as HIMEM.SYS. The x represents the station's version of DOS. XMSNET3.COM is used for DOS 3.x, XMSNET5.COM for DOS 5.x. Novell has also released a *universal* version of this program called XMSNETX.COM. (In this case, the X is the character "X," not representative of a number.) This version of the program works with DOS versions 3.x through 5.x. The file is automatically executed when the filename is included in the Autoexec.bat file. This has been replaced by VLMs in newer versions of NetWare.

X-ON/X-OFF

An abbreviation for Transmitter On/Transmitter Off. These are control characters used for flow control. They instruct a terminal to start transmission (X-ON) and end transmission (X-OFF).

X/Open

A group of computer manufacturers that promotes the development of portable applications based on UNIX. They publish a document called the X/Open Portability Guide.

Y

Yahoo

A search engine on the Internet that can be found at www.yahoo.com.

Yellow Pages

A directory of usernames, passwords, and machine names on a local network. It provides automatic machine addressing and facilitates managing databases distributed across a network.

YMODEM

A data transmission file transfer protocol. The protocol sends information in 1,024-byte (1-KB) blocks of data, which is a faster method of data transmission than XMODEM.

Y

Yahoo

A search engine on the Internet that can be found at www.yahoo.com.

Yellow Pages

A directory of user names, passwords, [illegible] names on a local network. It provides automatic machine addressing and facilitates managing databases distributed across a network.

[illegible]

A [illegible] XML [illegible]

Z

Z39.50 protocol

A National Information Standards Organization (NISO) protocol that provides a common command language used for bibliographic information retrieval of online systems, including online library catalogs. Using Z39.50, one computer can query another and transfer records for the purpose of information retrieval.

ZAP file

A file type used with the Windows Installer Service. ZAP files are similar to INI files and provide installation instructions.

Zero Administration for Windows (ZAW)

A Microsoft initiative to decrease the Total Cost of Ownership of Windows-family computers.

ZMODEM

A data transmission file transfer protocol. Generally regarded as the fastest and most efficient way to transfer data, as compared with XMODEM and YMODEM.

Zombie

A dead (or undead) process that cannot be completely removed from the operating system after it has been killed.

Zone

A grouping of logical devices on one or more networks.

Zone Information Protocol (ZIP)

Responsible for linking users and resources on the network with the appropriate zone.

Zone list

A list of zones (up to 255).

Acronyms

—A—

AAL	ATM Adaptation Layer
Abend	Abnormal end
ABR	Automatic Baud Rate Detection
ACDI	Asynchronous Communications Device Interface
ACE	Access Control Entry
ACF/VTAM	Advanced Communications Function/Virtual Telecommunications Access Method
ACK	Acknowledgment
ACL	Access Control List
ACPI	Advanced Configuration and Power Interface
ACSE	Association Control Service Element
AD	Administrative Domain
ADB	Apple Desktop Bus
ADMD	Administrative Management Domain
ADO	ActiveX Data Objects
ADSI	Active Directory Services Interface
ADSL	Asymmetric Digital Subscriber Line
ADSP	AppleTalk Data Stream Protocol
AEP	AppleTalk Echo Protocol
AES	Advanced Encryption Standard
AFP	AppleTalk Filing Protocol
AGP	Accelerated Graphics Port
AIFF	Audio Interchange File Format
ANI	Automatic Number Identification
ANSI	American National Standards Institute
AOW	Asia and Oceania Workshop
APA	All Points Addressable
API	Application Programming Interface
APM	Advanced Power Management
APPC	Advanced Program-to-Program Communication
ARA	AppleTalk Remote Access
ARCNET	Attached Resource Computer Network
ARP	Address Resolution Protocol
ARPA	Advanced Research Projects Agency
ARPANET	Advanced Research Projects Agency Network

ARQ	Automatic Repeat-Request
ASCII	American Standard Code for Information Interchange
ASD	Automatic Skip Driver Agent
ASIS	American Society for Industrial Security
ASMP	Asymmetric Multiprocessing
ASN.1	Abstract Syntax Notation One
ASP	Active Server Pages
ASP	AppleTalk Session Protocol
ATM	Asynchronous Transfer Mode
ATP	AppleTalk Transaction Protocol
AUI	Attachment Unit Interface
AUP	Acceptable Use Policy
AWG	American Wire Gauge
AWT	Abstract Window Toolkit

—B—

BBS	Bulletin Board System
bcp	Bulk Copy Process
BDC	Backup Domain Controller
BER	Basic Encoding Rules
BGP	Border Gateway Protocol
BIOS	Basic Input/Output System
BISDN	Broadband ISDN
bit	Binary Digit
BITNET	Because It's Time Network
BNC	British Naval Connector
BOC	Bell Operating Company
BootP	Bootstrap Protocol
Bps	Bytes per second
bps	Bits per second
BRI	Basic Rate Interface
BSC	Binary Synchronous Communications
BSD	Berkeley Software Distribution
BTAM	Basic Telecommunications Access Method

—C—

CAL	Client Access License
CAP	Competitive Access Provider
CATV	Community Antenna Television
CBR	Constant Bit Rate
CBT	Computer-Based Training
CCITT	Comite Consultatif International de Telegraphique et Telephonique (now the ITU)
CCL	Common Command Language

CCR	Commitment, Concurrency, and Recovery
CCTV	Closed-Circuit Television
CDF	Channel Definition Format
CD-ROM	Compact Disc Read-Only Memory
CERN	Laboratoire Europeen pour la Physique des Particules
CERT	Computer Emergency Response Team
CGA	Color Graphics Adapter
CGI	Common Gateway Interface
CICS	Customer Information Control System
CIR	Committed Information Rate
CISC	Complex Instruction Set Computer
CIX	Commercial Internet Exchange
CLBS	Component Load Balancing Service
CLI	Command=Line Interface
CLNP	Connectionless Network Protocol
CLTP	Connectionless Transport Protocol
CMIP	Common Management Information Protocol
CMOS	Complementary Metal Oxide Semiconductor
CMOT	CMIP over TCP
CN	Common Name
CO	Central Office
COM	Component Object Model
CONP	Connection-Oriented Network Protocol
COS	Corporation for Open Systems
COSINE	Cooperation for Open Systems Interconnection Networking in Europe
CPE	Customer Premise Equipment
CPI	Common Programming Interface
cps	Characters per second
CPU	Central Processing Unit
CRC	Cyclic Redundancy Check
CREN	Consortium for Research and Education Network
CRT	Cathode Ray Tube
CSMA	Carrier Sense Multiple Access
CSMA/CA	Carrier Sense Multiple Access/Collision Avoidance
CSMA/CD	Carrier Sense Multiple Access/Collision Detection
CSNET	Computer Science Network
CSP	Cryptographic Service Provider
CSU	Customer Service Unit
CU	Control Unit
CUPS	Common UNIX Printing System

—D—

DA	Desk Accessory
DAC	Digital-to-Analog Converter
DACS	Digital Access and Cross-Connect System
DAO	Data Access Objects
DARPA	Defense Advanced Research Projects Agency
DAV	Digital Audio Video
DB2	Database 2
DBCS	Double Byte Character Set
DBMS	Database Management System
DBO	Database Owner
DBOO	Database Object Owner
DCA	Defense Communications Agency
DCE	Data Communications Equipment
DCE	Distributed Computing Environment
DCOM	Distributed COM
DD	Double Density
DDE	Dynamic Data Exchange
DDI	Device Driver Interface
DDL	Data Definition Language
DDM	Distributed Data Management
DDN	Defense Data Network
DDNS	Dynamic Domain Name System
DDP	Datagram Delivery Protocol
DES	Data Encryption Standard
DET	Directory Entry Table
Dfs	Distributed File System
DFT	Distributed Function Terminal
DHCP	Dynamic Host Configuration Protocol
DHTML	Dynamic Hypertext Markup Language
DID	Direct Inward Dialing
DIG	Domain Information Groper
DIMM	Dual, In-Line Memory Module
DISA	Defense Information Systems Agency
DIX	Digital, Intel, and Xerox
DLC	Data Link Control
DLCI	Data Link Connection Identifier
DLL	Dynamic-Link Library
DMA	Direct Memory Access
DMI	Digital Multiplexed Interface
DML	Data Manipulation Language
DMZ	Demilitarized Zone

DNA	Distributed Internet Application Architecture
DNS	Domain Name System
DOS	Disk Operating System
DoS	Denial of Service
dpi	Dots per inch
DQDB	Distributed Queue Dual Bus
DRAM	Dynamic Random Access Memory
DS	Data Set
DS	Double Sided
DS1	Digital Signal Level 1
DS2	Digital Signal Level 2
DS3	Digital Signal Level 3
DSA	Directory System Agent
DSDD	Double Sided, Double Density
DSE	Data Switching Equipment
DSHD	Double Sided, High Density
DSP	Digital Signal Processing
DSU	Data Service Unit
DTC	Distributed Transaction Coordinator
DTE	Data Terminal Equipment
DTR	Data Terminal Ready
DTS	Data Transformation Services
DUA	Directory User Agent
DVD	Digital Video Disc or Digital Versatile Disc
DXF	Drawing Exchange Format
DXI	Data Exchange Interface

—E—

EARN	European Academic and Research Network
EBCDIC	Extended Binary-Coded Decimal Interchange Code
ECF	Enhanced Connectivity Facilities
ECP	Enhanced Capabilities Port
EDI	Electronic Data Interchange
EEHLLAPI	Entry Emulator High-Level Language Application Programming Interface
EFF	Electronic Frontier Foundation
EFS	Encrypting File System
EGA	Enhanced Graphics Adapter
EGP	Exterior Gateway Protocol
EIDE	Enhanced IDE
EISA	Extended Industry Standard Architecture
E-mail	Electronic mail
EMF	Enhanced Metafile
EMS	Expanded Memory Specification

EPS	Encapsulated PostScript
ER Model	Entity Relationship Model
ES-IS	End System-Intermediate System
ESDI	Enhanced Small Device Interface
ESF	Extended Super Frame
EUnet	European UNIX Network
EUUG	European UNIX User Group
EWOS	European Workshop for Open Systems

—F—

FAQ	Frequently Asked Questions
FARNET	Federation of American Research Networks
FAT	File Allocation Table
FCB	File Control Block
FCC	Federal Communications Commission
FCS	Frame Check Sequence
FDDI	Fiber Distributed Data Interface
FEP	Front-End Processor
FFAPI	File Format API
FHS	File System Hierarchy Standard
FIN	Finish (flag, TCP/IP)
FIPS	Federal Information Processing Standards
FM	Frequency Modulation
FNC	Federal Networking Council
FPU	Floating Point Unit
FQDN	Fully Qualified Domain Name
FRICC	Federal Research Internet Coordinating Committee
FSF	Free Software Foundation
FT1	Fractional T1
FT3	Fractional T3
FTAM	File Transfer, Access, and Management
FTP	File Transfer Protocol
FYI	For Your Information

—G—

GC	Global Catalog
GDI	Graphics Device Interface
GDT	Global Descriptor Table
GID	Group ID
GIF	Graphics Interchange Format
GINA	Graphical Identification and Authentication
GNU	GNU's Not UNIX
GOSIP	Government OSI Profile
GP	Group Policy

GPL	GNU Public License
GPO	Group Policy Object
GUI	Graphical User Interface

—H—

HAL	Hardware Abstraction Layer
HCL	Hardware Compatibility List
HCSS	High Capacity Storage System
HD	High Density
HDLC	High-level Data Link Control
HDX	Half-duplex
HFS	Hierarchical File System
HID	Human Interface Device
HLLAPI	High-Level Language Application Program Interface
HMA	High Memory Area
HPFS	High Performance File System
HTML	Hypertext Markup Language
HTTP	Hypertext Transfer Protocol
Hz	Hertz

—I—

IAB	Internet Architecture Board
ICM	Image Color Management
ICMP	Internet Control Message Protocol
ICS	Internet Connection Server
IDE	Integrated Drive Electronics
IDEA	International Data Encryption Algorithm
IEEE	Institute of Electrical and Electronics Engineers
IESG	Internet Engineering Steering Group
IETF	Internet Engineering Task Force
IFS	Installable File System
IGMP	Internet Group Management Protocol
IGP	Interior Gateway Protocol
IGRP	Internet Gateway Routing Protocol
IIS	Internet Information Server
IMHO	In My Humble Opinion
INTAP	Interoperability Technology Association for Information Processing
InterNIC	Internet Network Information Center
IONL	Internal Organization of the Network Layer
IP	Internet Protocol
IPX	Internetwork Packet Exchange
IPXODI	Internetwork Packet Exchange Open Data-link Interface
IRC	Internet Relay Chat
IrDA	Infrared Data Association

IRF	Inherited Rights Filter
IRM	Inherited Rights Mask
IRQ	Interrupt Request
IRTF	Internet Research Task Force
ISAPI	Internet Server Application Programming Interface (Microsoft)
ISDN	Integrated Services Digital Network
IS-IS	Intermediate System to Intermediate System
ISO	International Organization for Standardization (not an acronym)
ISODE	International Organization for Standardization Development Environment
ISP	Internet Service Provider
ITU	International Telecommunication Union
IXC	Interexchange Carrier

—J—

JANET	Joint Academic Network (U.K.)
JDBC	Java Database Connectivity
JDK	Java Development Kit
JPEG	Joint Photographic Experts Group
JUNET	Japan UNIX Network

—K—

KB	Kilobyte
Kb	Kilobit
KBps	Kilobytes per second
Kbps	Kilobits per second
KCC	Knowledge Consistency Check
KDC	Key Distribution Center
KDE	K Desktop Environment

—L—

L2PDU	Layer 2 Physical Data Unit
L3PDU	Layer 3 Physical Data Unit
LAN	Local Area Network
LAPB	Link Access Procedure Balanced
LAPD	Link Access Procedure on D Channel
LAPS	LAN Adapter and Protocol Support
LATA	Local Access and Transport Area
LCD	Liquid Crystal Diode
LDAP	Lightweight Directory Access Protocol
LDP	Linux Documentation Project
LDT	Local Descriptor Table
LEC	Local Exchange Carriers
LEN	Low Entry Networking
LILO	Linux Loader
LLAP	LocalTalk Link Access Protocol (Apple)

LMI	Local Management Interface
LPD	Line Printer Daemon
lpi	Lines per inch
LPR	Line Printer
LPRng	Line Printer, next generation
LSA	Local Security Authority
LSB	Linux Standard Base
LSL	Link Support Layer
LU	Logical Unit
LUN	Logical Unit Number
LVM	Logical Volume Management
LVS	Linux Virtual Server

—M—

MAC	Media Access Control
MAN	Metropolitan Area Network
MAP	Manufacturing Automation Protocol (GM)
MAPI	Message Application Programming Interface
MAU	Media Access Unit
MAU	Multistation Access Unit
MB	Megabyte
Mb	Megabit
MBps	Megabytes per second
Mbps	Megabits per second
MBR	Master Boot Record
MCGA	Multicolor Graphics Array
MDI	Multiple Document Interface
MHS	Message Handling System
MHz	Megahertz
MIB	Management Information Base
MIDI	Musical Instrument Digital Interface
MILNET	Military Network
MIME	Multipurpose Internet Mail Extensions
MIPS	Million Instructions Per Second
MLID	Multiple Layer Interface Driver
MMC	Microsoft Management Console
MOO	MUD Object Oriented
MPEG	Moving Pictures Experts Group
MPPE	Microsoft Point-to-Point Encryption
ms	Milliseconds
MSAU	Multistation Access Unit
MSI	Microsoft Software Installer
MTA	Mail Transport Agent

MTA	Message Transfer Agent
MTU	Maximum Transmission Unit
MUA	Mail User Agent
MUD	Multiuser Dungeon
MVS	Multiple Virtual Storage
MVS-CICS	Multiple Virtual Storage-Customer Information Control System
MVS/TSO	Multiple Virtual Storage/Time-Sharing Option

—N

NAK	Negative Acknowledgment
NAT	Network Address Translation
NBP	Name Binding Protocol
NCB	Network Control Block (NetBIOS)
NCC	NetWare Control Center
NCP	NetWare Core Protocol
NCP	Network Control Point
NCSA	National Center for Supercomputer Applications
NDS	NetWare Directory Services
NetBEUI	NetBIOS Extended User Interface
NetBIOS	Network Basic Input/Output System
NetWare DA	NetWare Desk Accessory
NFS	Network File System
NIC	Network Information Center
NIC	Network Interface Card
NIS	Network Information Service
NIST	National Institute of Standards and Technology (formerly NBS)
NLM	NetWare Loadable Module
NLQ	Near Letter Quality
NLSP	NetWare Link Services Protocol
NMS	Network Management Station
NNS	NetWare Name Service
NNTP	Network News Transfer Protocol
NOC	Network Operations Center
NOS	Network Operation System
NREN	National Research and Education Network
ns	Nansecond
NSAP	Network Service Access Point
NSEPro	Network Support Encyclopedia Professional Volume
NSEPro	Network Support Encyclopedia Professional Edition
NSF	National Science Foundation
NSFNET	National Science Foundation Network
NT	Network Termination
NT	New Technology (Microsoft Windows OS)

NT1	Network Termination 1
NT2	Network Termination 2
NTAS	Windows NT Advanced Server
NTFS	New Technology File System
NTLM	NT Lan Manager
NTP	Network Time Protocol
NWADMIN	NetWare Administrator

—O—

OBS	Optical Bypass Switch
ODI	Open Data-link Interface
OHCI	Open Host Controller Interface
OIW	OSI Implementors Workshop
OLE	Object Linking and Embedding
ONC	Open Network Computing
OOP	Object-Oriented Programming
OPAC	Online Public Access Catalog
OpenHCI	Open Host Controller Interface
OS	Operating System
OSI	Open Systems Interconnection
OSPF	Open Shortest Path First

—P—

PAD	Packet Assembler/Disassembler
PAM	Pluggable Authentication Module
PAP	Printer Access Protocol
PBX	Private Branch Exchange
PCI	Peripheral Component Interconnect
PCI	Protocol Control Information
PCL	Printer Control Language
PCM	Pulse Code Modulation
PCMCIA	Personal Computer Memory Card International Association
PDC	Primary Domain Controller
PDF	Portable Document Format (Adobe)
PDF	Printer Definition File (NetWare)
PDN	Packet Data Network
PDS	Processor Direct Slot
PDU	Protocol Data Unit
PGP	Pretty Good Privacy
PHP	Personal Home Page
PID	Process Identification Number
PIF	Program Information File
PIN	Personal Identification Number
Ping	Packet Internet Groper

PKI	Public Key Infrastructure
PMMU	Paged Memory Management Unit
POP	Point of Presence
POP	Post Office Protocol
POSI	Promotion of OSI
POST	Power On Self Test
POTS	Plain Old Telephone Service
ppm	Pages per minute
PPP	Point-to-Point Protocol
PPTP	Point-to-Point Tunneling Protocol
PRAM	Parameter Random Access Memory
PRI	Primary Rate Interface
PRMD	Private Management Domain
PROFS	Professional Office System
PSN	Packet Switching Node
PU	Physical Unit
PUC	Public Utility Commission
PVC	Permanent Virtual Circuit

—Q—

QMF	Query Management Facility
QoS	Quality of Service

—R—

RADIUS	Remote Authentication Dial-In User Service
RAID	Redundant Array of Independent Disks
RAM	Random Access Memory
RARE	Reseaux Associes pour la Recherche Europeene
RARP	Reverse Address Resolution Protocol
RAS	Remote Access Service
RBOC	Regional Bell Operating Company
RDP	Remote Desktop Protocol
REM	Remark
RFC	Request For Comments
RFS	Remote File System
RIP	Raster Image Processor
RIP	Routing Information Protocol
RIPE	Reseaux IP Europeene
RISC	Reduced Instruction Set Computer
ROM	Read-Only Memory
ROSE	Remote Operation Service Element
RPC	Remote Procedure Call
RPM	Red Hat Package Manager
RRAS	Routing and Remote Access Service

RST	Reset (flag, TCP/IP)
RTF	Rich Text Format
RTMP	Routing Table Maintenance Protocol
RTSE	Reliable Transfer Service Element
RUP	Roaming User Profile

—S—

SAA	Systems Application Architecture
SAP	Service Access Point
SAP	Service Advertising Protocol
SAPI	Service Access Point Identifier
SAPS	Service Access Point Stations
SAR	Segmentation and Reassembly
SATAN	Security Administrator Tool for Analyzing Networks
SCSI	Small Computer Systems Interface
SDH	Synchronous Digital Hierarchy
SDI	Storage Device Interface
SDLC	Synchronous Data Link Control
SDN	Software Defined Network
SDU	SMDS Data Unit
SFT	System Fault Tolerance
SGID	Set Group ID
SGML	Standard Generalized Markup Language
SGMP	Simple Gateway Management Protocol
SID	Security Identifier
SIMM	Single, In Line Memory Module
SIP	SMDS Interface Protocol
SLIP	Serial Line Internet Protocol
SMB	Server Message Block
SMDS	Switched Multimegabit Data Service
SMI	Structure of Management Information
SMP	Symmetric Multiprocessing
SMS	Storage Management Services
SMTP	Simple Mail Transfer Protocol
SNA	Systems Network Architecture
SNMP	Simple Network Management Protocol
SONET	Synchronous Optical Network
SPAG	Standards Promotion and Application Group
SPE	Synchronous Payload Envelope
SPX	Sequenced Packet Exchange
SQL	Structured Query Language
SRAM	Static Random Access Memory
SRPI	Server Requester Programming Interface

SS7	Signaling System 7
SSH	Secure Shell
SSL	Secure Sockets Layer
STDM	Statistical Time Division Multiplexing
STI	Still Image Interface
STM	Synchronous Transport Module
STS	Synchronous Transport Signal
SUID	Set User ID
SVC	Switched Virtual Circuit
SYN	Synchronization (flag, TCP/IP)
Sysop	System Operator

—T—

TA	Terminal Adapter
TAC	Terminal Access Controller
TBC	Transmit Buffer Count
TBZ	Transmit Buffer Size
TCP	Transmission Control Protcol
TCP/IP	Transmission Control Protocol/Internet Protocol
TDM	Time Division Multiplexing
TE1	Terminal Equipment Type 1
TE2	Terminal Equipment Type 2
Telex	Teleprinter Exchange
TIFF	Tagged Image File Format
TLI	Transport Layer Interface
TLS	Transport Layer Security
TNX	Teletypewriter Exchange Service
ToS	Type of Service
TP0	OSI Transport Protocol Class 0
TP4	OSI Transport Protocol Class 4
TSA	Target Server Agent
TSR	Terminate and Stay Resident
TTF	TrueType Fonts
TTL	Time to Live
TTS	Transaction Tracking System
TWX	Teletypewriter Exchange Service

—U—

UA	User Agent
UDF	Uniqueness Database File
UDP	User Datagram Protocol
UID	User Identifier
UMA	Upper Memory Area
UMB	Upper Memory Block

UNC	Universal Naming Convention
UPS	Uninterruptible Power Supply
URL	Uniform Resource Locator
USB	Universal Serial Bus
UUCP	UNIX-to-UNIX Copy

—V—

VBR	Variable Bit Rate
VC	Virtual Console
VCI	Virtual Channel Identifier
VDM	Virtual DOS Machine
Veronica	Very Easy Rodent-Oriented Network Index to Computerized Archives
VGA	Video Graphics Array
VLM	Virtual Loadable Module
VLSI	Very Large-Scale Integration
VM/CMS	Virtual Machine/Conversational Monitor System
VMM	Virtual Memory Manager
VNET	Virtual Network
VPI	Virtual Path Identifier
VPN	Virtual Private Network
VRAM	Video RAM
VRC	Vertical Redundancy Check
VRML	Virtual Reality Modeling Language
VSE/CICS	Virtual Storage Extended/Customer Information Control System
VT	Virtual Terminal

—W—

W3C	World Wide Web Consortium
WAIS	Wide Area Information Server
WAN	Wide Area Network
WATS	Wide Area Telecommunications Service
WDM	Win32 Driver Model
WHQL	Windows Hardware Quality Labs
WINS	Windows Internet Name Service
WOW	Windows on Windows
WWW	World Wide Web
WYSIWYG	What You See Is What You Get

—X—

XDR	External Data Representation
XMS	Extended Memory Specification
XNS	Xerox Network Systems

—Y—

Y2K	Year 2000
YP	Yellow Pages

—Z—

ZAW	Zero Administration for Windows
ZIP	Zone Information Protocol